JULIAN SYMONS

BLOODY MURDER

FROM THE DETECTIVE STORY
TO THE CRIME NOVEL:
A HISTORY

VIKING

VIKING

Penguin Books Ltd, Harmondsworth, Middlesex, England
Viking Penguin Inc., 40 West 23rd Street, New York, New York 10010, U.S.A.
Penguin Books Australia Ltd, Ringwood, Victoria, Australia
Penguin Books Canada Ltd, 2801 John Street, Markham, Ontario, Canada L3R 1B4
Penguin Books (N.Z.) Ltd, 182–190 Wairau Road, Auckland 10, New Zealand

First published by Faber and Faber 1972
First published in the United States of America under the title *Mortal Consequences* by
Harper & Row, Publishers, Inc., 1972
This revised and updated edition published by Viking 1985

Copyright © Julian Symons, 1972, 1985

Filmset in Monophoto Palatino by
Northumberland Press Ltd, Gateshead, Tyne and Wear
Printed in Great Britain by
Richard Clay (The Chaucer Press) Ltd,
Bungay, Suffolk

BRITISH LIBRARY CATALOGUING IN PUBLICATION DATA

Symons, Julian
    Bloody murder.——Rev. ed.
    1. Detective and mystery stories——History
    and criticism
    I. Title
    809.3′872   PN3448.D4

    ISBN 0-670-80096-1

    Library of Congress Catalog Card Number
    84-51885

FOR JOAN KAHN
WITH RESPECT, GRATITUDE, AFFECTION

• Contents •

• Preface to the Revised Edition •

This book was first published in 1972. When I set out to bring it up to date, I had in mind no more than the addition of an extra chapter in which I would discuss a dozen writers who had come to prominence in the past decade. On looking at the book more closely, however, I saw that more must be said here, and deletions made there; something had to be said about the continuing growth of the spy story; the idea of merely lumping new names into a final chapter seemed crass. I ended by revising the whole book.

In the first half the revisions are mostly minor, although few pages are left unchanged. Later on, however, there are many additions although few changes of opinion. The development of a truly American crime story is discussed in more detail, the chapter on Simenon has been rewritten. I have found curiosities unmentioned in the original edition, some worth pursuing. The later work of several writers is reconsidered, and I hope I have conveyed my own pleasure in reading those who have recently emerged, Van de Wetering and George V. Higgins, P. D. James and Ruth Rendell, Ross Thomas and Charles McCarry and P. B. Yuill – and the list is far from complete. In the last chapter I have looked at the predictions I made more than a decade ago, to see how far they were from the bull's eye.

I should emphasize, finally, what is said in the text: I am an addict, not an academic, and this is a record of enthusiasm and occasional disappointment, not a catalogue. Writers I find of no more than average interest stay unmentioned, unless they are sufficiently celebrated to warrant the expression of a contrary view. This is a book meant for reading, consultation, argument, reasoned contradiction: but more than anything else I hope it will convince a new generation of readers that the best crime stories are not simply entertainments but also literature.

Julian Symons, 1984

The Guilty Party

It is the author who creates the crime
And picks the victim, this blonde dark girl sprawled
Across a bed, stabbed, strangled, poisoned, bashed
With a blunt instrument. Or the young middle-aged
Old scandalous and respected beardless greybeard
Destroyed most utterly by some unknown means
In a room with doors and windows 'hermetically sealed'.

So victims and means are found. As for the motive
It is often impersonal, a matter of money,
An estate to be gained, a will cheated on, a secret
Within the family, a discreditable
Business about the building contract for the new school.
It is simple for Hawkshaw, whose life has been
Logically given to the pursuit of logic.
He reads the signs, dustmarks, thumbprint, human and animal blood,
And arrests the solicitor.

                    The author
Puts down his pen. He has but poisoned in jest,
Stabbed and strangled in jest, destroyed in jest
By unknown means the smiling neuter victim.
What has he done that could deserve the tap
Upon the door of his butter-bright smiling room
Where crimes are kept in filing cabinets
Well out of sight and mind, what has he done
To bring this horde of victim villains in,
One paddling fingers in her own bright blood
And staining his face with it, another
Revealing the great wound gaping in his side,
The sliced-up tart carrying a juicy breast,
Inviting him to kiss it: and the villains all
Crowding him with their horrid instruments,
The rope that playfully tightens round his neck,
The blue revolver used to mutilate,

Prologue

The dagger points to pierce out jelly eyes,
The saw and hammer at their nasty work,
The shapes of agony — and worst of all
The unnamed death that strips away the flesh
And melts the bone, a death unnamable
Yet clearly known.

              From all such visions,
Unreal, absurd, phantasmagorical,
We naturally wish to be preserved.
If for a moment this white neutral room
Is filled with smells of rotted or burning flesh
There is a specific by which a respectable
Writer may puff away such nastiness
And regiment like Hawkshaw the unruly
Shapes of life to an ideal order.

              He picks up his pen.

Julian Symons

What They Are and
Why We Read Them

(i) Is it a detective crime psychological analytical suspense police story? No, it's a hybrid

The first problem facing anybody writing about crime fiction is to stake out the limits of the theme. Historians of the detective story have been insistent that it is a unique literary form, distinct from the crime or mystery story, not to be confused with the police novel, and even more clearly separate from the many varieties of thriller. Those who believe as I do that such classifications are more confusing than helpful, and that the most sensible sort of naming is the general one of crime novel or suspense novel (and short story), have to begin by countering a considerable weight of opinion.

For most critics the detective story has been taken as the central theme on which other crime stories and thrillers play variations. Accepting their classification, what is a detective story? The two qualifications everybody has thought necessary are that it should present a problem, and that the problem should be solved by an amateur or professional detective through processes of deduction. So Monsignor Ronald Knox, laying down in 1928 his 'Ten Commandments of Detection', insisted that the criminal must be mentioned early on, ruled out the supernatural, said that the detective must not himself commit the crime, and added that 'no accident must ever help the detective, nor must he ever have an unaccountable intuition, which proves to be right'. So also the Detection Club in Britain, shortly after its foundation in 1930, asked its members to swear an oath promising that their detectives would 'well and truly detect the crimes presented to them' without reliance on 'Divine Revelation, Feminine Intuition, Mumbo-Jumbo, Jiggery-Pokery, Coincidence or the Act of God'. Since logical deduction was the heart of the detective story, it followed that there was little room for any depth of characterization or any flourish of style. R. Austin Freeman, writing in 1924 about 'The Art of the Detective Story', thought it a cardinal error to confuse it with 'the mere crime story', and not to understand that it differed from all other types of fiction in offering to the reader 'primarily an intellectual satisfaction'. Allowing that it might be permitted humour, characterization and a picturesque setting, he insisted that these must be 'secondary and subordinate to the intellectual interest, to which they must be, if necessary, sacrificed'. S. S. Van Dine, writing in his real name of Willard Huntington Wright, went further than this, asserting that characters in a detective story should 'merely fulfil the requirements of plausibility', because any deeper delineation would 'act only as a clog in the narrative machinery'. Wright placed a ban on love interest, and in this had the full agreement of Dorothy L. Sayers, who severely reproved 'the heroes who insist on fooling about after young women when they ought to be putting their minds to the job of detection', rapped Freeman over the knuckles for allowing his secondary characters to 'fall in love with distressing regularity' and concluded that, upon the whole, 'the less love in a detective story, the better'. The beauty of the form, she thought, was that it had 'an Aristotelian perfection of beginning, middle and end'. She was writing, again, in the twenties, but her words were echoed in 1944 by Joseph Wood Krutch, who called the detective story 'the one clearly defined modern genre of prose fiction impeccably classical in form'. And more recently W. H. Auden succinctly defined the detective story's limits: 'The basic formula is this: a murder occurs: many are suspected; all but one suspect, who is the murderer, are eliminated; the murderer is arrested or dies.' The point to which these ideas lead is made briefly by Howard Haycraft, in his *Murder for Pleasure*: 'The crime in a detective story is only the means to an end which is – detection.'

The effects of such views on the work of the writers who held them are discussed later, but what must immediately be obvious is that few books actually conform to them. Indeed, the lines so carefully drawn are crossed by the critics themselves as soon as they begin to make those lists of 'The Hundred Best' which are such an entertaining parlour game. Haycraft, for instance, is briskly dismissive about Wilkie Collins's *The Woman in White*, which was, he says, 'a mystery rather than a detective novel', and so need not concern him. But then what are Eric Ambler's *The Mask of Dimitrios*, Dashiell Hammett's *The Maltese Falcon*, Francis Iles's *Before the Fact* and Mrs Belloc Lowndes's *The Lodger* doing in his list of 'Detective Story Cornerstones'? Most people would call the first two of these thrillers, the third a crime novel and the fourth a sensational murder story. Certainly none contains a puzzle to be solved by detection. Auden specifically excludes *Malice Aforethought* from the canon, another critic refuses to consider *The Lodger*. Ellery Queen's *Queen's Quorum*, which offers a choice of the most important 'Detective-Crime' short stories, contains such books as *Get-Rich-Quick Wallingford* and O. Henry's *The Gentle Grafter*. These are not even what most people think of as crime stories, let alone having any association with detection.

This is not said to put Messrs Haycraft and Queen into the pillory, but to suggest that these rigid classifications simply don't work in practice. They are also often inadequate to the books they describe. In Hammett's *The Glass Key* Ned Beaumont does not solve the puzzle by any genuine reasoning process, and he is a near-gangster who would hardly have been recognized as a detective by Wright, with his desire that the detective should stand outside the action like a Greek chorus, or by Knox, who thought that every detail of his thought process should be conscientiously audited, or by any of those who want crimes solved by a detective who rationally detects. And further than this, to call *The Glass Key* a detective story and leave it at that, is to limit rather than announce its merits.

When one looks at the attempts at definition more closely, they can be seen to apply only to the detective stories written in what is often called the Golden Age between the Wars. Many of these books were written within a convention as strict and artificial as that of Restoration plays, but that does not make the detective story a unique literary form, any more than the Restoration play is a unique dramatic form. Theorizing about detective stories began in the twenties, and would have seemed incomprehensible to Poe or Wilkie Collins or Sheridan le Fanu. They would have been astonished, and perhaps indignant, to know that they were working in what Haycraft calls 'a frankly non-serious, entertainment form of literature'. The detective story pure and complex, the book that has no interest whatever except the solution of a puzzle, does not exist, and if it did exist would be unreadable. The truth is that the detective story, along with the police story, the spy story and the thriller, all of them immensely popular in the past twenty years, makes up part of the hybrid creature we call sensational literature. This hybrid has produced a few masterpieces, many good books, and an enormous mass of more or less entertaining rubbish.

Of course this is not to say that there are no distinctions to be made between amateur detectives and private eyes, but however unlike Sherlock Holmes and Philo Vance may be to Sam Spade and Superintendent Maigret, they all belong to the same kind of literature. When this has been accepted there are certainly distinctions to be made within the literature. Spy stories, and thrillers in general, do stand apart from books that pose a puzzle to the reader. The latter kind of book asks questions about Who or Why or How, sometimes about all three put together, where the thriller or spy story frequently just tells us How. But all deal with violent ends in a sensational way, and although spy stories and thrillers have been discussed separately, it would not have been right to ignore them. The tree is sensational literature, and these are among its fruits.

(ii) Where to draw a line

The reason most often advanced for the division into categories is that once the floodgates are opened almost any tale which has the faintest connection with crime will be let in, from *Little Red Riding Hood* (an interesting case of disguise and attempted murder) to *Arden of Faversham* or almost any play by Shakespeare. In theory this is true. In practice, readers will have no difficulty in drawing a line that separates books in which interest in the nature of, motives for, and results of, a crime are at the heart of a story, from those where the criminal interest is a subsidiary one.

It would be tedious to labour this point, but perhaps just one example should be given of a novelist often concerned with crime who is not a crime writer. Trollope's novels contain cases of fraud, assault and murder, and in at least two of them a crime or an apparent crime is the hinge of the plot. *The Last Chronicle of Barset* is concerned with the accusation against Josiah Crawley, 'the perpetual curate of Hogglestock', that he has stolen a cheque for twenty pounds. We know that Crawley is innocent, but the mystery of the way in which the cheque got into his hands is maintained almost to the end of the book. The theft of Lizzie Eustace's diamonds is the core of the novel with that title, and again a teasing mystery is offered which leaves us in doubt about exactly what has happened. Yet nobody could seriously consider that either of these books is a crime story. In other hands this could be the material of crime fiction, but Trollope is using the apparent thefts to show the agonies of Mr Crawley in one case and to illuminate the nature of Lizzie Eustace and her world in the other. The line, then, would be drawn by almost everybody to exclude Trollope, but this is not to say that it does not waver from person to person in relation to this or that book. The precise placing of the line is a matter of individual taste.

(iii) Why we read them: the psychological basis

Crime literature is almost certainly more widely read than any other class of fiction in the United States, the United Kingdom and many other countries not under Communist rule. In 1940 Haycraft said that in the United States crime stories represented a quarter of all new fiction, and that most of the copies were sold to rental or public libraries. The proportion is probably not much changed today, although in the United Kingdom rental libraries have almost ceased to exist, and the public library has become overwhelmingly the most important patron of crime fiction in hard covers. But the situation has been radically changed by the growth of paperback editions. No accurate figures are available, but any reasonably well-known crime writer can be assured of paperback sales, and the sales of the most popular writers of spy and adventure stories are enormous. The readership of this literature cuts across definition by class or income group. Politicians and statesmen in particular have found it easy to relax (the compliment is a dubious one) while reading crime literature. Abraham Lincoln admired Poe's work in 1860 and Joseph Stalin enjoyed it more recently. Woodrow Wilson is said to have 'discovered' the books of J. S. Fletcher, the now forgotten Yorkshire detective story writer and journalist. Lord Rosebery was proud to possess a first edition of *The Memoirs of Sherlock Holmes*, Prime Minister Stanley Baldwin greatly enjoyed Anna K. Greene's *The Leavenworth Case*, and John F. Kennedy is supposed to have preferred Ian Fleming to any other writer of his kind. Although it is an exaggeration to say, as one writer has done, that crime literature is the 'favourite of all that is most intellectual in the reading public', at least Freud liked the books of Dorothy L. Sayers. On a superficial level what these and other readers looked for was pleasurable excitement removed from the reality of their own lives. But why did these mostly respectable people want detective stories concerned with a crime and its solution, or thrillers in which the heroes often did things that in real life the readers would have strongly disapproved?

Psychiatrists have strangely neglected the question of our motives for reading crime literature, and historians of the *genre* have never shown much interest in it. The first psychiatric piece of interest is Dr Leopold Bellak's 'On the Psychology of Detective Stories and Related Problems', written in 1945. Dr Bellak says about the content of detective stories that 'the criminal and aggressive proceedings permit a *phantasy gratification of Id* impulses'. In other words, first, the reader is permitted to identify with the criminal. This can safely be done because 'it [the story] is sufficiently removed from reality, and because soon the *Super-Ego is satisfied* that detection and punishment will follow.' As any reader today will realize, this is true of detective stories *circa* 1945 and earlier, but different phantasies are often fulfilled today. Bellak remarks later that the detective is 'an Ego Ideal, with the primitive, wish-fulfilling characteristics of a superman', a view endorsed and elaborated later in this book.

These are fairly elementary insights. Much the most suggestive psychoanalytical view of detective stories is Dr Charles Rycroft's article in the *Psychoanalytical Quarterly* in 1957. Rycroft begins by considering the hypothesis of another psychoanalyst, Geraldine Pederson-Krag, that the detective story has its origins in the 'primal scene' of infancy. The murder represents parental intercourse, the victim is the parent, and the clues are representations of mysterious 'nocturnal sounds, stains, incomprehensible adult jokes'. The reader, according to Pederson-Krag, satisfied infantile curiosity by becoming the detective, thus 'redressing completely the helpless inadequacy and anxious guilt unconsciously remembered from childhood'.

Rycroft adds an interesting gloss to this idea. If the victim is the parent, who is the criminal? He must personify 'the reader's own unavowed hostility towards that parent'. Thus 'the reader is not only the detective; he is also the criminal', and 'in the ideal detective story the detective or hero would discover that he himself is the criminal for whom he has been seeking'. Rycroft's exemplification of his own and Pederson-Krag's ideas in relation to *The Moonstone* is not always happy, although it is full of what might be called psychoanalytical Holmesian remarks. ('It is not necessary here to ... point out the symbolism of the drawer in the Indian cabinet, of the decorative painting and the stain on the nightshirt, nor of the fact that Franklin gave up cigar smoking during his courtship of Rachel.') But the most important point of which Rycroft, probably through lack of familiarity with the form, seems unaware, is that in some periods the crime story has followed the pattern he suggests. In early crime fiction the hero is often identified with the criminal, and in much recent work the hero is a criminal, or pretends to be a criminal, or behaves like a criminal.

Apart from Rycroft, whose valuable piece deserves wider readership (it is included in a collection of his essays), we are left with the stimulating but casual speculations of writers interested in the psychology of crime stories. Roy Fuller has pointed out the similarities between the detective story and elements in the Oedipus myth, 'the illustrious victim, the preliminary riddles, the incidental love interest, the gradual uncovering of the past, the unlikeliest criminal', and has suggested that it is 'a harmless and purging surrogate for the Oedipus myth in every writer's and reader's life'. W. H. Auden, in an essay which shoots off suggestions as a catherine wheel sends out sparks, says that the detective story has a magical function and that its mirror image is the Quest for the Grail. According to Auden the most satisfying detective stories are those set in idyllic and preferably rural conditions, so that the corpse appears 'shockingly out of place, as when a dog makes a mess on a drawing-room carpet'. They contain the magical quality of easing our sense of guilt. ('The typical reader of detective stories is, like myself, a person who suffers from a sense of sin.') Auden suggests that we live under, and mostly accept, the rule of law. What we are looking for in the detective story ritual, through which the person whose guilt was presumed proves innocent and the person who appeared outside the circle of suspicion turns out to be guilty, is an escape from this reality and a return to an imagined primal innocence where we can 'know love as love and not as the law'.

The last decade has seen an immense increase in critical studies devoted to crime stories, the great majority of them American, but few are concerned with the crime story's origins. *The Mystery Writer's Art*, edited by Francis M. Nevins (1971), is chiefly concerned with individual writers, although it contains an interesting essay on 'The Detective Story as a Historical Source' by William O. Aydelotte; and although *Detective Fiction*, edited by Robin Winks (1980), contains a section promisingly entitled 'The Genre Examined', four of the examinations date back to the forties and the fifth, Gavin Lambert's prologue to *The Dangerous Edge*, does no more than suggest that the crime story is a form of escape for readers living in 'an increasingly regulated society'. There can be no doubt that a great deal remains to be said.

Auden's valuable, wayward essay is written from a specifically Christian point of view, accepting the concept of sin as personal. I think one can amplify his suggestions, and those of Fuller, by relating the satisfaction gained from reading crime literature to the principle by which the primitive tribe is purified through the transference of its troubles to another person or animal. Murder is in many societies seen as the act which makes its perpetrator finally unacceptable. He may be expelled or destroyed, but never pardoned. Even in those societies where a temporary suspension of law is sometimes declared in relation to non-violent offences like theft, murderers are taken into custody. The murderer is an appropriate villain, and society's permanent scapegoat. Evil has been committed, suffering has ensued, a sacrifice is necessary. The murderer is seen as a devil personified, and his death ensures the purification of the tribe. Nicholas Blake, also writing in the forties, imagined a future Frazer calling the detective story 'The Folk-Myth of the Twentieth Century' and examining it very much from this point of view.

19

In the beginning there was guilt: the basic motive for reading crime fiction is the religious one of exorcizing the guilt of the individual or the group through ritual and symbolic sacrifice. The attempt is never wholly successful, for the true addict is a sort of Manichee and his spirits of light and darkness, the detective and the criminal, are fighting each other for ever. Human tribal sacrifices might be regarded as sacred, and often appeared in disguise before death, the human features being replaced by those of the devil who had to be expelled. The detective story shows this operation in reverse, the criminal appearing at first as an accepted and often respected figure. This mask is stripped away at the end of the book, when his real features as law-breaker are seen. The detective is the equally sacred witch doctor who is able to smell out the evil that is corrupting society, and pursue it, through what may be a variety of disguises, to its source. The objection often made to stories in which the detective turns out to be the criminal is partly social (such an idea subverts the law) and partly religious, since it confuses the powers of darkness with the powers of light.

Much of what has been said above applies to the detective story, but not to the crime novel or the thriller. In a detective story good people and bad people are clearly defined and do not change (except for the bad person who is pretending to be good). Policemen will not beat up suspects, nor will the criminal's state of mind be considered interesting, since the policemen are on the side of light and the criminal on the side of darkness. The psychological reason for the weakening of the detective story in recent years is a weakening in the sense of sin. Where an awareness of sin in religious terms does not exist, the detective as witch doctor has no function.

(iv) Why we read them: the social reasons

One of the most marked features of the Anglo-American detective story is that it is strongly on the side of law and order. Yet this was not always true, and is not altogether true now. Dorothy L. Sayers puts it clearly when she says that some early crime stories showed admiration for the criminal's astuteness, and that detective stories could not flourish 'until public sympathy had veered round to the side of law and order'. This book examines in some detail the kind of stories written before 'sympathy had veered round', stories in which not a detective but the rogue or criminal is quite often the hero. But the detective story, as developed through Collins and Gaboriau to Doyle and twentieth-century writers, was certainly on the side of 'law and order'.

It is important to understand that what Sayers means by public sympathy is the sympathy of the better educated classes, or to put it in another way those above a certain income level, who have a stake in the permanence of the existing social system. The values put forward by the detective story from the time of Holmes to the beginning of the Second World War, and by the thriller and spy story up to the advent of Eric Ambler, are those of a class in society that felt it had everything to lose by social change. In this detective story world decent men played games and were not too highly intellectual, women slept only with their husbands and never drank too much, and servants knew their place – which was in the servants' hall. The thriller's code of conduct in the same period was similar but a good deal cruder, because, as Blake said, detective stories were mostly read by the 'upper and professional classes' and thrillers by those with less money and inferior social status. In the terms of early thriller writers no Hun, and later no Red, was likely to be an honourable man, and this was particularly true of Reds, whose allegiance to some abstract impractical theory led them to behave in an unsporting and ungentlemanly way. They were the opposite of Bulldog Drummond, about whom 'Sapper' said: 'He lives clean, loves sport, and fights hard. I don't think he's ever done anything dirty; I can assure you he never will.' Drummond sometimes seems to be a sporting tough parodying an English gentleman, but the rule about the wickedness of Radicals was hardly ever broken. Raffles was an acceptable character as gentleman burglar just because he was good at cricket and died fighting for his country against the Boers. In France Arsène Lupin atoned for his criminal career by joining the Foreign Legion.

On the social level, then, what crime literature offered to its readers for half a century from 1890 onwards was a reassuring world in which those who tried to disturb the established order were always discovered and punished. Society's agent, the detective, was the single character allowed to have high intellectual attainments. He might be by ordinary standards (that is, those of his readers) eccentric, quaint, apparently a bit silly, but his knowledge was always great, and in practice he was omniscient. He was most often an amateur, because in this way the reader was able easily to put himself in the detective's position, and he alone was upon occasion allowed to be above the law, and to do things which for a character less privileged would have been punishable. Behind the conscious Victorian and Edwardian adherence to a firmly fixed hierarchical society there lay a deep vein of unease about the possible violent overturn of that society, especially by Anarchists. The 'propaganda by the deed' actions of those who called themselves Anarchists in France and America, before and at the turn of the century, included the assassination of Presidents Carnot and McKinley, and many more or less successful bomb attempts to kill people and destroy property. Barbara Tuchman in *The Proud Tower* has suggested the thrill of horror which such actions caused to the respectable in every country. How could the machinery of justice operate successfully against somebody like the French Anarchist Émile Henry, who said: 'We inflict death; we will know how to endure it.'?

The aloof, super-intellectual and slightly inhuman detective like Holmes, who occasionally acts outside the law, was particularly attractive when posed against such terrifying figures because he was a kind of saviour of society, somebody who did illegal things for the right reasons, who was really one of us. An intelligent French critic, Pierre Nordon, has pointed out that the whole Sherlock Holmes cycle is 'addressed to the privileged majority, it plays on their fears of social disturbance and at the same time makes use of Sherlock Holmes and what he stands for to reassure them'. Typical detective stories of the period were remarkably free from the realities of violence. Victim, murder, investigation, all have a hieratic and ritual quality. What the stories assert is the static nature of society, the inevitability with which wrongdoing is punished.

The nature and appeal of crime literature did not change much in the years between the two World Wars, but its relationship to the world around was greatly altered. Before 1914 the exterior trappings of typical detective stories corresponded reasonably well to the world outside. The big country house still existed, with its lengthy visits by friends and relations, its mild local entertainments, its shooting and fishing, its small army of servants and its multiplicity of rooms, including the corpse-filled library. This world had pretty well vanished by 1939, but detective story writers pretended that it was still there. In a sense, obviously, all detective stories are games of let's pretend, but the imagination of writers grew feebler as it had less and less to feed on. There are still some readers who, like Auden, find it hard to read any detective stories except those set in a rural world belonging not to the present but to the past, but most people found it much more difficult to accept the pretences upon which they were based. By the end of the Second World War the reassurances offered by the classical kind of detective story had become very shaky indeed. The social and religious structure of society had changed so much that its assumptions seemed preposterous. The pretence that the world was static could no longer be maintained. The detective story with its closed circle of suspects and its rigid rules had always been a fairy tale, but the point and pleasure of fairy tales is that by exercising the imagination one can believe them to be true. In the post-war world this sort of story changed from a fairy tale to an absurdity. In America, where social stratifications had never been very firm, the pattern was broken much earlier than in England, through Hammett and his successors. The process by which the detective story changed into the crime novel, which fulfils quite different emotional needs, is set down in this book.

Perhaps the reaction of 'Plain Man' readers may be anticipated: 'So that's why I read crime stoies. And I thought they were just a bit of relaxation.' It is a natural comment, but even Plain Men and Women should understand that there are social and emotional reasons for the kind of entertainment they enjoy.

(v) Personal feelings and the double standard

If all this suggests an academic approach, that is an impression I should correct. Like the Plain Man and Woman I am an addict, with a passion for crime literature that survives any rational explanation of it. This book is the result of the addiction, which started at the age of ten or eleven with Sherlock Holmes and Father Brown, and survived the rigours of several years' reviewing of crime stories. My research has been that of an addict, rather than of an academic busy with his card indexes. It is based upon wide reading and re-reading, but not upon an attempt to read the whole bulk of crime literature, which is now so vast that to try to cover the whole of it would have resulted in a mere catalogue. The most noticeable omissions are probably the result of my preferences, but there will be others caused by ignorance. I hope that proper severity about my mistakes will be blended with an indulgence like that of Holmes in relation to the student who looked at the examination papers in advance, when he said that it is human to err.

So this is a book expressing personal preferences, as all such surveys do, although few admit it. My early enthusiasm for every sort of crime story has not remained unscathed. I can no longer read with any pleasure the work of those writers later labelled the Humdrums, although I did so once. I still enjoy enormously the best work of the Golden Age detective story writers, but I admire much more the finest books of those authors I have called crime novelists. At the same time I have done my best to be fair, and I have tried to produce a book which should offer for the first time some assessment of crime stories on literary grounds. For the first time? Well, certainly most of those who have written about crime novels and short stories have assessed them by extra-literary considerations. Auden, for instance, says flatly that for him 'detective stories have nothing to do with works of art', but have rather the function of sympathetic magic. He remarks on *The Trial* as a work of art in which 'it is the guilt that is certain and the crime that is uncertain', in distinction from the detective story which works the other way round. If one protests that such a comparison really tells us nothing, and that some books by Hammett and Chandler (among others) have at least some of the characteristics of art, Auden escapes by saying that such books are not detective stories by his definition, and that Chandler's 'powerful but extremely depressing books should be read and judged not as escape literature, but as works of art'. This does not seem to be right. Chandler's books are escape literature of a different kind, that is all. Chandler himself was evasive when asked who was the 'best mystery writer', replying: 'Can't answer, too many types. By sales Gardner and Christie. Can't read Christie, Gardner close personal friend. Carter Dickson I can't read but others love him ... Best plodding detail man, Freeman Wills Crofts. Best Latin and Greek quoter, Dorothy Sayers ... This is a lot of nonsense. You have to agree on definitions and standards.'

You have to agree on definitions and standards: but that is impossible. How can one weigh the puzzle interest of the detective story against the interest in characterization that marks the crime novel, especially when the detective story often contains some characterization and the crime novel often contains a puzzle? These two kinds of book are very much like each other, but they are not the same thing. If detective stories are assessed by any recognizable literary standards most of them seem at first sight of negligible interest. But nobody condemns Restoration comedy outright because it lacks the profundity of Jacobean drama. It is an inferior thing, but a thing with its own particular and unique merits. In the same way the detective story is an inferior thing to the crime novel, but it has wholly individual merits for all except the most priggish. A double standard of judgement has to be used here, so that one can say first of all that the characteristic detective story has almost no literary merit, and second that it may still be an ingenious, cunningly deceptive and finely constructed piece of work. The parallel with Restoration comedy holds. And there are gradations within the detective story itself, so that just as it would be an erratic taste that preferred Vanbrugh to Congreve, so it would be a mistake to equate any other writer with John Dickson Carr as a master of the locked-room mystery. When Edmund Wilson says that 'with so many fine books to be read ... there is no need to bore ourselves with this rubbish', he is denying the *convention* of the detective story any interest or attraction at all.

Most of the form's historians or critics err by applying a single standard of the opposite kind. They are so delighted by puzzles and problems that they confuse the undoubted interest such things possess with that of literature, claiming by implication that if *The Moonstone* is a work of literature then the books of X Y Z, which are just as cleverly plotted and much more baffling, must be literature too. By mixing the names of writers of unquestioned talent who have been interested in the form, like Poe and Faulkner, with those of hacks who have clever ideas, all criminal coinage is debased. The assumption made here is that if we are to say what is good in crime fiction we should say also what is less good, commonplace, or poor; that the best crime stories are novels of quality; and that clever ideas and tricks are positive virtues, although they may be cancelled by writing that is crude and slovenly.

(vi) Sources and style

Many of my debts to the historians and chroniclers of the crime story are acknowledged in the text, but I may as well make them explicit here in lieu of a Bibliography.

Howard Haycraft's *Murder for Pleasure* (1941) is the best and most comprehensive survey of detective fiction up to the year of its publication, and if it shows a bias towards American writers, very likely this volume provides a corrective. The collection of essays edited by Haycraft, *The Art of the Mystery Story* (1946), contains much important critical writing about crime stories, including pieces by Chandler, Wright, Sayers and others, which first appeared elsewhere. *Crime in Good Company* (1959), edited by Michael Gilbert, contains a number of interesting essays of a later date. Ellery Queen's *Queen's Quorum* (1951) and *In the Queen's Parlor* (1957) have been informative. A. E. Murch's *The Development of the Detective Novel* (1958) contains a lot of detailed and valuable material about nineteenth-century crime fiction, not easily found elsewhere.

In the last decade a number of critical studies have appeared, most of them American and in flavour scholastic. William Ruehlmann's *Saint with a Gun* (1974) and the collection of essays in *Tough Guy Writers of the Thirties*, edited by David Madden (1968), have considerable historical and critical interest. In *Detective Fiction* (1980) Robin Winks gathered together more than a dozen critical pieces, most of them to be found elsewhere. Several books about individual crime writers have appeared, again mostly

American and dealing with American writers, although Dorothy L. Sayers and P. D. James have been the subjects of individual studies. In *Designs of Darkness* (1983) Diana Cooper-Clark carried out long and probing interviews with a number of writers, including James, Ross Macdonald and Highsmith. I have used all these works sparingly, and recent biographies of James M. Cain, Chandler, Hammett and Sayers hardly at all. This is primarily a critical book, which would be unbalanced by a mass of personal detail.

Allen J. Hubin's immense bibliography of everything in the genre (well, not quite everything) up to the year of its publication, 1975, is of value to every student, more or less superseding the late Ordean A. Hagen's erratic guide list *Who Done It?* (1969). Several encyclopedias have appeared, all useful but none completely to be trusted. They include Chris Steinbrunner's and Otto Penzler's *Encyclopaedia of Mystery and Detection* (1976), H. R. F. Keating's *Whodunnit?* (1982) and *Twentieth-Century Mystery and Crime Writers*, edited by John M. Reilly (1980). Many hands have been involved in all of these works. More personal, and by my standards often wayward, is Jacques Barzun's and Wendell Hertig Taylor's *A Catalogue of Crime* (1971), a listing and assessment of some 7,500 books, named by the editors 'a *catalogue raisonné* – a list with reasons'. An excellent account in English of *The Swedish Crime Story*, was written by Bo Lundin (1981).

These have all been consulted, but of course there is no substitute for the actual reading of books, and the reader will find things here that are not mentioned in any of the works listed above. This revised version, like the original edition, is very little cluttered by footnotes. It is a book to be dipped into and read for pleasure first, information second, and I think readers should be prepared to search out the origins of phrases and references for themselves. And, as before, I have not consulted any colleagues, British or American, feeling that it would be better to stand by my own opinions rather than be drawn into friendly arguments which might have ended in tame modifications. I have moved occasionally from third to first person when that seemed useful or desirable, and after the first reference to a writer have generally used only the surname, whether of man or woman.

• 2 •

The Two Strands:
Godwin, Vidocq, Poe

Historians are divided between those who say that there could be no
detective stories until organized police and detective forces existed, and
those who find examples of rational deduction in sources as various as the
Bible and Voltaire, and suggest that these were early problems in detection. For the first group the detective story begins with Edgar Allan Poe,
for the second its roots are in the beginnings of recorded history. Into the
mud of this tiresome controversy I propose to dip no more than one long
paragraphic toe.

The decisive point is that we should be talking about crime literature,
while those who search for fragments of detection in the Bible and
Herodotus are looking only for puzzles. The puzzle is vital to the detective
story but is not a detective story in itself, and its place in crime literature
generally is comparatively small. If we consider what Sayers calls the first
four detective stories, we find that they involve the use of natural cunning
rather than detective skill. In the tale of Susanna and the Elders, Daniel
traps the Elders by an adroit question, but he has no means of knowing
that Susanna is innocent and they are guilty, and in the story of the priests
of Bel the reason for supposing them to be lying is theological, the fact
that Bel is a heathen idol. The tale of King Rhampsinitus' attempts to catch
the thief who stole from his treasure house is no more than a battle of
wits with the rogue coming off best, and although the affair of Hercules
and Cacus contains a deception about footprints, it bears no other relation
to detection. The histories and fairy tales of which these are fragments are
quite different in nature from crime literature. The trick or puzzle element
is present in several of the Arabian Nights stories, often as an example
of natural cunning used to escape a trap, on the level of the cock caught
by a fox in Chaucer's 'The Nun's Priest's Tale' (mentioned by one historian) who persuades the fox to open his mouth and then flies away. The
most interesting of these exercises is in Voltaire's *Zadig* (1747). Without
seeing the Queen's bitch or the King's horse, both of which have disappeared, Zadig is able to say that the bitch recently had puppies, limps

in the left foreleg and has long ears, and that the horse is five feet high, with very small hooves and a tail three and a half feet long. He adds that the horse is shod with silver of eleven deniers proof, with bosses on its bits of twenty-three-carat gold. When he insists that he has never seen the animals, Zadig is sentenced to be flogged. His explanation, made after the animals are found, is a piece of true deduction. In the case of the bitch, hanging dugs and earmarks traced in the sand, with one paw more deeply impressed than the others, provided the clues. The horse had brushed off some leaves in an arcade at a height of five feet, and its tail had wiped away dust at a distance of three and a half feet. Marks left on stones showed the details about the bit and shoes. This brilliant fragment was borrowed by Voltaire from a romance by the Chevalier de Mailly published thirty years earlier, and at a further distance from the *Arabian Nights*, of which Zadig is an ironical imitation. Voltaire's prime concern is not to show the power of reason, but its inadequacy in dealing with all the unreasonable people in the world. This ingenious piece of analytical deduction is a flirt of the imagination in a book that does not bear the slightest resemblance to a crime story.

If we leave aside such puzzles and riddles, there is a great deal of fiction concerned with crime which goes back at least to the eighteenth century, including Fielding's *Jonathan Wild* and the tales of mystery and terror written by Mrs Radcliffe, Maturin and 'Monk' Lewis. But Fielding's book belongs to the tradition of the picaresque novel about the adventures of a rogue rather than to the genre of crime story, and although the Gothic novel bears a relationship to the detective story in the sense that it often poses a mystery to be solved, the solution is never in itself of much interest. The Gothic novelists wanted to arouse in their readers feelings of terror and delight at the horrific plight of the central character, and they used mysterious events to enhance these feelings. The solution of a puzzle was not for them the main object of a book. The characteristic note of crime literature is first struck in *Caleb Williams* by William Godwin (1756–1836), which appeared in 1794.

'Psychological novel, detective, adventure or pursuit novel, and political novel – these are the labels most often attached to Caleb Williams,' says Professor McCracken, introducing a modern edition of the book. The novel points up the weakness of any attempt to fit crime stories too closely into separate compartments. *Caleb Williams* is about a murder, its detection, and the unrelenting pursuit by the murderer of the person who has discovered his guilt. It was also for Godwin a means of expounding his Anarchist beliefs, and because of this is not usually considered as coming within the crime story's critical canon. Yet one has only to consider the account he gives of the book's conception to see how close he was in spirit to the modern crime story. He invented the last volume first, he says, as a volume of flight and pursuit with 'the fugitive in perpetual apprehension of being overwhelmed with the worst calamities, and the pursuer, by his ingenuity and resources, keeping his victim in a state of the most fearful alarm'. But how was he to account for this pursuit, why did it happen? He devised, as the material of the second volume, 'a secret murder, to the investigation of which the innocent victim should be impelled by an unconquerable spirit of curiosity'. And then, to make the implacable pursuit plausible, the first volume must show 'the pursuer ... invested with every advantage of fortune, with a resolution that nothing could defeat or baffle, and with extraordinary resources of intellect'. This manner of working back from effect to cause, from solution to problem, is at the heart of crime literature, and no writer before Godwin had attempted it with his conscious deliberation.

Hazlitt thought that nobody who began *Caleb Williams* could fail to finish it, and that nobody who read it could possibly forget it, yet a summary of the plot may be useful. Falkland, a generous and charming country squire, is accused of stabbing to death his atrocious neighbour, Tyrrell. He is tried and acquitted. A tenant of Tyrrell's, named Hawkins, is then arrested, together with his son, and they are both tried and hanged. One principal piece of evidence against them is a knife found in their lodgings, the broken blade of which precisely fits the piece left in the wound. Caleb Williams is the narrator of the story – or most of the story, for Godwin introduces another narrator in a way that slightly anticipates *The Moonstone*. Caleb is a poor boy who enters Falkland's service as secretary at a time when the murder lies in the past. He suspects that his master had something to do with the crime, and pursues his investigation with the unquenchable curiosity of the amateur detective. After Caleb has discovered the truth, that Falkland killed Tyrrell and then planted clues against Hawkins, he is dismissed, put in prison on a charge of theft (Falkland has secreted jewellery among his belongings), and then pursued and persecuted by Falkland and his agent, Gines. The pursuit is relentless, frustrating Caleb's attempts at escape by disguising himself as an Irish beggar, a lower-class farmer and a Jew. In the end Caleb brings Falkland to trial and the squire, now a dying man, admits his guilt and praises his accuser.

Caleb Williams is a remarkable rather than a great novel. The second and third volumes are absorbingly interesting but the first, in which the nobility of Falkland's nature is contrasted with the brutishness of Tyrrell's, is heavy going for a modern reader. And Godwin's object in writing the book was political. In 1793 his *Enquiry concerning the Principles of Political Justice* had appeared, and this outline of an ideal Anarchism, the book by which he is now remembered, at once made him famous. In it Godwin attacked practically all the institutions of the state, including the legal system, opposing to them the vision of a world in which 'there will be no war, no crimes, no administration of justice, as it is called, and no government'. In the bright dawn of the French Revolution this vision found many sympathizers, and Godwin became for a time the intellectual leader of the English Radical movement, as Tom Paine was its leader in action. *Political Justice* was an account of things as they might be, an expression of faith in the perfectibility of man. The original title of *Caleb Williams* was *Things As They Are*, and it is meant to show the corruption inherent in any legal system through which one man has power over another. Falkland is a good and generous man, and in Godwin's eyes his villainy springs from his trust in social institutions, which betray him until he commits and then has to conceal the ultimate crime of murder. Caleb's sufferings, in prison and throughout his wanderings, are forced on him directly by Falkland but indirectly through the authoritarian power exerted by evil institutions over the virtuous individual. And the climactic scene of Falkland's exposure is later seen by Caleb as his own terrible mistake. In desperation at the sufferings inflicted on him he too has invoked the force of law, where he should have attempted 'the just experiment' by confronting Falkland privately: 'I despaired, while it was yet time to have made the just experiment; but my despair was criminal, was treason against the sovereignty of truth.'

The particular importance of *Caleb Williams* is that it denies all the assertions to be made later through the detective story. In the detective story the rule of law is justified as an absolute good, in Godwin's book it is seen as wholly evil. The important strand in modern crime fiction which looks for corruption in officialdom and bureaucracy, and often suggests a close alliance between police and gangsters, was expressed here by the crime story's most significant ancestor. Godwin's attitude often gives extraordinary power to his assertion of the heroic nature of the outlaw. At times he might be speaking with the voice of Brecht, as in the credo of Raymond, leader of a gang of thieves joined by Caleb: 'We, who are thieves without a licence, are at open war with another sort of men, who are thieves according to law.' And the proto-typical figure of the law-breaker turned thief-taker appears here for the first time in the person of

Falkland's agent, Gines, who has been expelled from Raymond's band for his brutality, but becomes perfectly acceptable to society as an upholder of the law. There are some passages of biting sarcasm about the code of honour adhered to by such a figure as Gines.

It is a mark of Godwin's perceptiveness that he should have created such a character more than thirty years before the publication of the *Mémoires* of Eugène François Vidocq (1775–1857), the criminal who became in 1811 the first chief of the Sûreté, and later started the first modern detective agency, Le Bureau des Renseignements. We do not know much about Vidocq's criminal activities apart from what is said in his own highly coloured and ghosted autobiography. According to this he began by stealing 2,000 francs from his mother while in his early teens, joined the army and fought fifteen duels in six months, and then at the age of twenty-two received an eight-year prison sentence. He decided to become a police informer 'for the interest of honest men' and wrote to 'Papa' Henry, a divisional chief at the Paris prefecture, to offer his services. Dates and details are confused in the *Mémoires*, but there is no reason to doubt the substantial truth of Vidocq's story. He says that he spent twenty-one months as a police spy in prison, and during this time he proved his loyalty to the police. His 'escape' was arranged, and he was appointed Chef de la Sûreté with a staff originally of four men, a number eventually increased to twenty eight.

Almost all of his agents were ex-convicts and there were persistent rumours that some of them, and perhaps Vidocq himself, engineered robberies that they later solved, instigated to do so by the arrangement through which they were paid no salary but received a fee and expenses for every arrest. These essentially probable offences were never proved, but in 1827 Vidocq's resignation was forced by his superior in the second Division, the Chevalier Duplessis. He was replaced by one of his most dubious ex-criminal agents, Coco Lacour, and although he returned to power in March 1832, he was never really trusted. In November he resigned again after a case in which one of his agents was accused of acting as *agent provocateur* in a case involving the arrest of several thieves. After this the authorities pursued him intermittently, and eventually succeeded in wrecking his Bureau. He lived on for more than twenty years after its destruction, writing, or at least producing, books, doing some private detective work, even still acting occasionally as a police agent.

The influence of Vidocq on writers of crime fiction in his own lifetime, and on detective story writers after his death, was immense. It did not rest on his skill in analytical detection, for he had none. He started a card index system at the Sûreté, and his *Mémoires* mention at one point taking impressions of footmarks, but it cannot be said that he was in any way a forerunner of later police methods, his perceptiveness being confined to such general observations as that many criminals are bow-legged. Vidocq's importance rested in his nature as the archetypal ambiguous figure of the criminal who is also a hero. The interpenetration of police with criminals, and the doubt about whether a particular character is hero or villain, is an essential feature of the crime story, and Vidocq embodied it in his own person. A typical passage in the *Mémoires*, relating to his own early days as a police spy, runs:

> I frequented every house and street of ill fame, sometimes under one disguise and sometimes under another, assuming, indeed, all those rapid changes of dress and manner which indicated a person desirous of concealing himself from the observation of the police, till the rogues and thieves whom I daily met there firmly believed me to be one of themselves.

The capacity for physical disguise is of course a mark of ambiguity, and there is no doubt that Vidocq was very successful in disguising himself. His ability to do so fascinated several contemporary writers, including Balzac and Bulwer-Lytton. Balzac heard from Vidocq's own mouth, and Lytton read in the autobiography, stories about the false wrinkles, pigtail, snowy ruffles and three-cornered hat that helped him to become a 'very respectable gentleman' when necessary, of the time when he had his hair and beard dyed black, stained his face with walnut liquor, and garnished his upper lip with coffee grounds plastered on with gum arabic, and of the mock blisters and fetter marks made on his feet and legs when he impersonated a criminal named Germain. When, in old age, he paid a visit to London, *The Times* gave his height as five feet ten inches 'when perfectly erect' (he was in fact five feet six inches tall), and added that 'by some strange process connected with his physical formation he has the faculty of contracting his height several inches, and in this diminished state to walk about, jump, etc.' The climactic emotional moment at which the man who has seemed to be bad is revealed as good and the true villain is exposed, comes often in the *Mémoires*, when Vidocq abandons disguise and proclaims 'I am Vidocq', and of almost equal symbolic importance are such occasions as those when Vidocq in disguise is set to search for and destroy himself. Vidocq started a tradition of disguise in the French detective force which persisted at least until the end of the century.

It was the criminal rather than the maintainer of law who fascinated Vidocq's contemporaries, and whom in some cases they admired. Balzac was a friend of Vidocq's and based upon him the character of Vautrin, who appears in *Le Père Goriot* and other books. Vautrin, alias Jacques Collin, is, like Vidocq, a master of disguise, and like him also is a figure both genial and sinister. He gives up criminal activities and enters the police. Balzac's interest, however, was not in painting a portrait of Vidocq but in using him to create a major character whose philosophy transcends the conventions of legality. 'In every million men there are ten who put themselves above everything, even the law, and I am one of them,' Vautrin says, and on the occasion of his arrest he is allowed a splendidly forceful declaration: 'Have you never seen a convict before? A convict such as I am is a man less cowardly than the rest, who protests against the hypocrisy of the social contract, as says Rousseau, whose disciple I am proud to call myself.' As A. E. Murch has pointed out, Balzac sometimes gave a hero's role to the criminal, but never made a hero out of a detective. His conception of the ethical relationship between crime, order and society is nearer to Godwin than to Wilkie Collins.

The most famous work of Eugène Sue (1804–57), *Les Mystères de Paris*, is a sensational novel owing a great deal to the Vidocq tradition, and indeed directly to the *Mémoires*, as well as something at a further distance to the horrors of Mrs Radcliffe. An impossibly virtuous aristocratic hero living in the Paris slums becomes mixed up in the activities of a gang of thieves and murderers. The adventures are often absurd, and although there is a great deal of information about criminal habits, the 'mysteries' hardly exist in a modern sense. There are several passages of deductive reasoning in the works of Alexandre Dumas Père (1802–70), including one by d'Artagnan in *Le Vicomte de Bragelonne* which closely resembles Zadig's reasoning about the horse and the bitch. Dumas was also the first writer to point out that an impression may be left on the second sheet of a pad of paper when the first has been torn off. But for the most part Dumas recounts ingenious tricks, like those featuring in the eighteenth-century picaresque novel, which are no more than deceptions practised on gulls.

In one or two of James Fenimore Cooper's romances there are similar incidents which anticipate the deductive methods of the detective story, the best known of them relating to the tracking exploits of the scout Hawkeye, as he points out the difference between one moccasin and another, but essentially these are repeating in a different time and country the feats of Zadig.

In England Edward Bulwer-Lytton (1803–73), later Lord Lytton, also stressed the romantic qualities of the criminal. Murch picks out for particular discussion his second novel, *Pelham* (1828), pointing out that Lord Pelham is confronted by a characteristic detective problem when his friend Sir Reginald Glanville is to be committed for trial on a charge of murder unless Pelham can 'by the day after to-morrow, ascertain any facts to elucidate this mysterious crime and point the inquiries of justice to another quarter'. This subsidiary plot, however, is far from being at the heart of the book, as murder is the central fact of *Caleb Williams*, but is rather evidence of Lytton's absorption in the world of the criminal as opposed to the world of authority. In Lytton's four genuine crime novels the hero is also a criminal. The best of them, *Night and Morning* (1841), points up frequently the distinction between Gawtrey, who commits crimes but is shown as essentially a good man led astray, and Lord Lilburne who breaks no laws but ruins the lives of others in pursuit of his own pleasure. *Eugene Aram* (1832) was based upon an actual case in which the scholarly and virtuous Aram was convicted and executed for a murder committed fourteen years earlier. But although these books of Lytton's have a genuine connection with modern crime stories, one should not overstate the case. The books sprang from the conception of the criminal as a romantic outsider, a man condemned to the life he led by the cruelty of an unjust society and a corrupt or ignorant judiciary, that was prevalent during the first half of the nineteenth century. Lytton's early Radicalism and his unhappy marriage led him to create characters who were outcasts from the respectable world, and to show them as sympathetic, but the point for him (in the case of Eugene Aram, that a single act can be 'at war with a whole life – blasting for ever the happiness') can hardly be the point for us.

The idea that detective fiction could not be written until organized detective forces existed is logically persuasive but not literally true, for the first detective stories were written by Edgar Allan Poe (1809–49), before a Detective Office had been established at Scotland Yard, and at a time when few American cities had any kind of police system. The relationship between detective stories and the development of detective branches in police forces is discussed in the next chapter, but it is a tribute to Poe's inventive genius that his stories had so little to do with actual police operations. He had read Vidocq, and it is right to say that if the *Mémoires* had never been published Poe would not have created his amateur detective, but one should immediately add that Poe owed to Vidocq only the inspiration that set light to his imagination. Almost every later variation of plot in the detective story can be found in the five short stories he wrote which, with a little stretching here and there, can be said to fit within the limits of the form. He is the undisputed father of the detective story, although he would have been disconcerted by many of his children and grandchildren.

It should be recognized also that Poe did not think of himself as writing detective stories (the word 'detective' was unknown at the time the first of them, 'The Murders in the Rue Morgue', appeared), or regard these particular stories as of much importance. Poe's roots as a prose artist lay, like those of Lytton and others at the time, in the romantic tale of terror. As Edmund Wilson has said, he was, far from being alien to the spirit of his age, one of its most typical figures, 'a thorough romantic, clearly akin to his European contemporaries', and it was probably fortunate for him as an artist that he spent his adult life in the tame literary enclosure of the United States. His work looks longingly towards Europe, but it was the irritant influence of the philistines surrounding him that helped to mature the pearl in this oyster. When T. S. Eliot calls Poe provincial, and Henry James says that 'to take him with more than a certain degree of seriousness is to lack seriousness oneself', they undoubtedly have in mind the endless endeavour he made to sound the artistic note of a civilization from which he was separated by the Atlantic. In prose, as in verse and science, he longed always to produce something new, and his curiosity was endless. To quote Eliot again:

The forms which his lively curiosity takes are those in which a pre-adolescent mentality delights: wonders of nature and of mechanics and of the supernatural, cryptograms and cyphers, puzzles and labyrinths, mechanical chess-players and wild flights of speculation. The variety and ardour of his curiosity delight and dazzle: yet in the end the eccentricity and lack of coherence of his interests tire.

Eliot's remarks are often taken as being in dispraise of Poe, but they should be regarded rather as outlining the limitations of his genius. The ingenuity and freshness of his mind were extraordinary, and throughout his writing life he was searching for new forms in which to express the ideas that crowded in on him, and in the horror stories to blend these with the neuroses by which he was increasingly obsessed. In these stories Poe was always driving towards perverse sexual themes with which he could not deal directly because of the limitations imposed by his society. The result can often be grotesque, as in 'Berenice', where the narrator is driven by some unspecified guilt not only to murder his epileptic cousin, but after she has been buried alive during a fit, to fulfil his obsession with her teeth by digging the living body out of the grave and extracting the thirty-two teeth with 'some instruments of dental surgery'. What he called the 'tales of ratiocination', like those involving his interest in cryptography, and his discovery that the Lamentations of Jeremiah were written in acrostic verse, are the obverse of this horrific romanticism. If we ask, as some writers have done, why he did not exploit the ratiocinative vein further, the answer is simply that it did not interest him enough – or, to put it another way, that his obsessions eventually became so overwhelmingly important that they did not permit the production of purely rational work.

What he did may be summarized briefly. 'The Murders in the Rue Morgue', which appeared in 1841, was the first of those hundreds of locked-room mysteries that propose the puzzle of a dead body found in a room which seems to be effectively sealed. Sometimes the problem in such stories concerns the murder method (how was X stabbed, shot, poisoned, when nobody could have entered the room and there is no trace of a weapon or the poison?), and sometimes the means of entry or exit. One common form of solution is that in which the murder was committed before the door was locked or after it had been re-opened, another depends upon some mechanical device like a murder weapon which will operate at a particular time, and another still is related to some possible means of entry which is not apparent. In Poe's story the investigator, Dupin, deduces that the murderer must have come in through the apparently securely nailed windows, and finds that the nail of one window is broken, so that it only appears to be holding the window, which is also retained by a concealed spring. The police, thinking that the nail was completely driven through the window, did not trouble to look for the spring. By various other deductions Dupin comes to the correct conclusion that the murders were committed by an orang-utan which must have escaped from its owner.

'The Mystery of Marie Rogêt' was written and published in magazine form during the following year. It follows closely the murder of a girl named Mary Cecilia Rogers in New York. She was killed in July 1841, and the case remained a mystery at the time Poe wrote of it, changing the scene from New York to Paris and putting forward a solution through the comments of Dupin. The innovation here is that the story is told through newspaper cuttings which, although attributed to French papers, are similar to those in the New York press. The cuttings are interspersed with the comments and conclusions of Dupin, who relies for his evidence wholly upon this sometimes contradictory press information, so that this story is the first piece of 'armchair detection', the precursor of all those tales in which the detective solves a crime simply by analysis of and deduction from the material with which he is presented.

The third of the Dupin stories, 'The Purloined Letter', first appeared in the American annual *The Gift*, and was dated 1845 but published in September 1844. The story was the prototype of detective novels and short stories based on the idea that the most apparently unlikely solution is the correct one, with the ingenious addition in Poe's story that what seems most unlikely is really perfectly obvious. A document 'of the last importance' has been 'purloined from the royal apartments'. The identity of the person who took it is known, but he is a Minister, too important to be arrested without proof. The police search without success, every night for three months, the hotel in which the Minister lives. They probe cushions with needles, remove table tops, look for cavities in bed legs, examine the rungs of every chair and the moss between bricks, measure the thickness of book covers to see if the bindings have been tampered with. At the end of all this Dupin pays a visit to the hotel and sees the letter at once. It is in full view, placed in 'a trumpery filigree card-rack of pasteboard', soiled and crumpled and torn nearly in two across the middle. It has been put into a place so obvious that the police have ignored it. Dupin goes to see the Minister again, and takes the letter when a diversion is created in the street with a musket by a man in his pay.

These three tales are directly associated with the detective story as we know it, but 'The Gold-Bug' and '"Thou Art The Man"' are so evidently the forerunners of much in later fiction that they should not be ignored. 'The Gold-Bug' is a puzzle story, the interest of which is linked to the mystery of the apparently sane Legrand's insistence that the Scarabaeus he has discovered is 'a bug of real gold'. We know from the beginning that Legrand will somehow be able to justify this statement, and he does so by deciphering a code on a scrap of paper left by the pirate Captain Kidd. Looked at in one way, the story is no more than a fictional exemplification of the principles laid down by Poe in his entertaining essay on cryptography, although the protagonist and the marshy island on which the bug is found have his characteristic imaginative strangeness, but many later writers are in debt to it. The directions for finding the pirates' treasure in *Treasure Island* and the Sherlock Holmes code story 'The Dancing Men' (in which the cipher is a simple one, like that of 'The Gold-Bug', based on the predominance of the letter 'e') are among the first of the many stories and passages in books that would not have been written but for the example of Poe. '"Thou Art The Man"' blends Poe's interest in detection with the obsession about the narrow barrier between life and death shown in such a story as 'Facts in the Case of M. Valdemar', in which the body of a man who has been in a coma for seven months is roused to speech by mesmerism before disintegrating into 'a nearly liquid mess of loathsome – of detestable putrescence'. '"Thou Art The Man"' is a murder mystery. The wealthy Barnabas Rattleborough has disappeared, and several clues indicating that he has been murdered are found by his friend Charley Goodfellow, all of them leading to the conclusion that Rattleborough has been murdered by his dissipated nephew, Pennifeather. They include a bloodstained waistcoat and knife, both belonging to the nephew, and a bullet found in Rattleborough's dead horse, 'exactly adapted to the bore of Mr Pennifeather's rifle' and containing 'a flaw or seam' which 'corresponds precisely with an accidental ridge or elevation in a pair of moulds acknowledged by the accused himself to be his own property'. At a party given by Goodfellow to celebrate the arrival of a case of Château-Margaux, however, the case proves to contain not wine but the 'bruised, bloody and nearly putrid' corpse of Rattleborough, who sits up, looks at Goodfellow, and says clearly, 'Thou art the man.' A confession follows, with the revelation that all the false clues have been planted by Good-fellow, and the further revelation by the narrator that he had found the body, obtained the jack-in-the-box effect by thrusting whalebone down the corpse's throat and then doubling it up in the case, and used his ventriloquial ability to produce the few words of accusation. The original-ity of this improbable story from the detective point of view rests in the laying of false clues, in the fact that this is the first use of elementary ballistics, and in the commission of the crime by the most unlikely person. (Although actually the tone is one of such insistent levity about the absolute straightforwardness of 'old Charley Goodfellow', and indeed of anybody named Charles, that Poe clearly did not intend to deceive his readers.)

Here, then, is the announcement of the themes which later writers were to use, expand, elaborate: but Poe's originality does not end with the provision of material for plots used by writers who may well not have read his stories. He invented also the first detective of fiction, the Chevalier C. Auguste Dupin, and established the convention by which the brilliant intelligence of the detective is made to shine more brightly through the comparative obtuseness of his friend who tells the story. For nearly a century this was to be a fixed pattern for most detective stories. The friend might be exceptionally thick-headed like Dr Watson, Poirot's companion Captain Hastings, or Philo Vance's District Attorney, John F.-X. Markham, he might be a more or less neutral receiver of the detective's bright ideas like Ellery Queen's father the Inspector, or Thorndyke's friend Jervis, he might even be allowed his share of natural shrewdness like Hanaud's urbane dilettante, Mr Ricardo, but he had to be there as a recorder. At least that is one's first impression, although like all categorical statements this one has its exceptions. But still, the Dupin pattern of the omniscient amateur detective and his clumsy coadjutor was the one that nine out of ten writers were to follow.

Poe made Dupin in his own image, or rather in the image of what he desired to be. He was 'of an excellent – indeed of an illustrious family', partly because Poe detested the levelling idea of democracy, and partly as compensation for his own upbringing in the care of an unsympathetic foster father. He was poor, but like a romantic hero (and unlike Poe) regarded this very little, managing 'by means of a rigorous economy, to produce the necessaries of life, without troubling himself about its super-fluities'. He believed, as Poe did, in the supreme importance of the intellect, yet a strain of wild romantic feeling led him to close the shutters of the apartment in which he lived at dawn, and to go out into the streets only when 'warned by the clock of the advent of true Darkness'. Like Sherlock Holmes later on (and Conan Doyle fully acknowledged his debt), Dupin is able to interpret the thoughts of his companion by the way in which he reacts to exterior events like being pushed aside by a fruiterer carrying a basket on his head. He solves the problems presented to him by pure analytic deduction. Aristocratic, arrogant and apparently omniscient, Dupin is what Poe often wished he could have been himself, an emotion-less reasoning machine.

A reasoning machine would not be interested in the motives and psychology of people, but only in making correct deductions about their actions. It should be repeated that Poe himself did not regard these stories very seriously. 'These tales of ratiocination owe most of their popularity to being something in a new key,' he wrote to a corres-pondent in 1846. 'I do not mean to say that they are not ingenious – but people think them more ingenious than they are – on account of their method and air of method.' The stories were exercises in analysis on matters that caught the interest of his brilliant mind, and he was right in mentioning their *air* of method, for all of the Dupin stories reveal under examination mistakes that are damaging to them as pieces of rational deduction.

The most notable, and least-known, of these are the criticisms made by Laura Riding of 'The Murders in the Rue Morgue'. They concern the way in which the ape got in and out of the window fastened by a secret spring undiscovered by the police. As she points out, this is in itself a most unlikely arrangement – why should such a mechanism be fitted in a fourth-storey room of an old shabby house? In relation to the window, one cannot do better than quote Miss Riding:

The ape reached the window from the lightning-rod which was five and a half feet away, by a shutter three and a half feet broad which could shut like a door to cover the whole window and was now lying flat against the wall. He grasped the 'trellis-work' on the upper part of the shutter and swung himself into the room, landing unobserved directly on the head of the bed. [The head of the bed partly obstructed the window. *J.S.*] This is impossible. Poe at one point suggests that it was a double-sashed window: he speaks of the 'lower sash'. But he does not say, whether only the lower sash moved, or both sashes, or whether the two sashes were really one single piece. If only the lower sash moved, then the ape, grasping the shutter and kicking himself backwards (frontways is impossible) into the room, would have been obstructed by the upper half of the window from landing directly on the head of the bed, which was pressed close against the window. If only the lower half moved, then it was only the lower half that was open. If, however, the upper sash moved too, the ape, on climbing out and shutting the window behind him, as he is said to have done, could not have fastened this upper sash by the secret 'catch' ... The window would have remained open.

I have never seen any answer made to this detailed criticism by writers about the detective story, who seem to be unaware of it. Poe made corrections in later versions of the story. He increased the length of the broken nail in the window frame, and reduced the distance between house and shutter, but the changes do not dispose of the criticism.

'The Mystery of Marie Rogêt' takes its flavour from the fact that it followed so closely an actual murder case. 'I have handled my design in a manner altogether novel in literature,' Poe wrote on 4 June 1842. 'I believe not only that I have demonstrated the fallacy of the general idea – that the girl was the victim of a gang of ruffians – but have indicated the assassin in a manner which will give renewed impetus to investigators.' Three years after the story's appearance he claimed in a footnote that 'the confessions of two persons ... confirmed, in full, not only the general conclusion, but absolutely all the chief hypothetical details by which that conclusion was attained'. With one or two exceptions critics have taken this statement as being correct, and have said that Poe 'solved' the mystery. In fact he cheated by changing the newspaper stories when he needed to do so, and the case remained unsolved, with the balance of probability being that Mary Rogers died accidentally following an abortion. A year before his death Poe, who had said in the story that 'it was at once evident that murder had been committed', admitted this in a letter: 'The "naval officer" who committed the murder (rather the accidental death arising from an attempt at abortion) confessed it ... but, for the sake of relatives, I must not speak further.' The naval officer existed, although we have only Poe's word for his confession: but the point really is that the story was based upon the idea that Mary Rogers had been murdered, and if she died accidentally the logic of the argument is destroyed.

Poe thought 'The Purloined Letter' to be 'perhaps the best of my tales of ratiocination', and he is probably right. The flaw here, noted by several writers, is not seriously damaging to the story. It lies in the fact that Dupin could have seen only the front or the back of the letter, and therefore could not possibly have observed at the same time the 'large black seal' (on the back) and the address 'in a diminutive female hand' (on the front).

Does such detailed criticism weigh too hard on Poe? It does, in the sense that almost any 'tale of ratiocination' would wilt if subjected to similar examination. Yet the criticism is important, because the prime merit claimed by Poe for his puzzle stories was that they were model exercises in reasoning. If the reasoning is faulty the merit of the stories is reduced. For Poe these stories were above all an expression of his desire to oppose the forces in himself that were, as he said of Dupin, 'enamoured of the night for her own sake'. Against them is posed that longing for the morbid and perverse expressed in stories about a burden of unnamable personal guilt, like 'William Wilson', in which the central character feels himself responsible for 'unspeakable misery and unpardonable crime' and commits moral suicide when he stabs his black-masked double. In the pursuit of some completely original form by this figure of unmistakable genius, the detective and puzzle stories played a small part. Poe's paternity of the detective story is not in dispute, but his fatherhood was unintended. He thought his mistress was Art, but really she was Sensation.

• 3 •

Dickens, Collins, Gaboriau:
The Pattern Forms

(i) The 'Unknown Public'

Poe was the founding father whose genius suggested the themes to be followed by other writers: but the pattern of the detective story as it formed in the eighteen-fifties and -sixties was closely related to the rise in Britain and America of a middle class with increasing leisure, the spread of reading, and the development of detective forces in several countries. Given these social factors, detective stories must inevitably have been written. The form they took was derived from Poe, but a look at their development in Britain shows how well the detective story was suited to the emotional needs of the growing middle class.

In 1858 Wilkie Collins wrote an essay on 'The Unknown Public', which was, he said, 'in a literary sense, hardly beginning, as yet, to read', and suggested that 'the future of English fiction may rest with this Unknown Public which is now waiting to be taught the difference between a good book and a bad'. The Unknown Public had been born with the Industrial Revolution, which brought with it a certain amount of education, strongly opposed by many who felt that to teach farm workers and domestic servants to read was no service either to them or to the country in which they lived. In the Sunday schools set up at the end of the eighteenth century only works tending to the improvement of religious education were read, but the creation of a semi-literate class of skilled workers, small shopkeepers, clerks and domestics had results not intended by Hannah More, who wanted everybody to be able to read religious books, or by the Utilitarians, who thought that 'the diffusion of useful knowledge' must be conducive to 'the future welfare of mankind'.

In the early part of the nineteenth century the high price of novels limited their circulation (the price was often a guinea and a half for a new work, and the sale usually not much more than 1,000 copies) and kept them out of the hands of the new readers, but as always demand created supply. A sub-literature sprang up to satisfy the needs of those who would in any case have found Scott, the best-selling novelist of the time, beyond their scope. It took the form of broadsheets and pamphlets, some of them political, but more concerned with crime. James Catnach published broadsheets and ballads about murders and executions, many of which sold up to a million copies, and other publishers and printers issued what were called 'blue books', abridgements or imitations of Gothic novels in thirty-six or, less often, seventy-two pages, which sold at sixpence. In 1841 Edward Lloyd, later the founder of *Lloyd's Weekly Newspaper*, put out books in weekly parts sold at a penny, which were called 'penny dreadfuls'. The dreadful thing about them was supposed to be their subject matter, although the stories were no more than amalgams of excitement and romance, often belying the promise of such titles as *Vice and its Victim: or, Phoebe, the Peasants' Daughter*. Some stories had a more directly violent or sexual content. G. W. M. Reynolds, who founded first of all *Reynolds' Miscellany* and later, like Lloyd, his own newspaper, wrote a series of enormously long 'Mysteries' which were issued in penny numbers with titles like *Mysteries of the Inquisition* and *Mysteries of the Court of London*. They were no more mysterious than Sue's work on which they were based, but Reynolds's early serials in particular are much concerned with torture and violence, up to the point of what Victorians considered permissible in open publication. In an obituary notice of Reynolds, who died in 1879, the *Bookseller* called him 'the most popular writer of his time'.

By the eighteen-fifties penny dreadfuls were being aimed more particularly at a juvenile market. Their readership changed largely because of the spread of subscription and public libraries, which in its turn reflected the rise of the new class created by the pressures of an increasingly industrial and urban civilization. Circulating libraries had existed in England for a long time, but they were given wide popularity by Charles Edward Mudie, who offered a yearly subscription for one guinea instead of his competitors' two, and arranged for an efficient delivery service in town and country. He found that the greatest demand was for novels, and although of course many of his country subscribers were the clergymen and gentry who had formerly bought books, in towns they were often the families of the highly respectable tradesmen and small businessmen who were anxious to move away from their origins and to assert their recently won privileges. All of these subscribers were able to feel assured that no work of a morally doubtful kind would be offered to them by Mudie, who was a Dissenter and had no hesitation in refusing to stock any book of which he disapproved.

So Mudie's, and other subscription libraries, helped to diffuse reading matter, if not always useful knowledge. They were supplemented by the free – that is, rate-supported – libraries which, after a good deal of opposition in the House of Commons on such grounds as that if the working classes read more they would damage agricultural interests by drinking less, were approved in 1850. Between Parliamentary approval and local readiness to establish libraries at the expense of ratepayers there was a considerable gap, and as late as 1887 only two parishes in London had rate-supported libraries. Their opponents felt that they were a sure road to ruin, and in the early eighteen-nineties a correspondent of the *Evening Standard* wrote of a young man in Brighton who spent all his time at the Public Library 'perusing light literature' and did no work. Another visitor to Brighton library said that 'no greater curse existed than these libraries', and he 'had rather see a young man hanging about a public-house than spending his time in these places'. The free libraries were not used by the gentry. A breakdown of borrowers by occupation at Manchester in the eighteen-fifties showed that 'artisans and mechanics' were by far the largest group of borrowers. Many of them wanted useful or improving books, but the demand for fiction was immediate and grew by what it fed on. As early as the mid fifties about half of the books lent or read at Sheffield Public Library were novels, and as the decades passed it was accepted that the purpose of libraries was to provide entertainment as well as education. Circulating and free libraries presented a threat to ordinary publishing which was countered by the issue of novels in monthly parts, and by the publication of still cheaper editions. The immense success of *Pickwick Papers* in monthly parts was the signal for much popular fiction to appear first in this form, sometimes simultaneously with publication in the new magazines that appeared at the end of the fifties. The first issue of the *Cornhill*, which included an instalment of Trollope's *Framley Parsonage* and Thackeray's *Roundabout Papers*, sold 120,000 copies. Cheap editions flourished too, encouraged greatly by the spread of rail travel and the length of the journeys. Every station of any size had its bookstall, and 'railway novels', most of them yellowbacks with a picture on the front and advertisements at the back, were immensely successful. They sold at a shilling or one and sixpence, which may not seem cheap in comparison with modern paperbacks, but was within the price range of those who travelled by rail and ignored the free library.

This, then, was what Collins called the Unknown Public: a new generation of readers possessing literacy and some leisure, and with a vague but pressing need to read for amusement books which would in some degree confirm the permanence of their own newly won position in society. There were plenty of books in the Railway Library or the free libraries that were written from a social attitude with which they agreed, but not many that expressed the concern they felt about the importance of law and order, their interest in the prevention and punishment of crime.

(ii) The development of the police and detectives

There is a common impression that the Victorian age in Britain was one of settled calm, but that is not the way the early part of it looked to those who lived through it. It was not merely that the existing social order seemed threatened by the Chartist movement, but that the country was in fact a lawless place. Certain areas of London, as of New York and other big cities, were practically immune from visits by the police, and the detection of crime was in the hands of the Bow Street Runners, who were in effect private detectives operating partly for private reward, and widely thought to be susceptible to bribery. Even when a professional paid police force came into existence after the Metropolitan Police Act of 1829, the Bow Street Runners survived for another ten years. They were replaced in 1842 by the Detective Department, which consisted of two inspectors and six sergeants. The first head of the Department had distinguished himself two years before its foundation by what was then an unusual piece of detective work, when he noticed that apparent marks of forcible entry into a house had been faked, and that what appeared to be an 'outside' crime was really an 'inside' one.

It is impossible to understand the romantic aura which spread around detective departments and bureaus without realizing the thankfulness felt by the middle class at their existence. As they grew, the strand in crime writing represented by Godwin, Lytton and Balzac, in which the criminal was often considered romantic and the policeman stupid or corrupt, almost disappeared, although it could still be found in the penny dreadful. The detective, as the protector of established society, gradually replaced the criminal as hero.

In this capacity he was celebrated by Charles Dickens (1812–70), whose articles about various members of the Detective Department in *Household Words* were often expressed in terms of hero-worship. Dickens's ambivalent fascination with crime extended to the psychology of the criminal and the conditions of prison life. In several novels and short stories the idea of murder and its attendant guilt is examined, fretted over, viewed with distaste and even horror, yet considered as an act to which an evil character may be magnetically drawn. The psychological insight in the depiction of a figure like Bradley Headstone in *Our Mutual Friend* sprang no doubt from Dickens's deepening awareness of his own criminal instincts. Our responses to the crimes of violence committed or attempted in the novels, from those of Bill Sikes and Jonas Chuzzlewit onwards, are all marked by our sense of the writer's own involvement.

Dickens's interest in prison conditions and his attempts to ameliorate their harshness were perfectly genuine, although his preference for the Silent System (by which all communication between prisoners was forbidden and infringements severely punished) over the Separate System (by which prisoners occupied individual cells and were masked or veiled when leaving them for religious instruction or any other purpose) may seem to us a liking for one form of barbarism over another. He viewed prisoners with the wrath and fear of one who senses a potential threat to his own social position, and echoed Carlyle in stressing the virtues of purposeless punishment: 'It is a satisfaction to me to see [a] determined thief, swindler, or vagrant, sweating profusely at the treadmill or the crank, and extremely galled to know that he is doing nothing all the time but undergoing *punishment*.'

It was natural that a man holding such views should extol the police, with whom he went out on expeditions, not only in London but also in Liverpool and New York. The articles that Dickens wrote, and others that he sponsored in his magazine *Household Words*, played a considerable part in forming the public view of detectives and changing the hostile or critical working-class attitude to the police. This hostility was based on two grounds: first that the police might be used as the state's arm to suppress reform movements, and second that they were inefficient. When a policeman was stabbed to death while helping to disperse a crowd at a political meeting in the eighteen-thirties the jury brought in a verdict of justifiable homicide. The efficiency in the early days of this collection of out-of-work tradesmen and unskilled labourers may be judged from the fact that in the first eight years of the Metropolitan Police Force's existence 5,000 men were dismissed and another 6,000 resigned. But by Dickens's time these growing pains were almost over, and he praised the imperturbability of the men in blue, although his greatest admiration was reserved for detectives. They were, he found, men of good deportment and unusual intelligence, never lounging or slinking about, showing signs of 'strong mental excitement', and (a common although unreliable test of honesty) 'they all can, and they all do, look full at whomsoever they speak to'. Dickens's particular hero was Inspector Field. When he entered a thieves' den 'every thief here comes before him, like a schoolboy before his schoolmaster'. His eye was keen and roving, he saw everything, he appeared to know everybody and to have access everywhere in criminal society. In the keenness and sagacity of Field (or Wield, as he appeared in other articles), and in his tricks of behaviour like 'the corpulent forefinger which is constantly in juxtaposition with his eyes or nose', we can see the outline of the professional detective of fiction, the bloodhound counterpart to Poe's aristocratic amateur. It is fitting that Dickens should have created the first English fictional police officer, natural that he should have been made in Field's image.

(iii) The pattern forms

'Inspector Bucket of the Detective', as he calls himself, was not precisely the first detective, even in Dickens. Before Bucket there was the insurance company investigator Nadgett in *Martin Chuzzlewit*, who carries cards saying that he follows all sorts of occupations from coal merchant to commission agent. Nadgett runs Jonas Chuzzlewit to earth, although he has to call on the police to make the arrest. Nadgett is a minor character, however, Bucket a major one. He makes his appearance about a third of the way through *Bleak House* (1853), in a manner appropriately unobtrusive, and indeed almost magical. Snagsby the stationer is talking to the lawyer Mr Tulkinghorn, when he is aware of a third person in the room, 'who was not there when he himself came in, and has not since entered by the door or by either of the windows. There is a press in the room, but its hinges have not creaked, nor has a step been audible upon the floor.'

Bucket has several physical resemblances to Field, including his use of a fat forefinger to make points. Like Field he is on familiar terms with law-breakers, has an encyclopedic knowledge of their habits, and is greatly respected by them. He is able to disguise himself when necessary, an attribute no doubt derived from Vidocq. He is not at home among the upper classes, as is shown by his invariably addressing Sir Leicester Dedlock as 'Sir Leicester Dedlock, Baronet', but his plodding assurance is untouched by Sir Leicester's supercilious attitude. He is sympathetic to the poor, and capable of genially offering to fit a second pair of handcuffs on to an arrested man's wrists in case the first pair is uncomfortable. Bucket engages in no spectacular feats of detection, but is shown as a shrewd and sympathetic man. In a general way he serves as a model for many later professional detectives.

Dickens's unfinished last novel, *The Mystery of Edwin Drood*, is sometimes classed as a mystery or detective story. It was left unfinished at a peculiarly tantalizing point, when Drood has disappeared and the movements of the sinister John Jasper are being watched by several people, among them the obviously disguised Datchery. Had the book been finished these puzzles would of course have been resolved, and fascinating though they are in themselves they do not mean that the novel was intended to be, or would have appeared when completed as, a mystery story. An immense amount of ingenuity has been expended in solving these fortuitous puzzles, and the clues left by Dickens (who did not, one should perhaps stress, intend them as clues) and his illustrators can be interpreted in several ways. On the balance of probabilities Mr J. Cuming Walters is reasonable in suggesting that Datchery was Helena Landless in disguise, and that Jasper had killed Edwin, or at least believed that he had killed him, although I would have a small saving bet on the possibility suggested by Mr Michael Innes that Datchery may have been somebody who had not previously entered the story, but was closely connected with one of the leading characters. But these are mysteries related to Dickens's intentions, and probably the completed book would have been a mysterious thriller rather than a detective story, resembling *The Woman in White* rather than *The Moonstone*.

It is by these two books that Dickens's close friend Wilkie Collins (1824–89) is remembered today. Collins is generally regarded, as he was in his own lifetime, as a writer whose merits lie purely in the field of melodrama. 'Mr Collins is in the habit of prefixing prefaces to his stories which might almost lead one to think he looks on himself as an artist,' said the *Pall Mall Gazette* contemptuously in reviewing *The Moonstone*. 'A conjurer at a county fair has as much right to prate about his art ... Is this, then, what fiction has come to? We scarcely see how anything could be meaner.' Yet, as T. S. Eliot has pointed out, in Collins's time 'the best novels *were* thrilling', and neither Collins nor his readers thought of him as writing down to them. In the preface to his second novel, *Basil*, Collins stated a creed from which he never wavered when he said that 'the business of fiction is to exhibit human life' and that it was permissible to depict 'misery and crime' if they were turned to 'a plainly and purely moral purpose'. The intentions of Collins were no less serious than those of Dickens. Both of them pursued, and indeed captured, the Unknown Public, and although Collins was not a genius like his friend, he was a melodramatic writer of the highest class, and perhaps the most skilful plot-constructor of the century.

His first novel which shows any detective element is *Hide and Seek* (1854), in which, as one critic has said, he borrowed Fenimore Cooper's

Leatherstocking, had him scalped by Indians and set him down in London. The element of detection in the story, which relates to the unravelling of the history of an orphan and her mother, is real but slight. Some of the stories in the two collections *After Dark* (1856) and *The Queen of Hearts* (1859) also have a small claim to consideration. 'A Stolen Letter' in the first collection follows Poe's device in 'The Purloined Letter' so closely that it can almost be called a crib, and in the second 'Anne Rodway' is a murder story with an unusually convincing low-life background, and 'The Biter Bit' a comic detective story about a lawyer's clerk who has been accepted as a recruit for the 'Detective Police' and makes an appalling mess of his first and only case. Collins was particularly good at depicting bumptiously self-important characters, and this is one of the few successful comic detective short stories.

The Woman in White (1860) is the liveliest of Collins's crime stories, and the one most full of memorable characters. Upon the basis of an eighteenth-century French case, in which a woman was drugged and imprisoned so that she should be presumed dead and her estate pass to her brother, was built the idea of the substitution of one person for another, effected with the aid of a private asylum. In the interesting article about the book's construction Collins wrote a couple of years before his death, he discussed in detail the development from this original germ, the invention of the Italian Fosco because the crime was too ingenious for an English villain, the obesity which Fosco was given after the story had been begun because this was 'in opposition to the recognized type of villain' (in Victorian days fat men were jolly though sometimes unctuous, for us to be overweight is in itself sinister), the various false starts, and the ingenious shifts of viewpoint by which interest is maintained. But analysis of this kind does not fully account for the quality of the book. Marion Halcombe, almost the only moustached heroine in English fiction, and Fosco come through more clearly than any other Collins characters, and they do so because something about Marion's indomitable determination and about Fosco's charm struck a chord of romantic feeling in their author. This mild, genial little man, whose feet were so tiny that they were too small for women's shoes, had an obsession with physical deformity that is often ludicrous or disagreeable, but is urbanely comic in the picture of Fosco's monstrous fatness. The feeling was accompanied by a penchant for dominating ladies, seen at its most pleasant in Marion. Beyond this, the book has a high-spirited inventiveness that was uncommon even in Victorian fiction. The turns of the plot are always ingenious and often unexpected, and it is not surprising that Collins chose as a summary of his career on his tombstone: 'Author of *The Woman in White* and other works of fiction'.

From the beginning the book was a great success. In England Dickens's *All the Year Round* and in America *Harper's Magazine* began to carry it on the same date, 29 November 1859. On publication day the London crowds queued outside the magazine offices for it. Cloaks, bonnets and perfumes, waltzes and quadrilles, were called by its name. Gladstone cancelled a theatre engagement to go on reading it, and Prince Albert sent a copy to Baron Stockmar. The book established Collins, in the minds of some readers, as a rival to Dickens. It is possible that some feeling of this kind was in Dickens's own mind, for although he published the book as a serial, he animadverted on it with unusual sharpness in a letter saying that 'the construction is wearisome beyond endurance, and there is a vein of obstinate conceit in it that makes enemies of readers'. In spite of a cool critical reception, the first edition of 1,500 copies (in the expensive three-volume form, it should be remembered) was quickly sold.

Judged purely as a novel of event and character, *The Moonstone* (1868) is not as good a book as *The Woman in White*. There are no characters in it equal to Fosco or Marion, and although Drusilla Clack, the spinster with her religious tracts, is a distinct comic figure, many readers have felt that they have had enough of her after a few pages. If we look at the originality of the conception, however, and at the skill shown in ordering the plot, *The Moonstone* is a masterly performance, a feat all the more memorable because shortly after beginning the book Collins was distressed by the illness and death of his mother, and during much of the later writing he was tortured by rheumatic gout so intense that several young men employed to take down from his dictation found his cries of pain unendurable and had to leave. Nothing of this comes through in a narrative told with an assurance, and a skill in varying style and tempo, equal to anything in Victorian literature.

But of course *The Moonstone* is not now judged primarily by these lights, but as the first detective novel written in English. Originality of this kind is something that doesn't last. As Sayers has said in writing about the book, 'when we have grown familiar with its successors and imitators the original classic no longer appears to us to have anything original about it'. This is not, however, quite true of *The Moonstone*. Collins's mind was so ingenious, and his skill in maintaining the deception about the jewel so great, that a reader who has been brought up on modern detective stories and then comes to the book is not likely to feel that this period piece was no doubt very good in its day, but rather that he is reading one of the few crime stories which combine great ingenuity in devising a puzzle with the ability to tell an absorbingly interesting story. The solution to the puzzle is perfectly fair, although its laudanum inspiration may now seem a little unsophisticated, and, as Sayers has said, the foundation for everything that happens later is laid in the first few chapters. The shifting of suspicion from one character to another is done with great adroitness, and the theft of an immensely valuable diamond, with its implied contrast between the mysterious East and the humdrum reality of Victorian life, gives full play to Collins's subdued romanticism. And, as a corrective to this, bringing what Collins sometimes called 'a breath of the Actual', there is Sergeant Cuff.

Cuff was founded upon Inspector Jonathan Whicher of the Detective Department, who appears in his days as a sergeant as 'Witchem' in a *Household Words* article. Whicher's career at the time Collins wrote had been a chequered one. In 1860 he had arrested Constance Kent on a charge of murdering her small brother Francis, and had suffered a blot on his reputation at her acquittal which was not quite wiped away when she confessed five years later. In 1861 he had been responsible in another murder case for the arrest of a man who was undoubtedly innocent. It is likely that the skills of Whicher, who was known before these calamities as 'the Prince of Detectives' were, like those of Field, much exaggerated, but Collins may have had in mind his rehabilitation. He used several details from the Constance Kent case and some of Cuff's deductions resemble those of Whicher, although there was no physical resemblance. Whicher was short, thick-set, pockmarked. Collins's portrait of Cuff, as described by the house-steward Gabriel Betteredge, shows what a splendid eye he had for externals:

A fly from the railway drove up as I reached the lodge: and out got a grizzled elderly man so lean that he looked as if he had not got an ounce of flesh on his bones in any part of him. He was dressed all in decent black, with a white cravat round his neck. His face was as sharp as a hatchet, and the skin of it was as yellow and dry and withered as an autumn leaf. His eyes, of a steely light grey, had a very disconcerting trick, when they encountered your eyes, of looking as if they expected something more from you than you were aware of yourself. His walk was soft; his voice was melancholy; his long lanky fingers were hooked like claws. He might have been a parson, or an undertaker – or anything else you like, except what he really was.

Cuff is, like many later detectives, a master of the apparently irrelevant remark, the unexpected observation. Faced with a problem and asked what is to be done, he trims his nails with a penknife and suggests a turn in the garden and a look at the roses; asked who has stolen the moonstone he says blandly that nobody has stolen it. The fascination of such remarks is that their meaning just eludes us. We feel that we should be able to grasp it by making the proper deductions.

'The first, the longest and the best of modern English detective novels': that was Eliot's description of *The Moonstone*, but its designation as 'the first' should certainly be corrected. Some of the claims for other books have been mentioned, but there is no doubt that the first detective novel, preceding Collins and Gaboriau, was *The Notting Hill Mystery*. This was published in book form in 1865, three years before *The Moonstone*, but first appeared in the magazine *Once a Week*, where publication began in November 1862 and continued well into the following year. Its primacy is thus unquestionable.

Its author, Charles Felix, remains mysterious. He wrote at least three other books, none of them a mystery, and although the name sounds like a pseudonym, research has not revealed another identity. *The Notting Hill Mystery* was no doubt an attempt to repeat the success of *The Woman in White*, with a sinister Baron playing the Fosco role, and although Felix had few of Collins's gifts as a story-teller, his book is in several ways an original work. It includes a map, a practice which was not to become common for a good many years, as well as facsimiles of a marriage certificate and of a fragment torn from a letter. The plot is in some ways strikingly modern in tone. The story is told in letters and reports sent to his employers by Ralph Henderson, investigator for a life assurance company. Their suspicions have been aroused after the death of Madame R by the fact that her husband, the Baron R, has taken out not one but five policies on her life, each in the sum of £5,000. Antimony is suspected as the cause of her death, but the Baron is able to prove that he never himself gave her food or drink. Henderson discovers that the 'Baron' is really a German named Carl Schwartz, and his conclusion is that Schwartz employed mesmeric powers to poison his wife through the sympathetic feeling existing between two sisters, so that poison given to one killed the other. The idea, preposterous to us, seemed less ridiculous to Victorians. The book ends with Henderson asking his employers what, if anything, can be done about a murder committed in this way. The level of the writing is far above Victorian hackwork, although equally far below that of Collins. But the essential point is that the book is a true detective novel, and the first of its kind.

This bow to the ghost of Charles Felix should not reduce appreciation of Collins. The combination of his particular gifts is rare. Perhaps if

Somerset Maugham had written a detective story, instead of a spy story, and if he had been at the top of his form, the result might have been something like *The Moonstone*. Collins himself, in the two decades left to him, never wrote anything approaching in merit his two finest books, although historians of the detective story have surprisingly neglected *The Law and the Lady* (1875). The plot here owes something to the Scottish trial of Madeleine Smith, with its 'Not Proven' verdict. Eustace Macallan, like Madeleine, is tried for poisoning by arsenic and set free by a similar unsatisfactory verdict, and the story is concerned with the efforts of his second wife, Valeria, one of Collins's determined heroines, to prove him innocent. There is a genuine puzzle to be solved, and some parts of the book are excellent, particularly the long account of Eustace's trial. The quality of the writing, however, is very uneven, and the book is marred by one of his more unsuccessful grotesques, the self-styled poet Miserimus Dexter, a sort of legless Quilp.

Collins admired and kept upon his shelves the crime stories of Émile Gaboriau (1833–73), and *The Moonstone* may have been influenced by the French writer's first three crime stories, *L'Affaire Lerouge* (1863), *Le Crime d'Orcival* and *Le Dossier No. 113* (1867) – dates given are those of the original serial publications in which Collins may have seen them, although *L'Affaire Lerouge* first appeared in book form in 1866. Gaboriau was a hack writer of historical and sensational serials whose work was transformed by his discovery of the possibilities of the detective story. Gaboriau, like Dickens and Collins, was fascinated by police work and knew a great deal not only about the operations of the Sûreté, but about the functions of the interrogating judge and the local policeman. A passage in his finest work, the posthumously published long short story, *Le Petit Vieux de Batignolles*, shows that he was aware of the difficulty involved in making his hero a policeman. The narrator, an amateur detective on his first case, accompanies a professional named Méchinet into the Prefecture:

This was the first time in my life that I crossed the threshold of the Prefecture of Police, against which I had hitherto been quite as prejudiced as any other Parisian. Those who study social questions may well ask how it happens that the French police are so generally hated and despised. Even the ordinary street policeman is the object of aversion; and the detective is loathed as intensely as if he were some monstrous horror, in lieu of generally being a most useful servant of society.

It was, then, a daring stroke to create a policeman hero, and Gaboriau sugared the pill by providing an amateur detective who often keeps him company. In *L'Affaire Lerouge*, Gévrol, Chief of the Sûreté, is quickly replaced as the chief investigator by an elderly retired pawnbroker named Père Tabaret, known as 'Tir-au-clair'. It is Tabaret who makes the brilliant deductions by which the crime is solved, explaining them as he goes along to a young policeman named Lecoq, first introduced as a minor character, 'an old offender reconciled with the law'. But although Père Tabaret does not disappear completely – at the end of *Monsieur Lecoq* (1869) he points out to the professional detective the clues he has missed – he moves into the background and Lecoq becomes the central figure, with Gévrol as his butt, and sometimes with a companion of inferior intelligence as his assistant. Gaboriau makes it clear that his hero was nothing like the hated detective of reality. 'The most obtuse shopkeeper is sure that he can scent a detective at twenty paces; a big man with moustaches, and a shining felt hat, dressed in a black, threadbare surtout, carefully buttoned up on account of the absence of linen. Such is the type.' Lecoq is nothing like that. His face is so mobile that he is able to 'mould his features according to his will, as the sculptor moulds clay for modelling'. He is a master of disguise, and on one occasion bitterly reproaches an agent for the inadequacy of his attempt to change his appearance. Unlike Cuff, Bucket or Dupin, he has a distinct eye on the main chance. When as a young detective he writes a report which by implication criticizes the inefficiency of Gévrol and does not sign his name to it, Gaboriau explains that the reason is not modesty but calculation, because 'by hiding oneself on well-chosen occasions, one gains greater notoriety when one emerges from the shadow'.

Lecoq is self-seeking and vain, but he is also honest – it is explained in a later story that the original mention of him as 'an old offender' was the result of a misunderstanding. He has reason to be vain, for his deductive feats are notable. He is the first detective of fiction to make a plaster cast of footprints, improvising for the purpose some old boxes, an earthen dish, plaster which he knocks off a wall, and water. He is the first also to observe that a striking clock may be used to tell the time a crime was committed, when he pushes the long hand of a clock round to half past three and it strikes eleven. He realizes in *Le Crime d'Orcival* that the criminal has deliberately planted the material clues, so that 'I had only, to reach the truth, to take the contrary of that which appearance had indicated'. Since five glasses were on the table the number of people present was 'more or less than five, but they were not five', and since the remains of supper lay on the table, they neither ate nor drank. He is able to tell his assistant that a man they are following is 'of middle age and tall, wore a shaggy brown overcoat, and was probably married as he had a wedding ring on the little finger of his right hand'. The points are explained: his 'heavy and dragging step' shown in convenient snow marked middle age, his height was marked by a block of granite on which he had leaned, the ring appeared through the imprint of his hand in snow, the colour of his coat was indicated by a few flakes of brown wool torn off by a wood splinter. Dupin might at this point have sat back and solved the case, but Lecoq is not an armchair detective. 'We hold the clue; we will follow it to the end. Onward, then,' he cries.

Gaboriau's highly sensational themes often contrast oddly with the sobriety of his detection. The murder has usually been committed to prevent the revelation of a scandal, and passages of detection are interspersed with long explanatory flashbacks about family history. Sometimes the villain turns out to be an aristocrat. In *Monsieur Lecoq* the detective in disguise pursues the murderer on an immense tour of Paris. He conducts a search of a grand mansion but goes away baffled, unable to believe that the nobleman who receives him with weary courtesy is the man he wants. Much of this is tiresome today, but there are compensations other than the passages of detection in the accurate and interesting accounts of aspects of the French legal system and the battles of wits in the dialogues between examining magistrate and accused, from which Simenon probably learned something. And in *Monsieur Lecoq* the detective plays a fascinating game of cat and mouse with the prisoner, which ends with his realization that somehow he has been betrayed, and that the mouse knows exactly what the cat is doing. This is the best of the novels: but *Le Petit Vieux de Batignolles* is undoubtedly his finest piece of work, a story full of tricks and turns, in which the murderer overreaches himself in thinking that the police are certain to discover that his victim is left-handed. They fail to do so, and arrest the right man on a completely false basis of argument. Gaboriau lacked humour, and skill in characterization, but it is going much too far to talk as one critic has done of his tawdry puppetry, dull and irrelevant digressions, and dreary and artificial verbiage. He remains an interesting and still underrated writer, whose crime stories are rooted in sound knowledge of police procedure and marked by a keen analytical intelligence.

Collins and Gaboriau: after Poe, they set the pattern in which detectives were made. Poe created the aristocratic amateur who was to endure, and upon the whole to be supreme, until the Second World War. Collins and Gaboriau gave us the honest professional, often disdained by the amateur, who, as Auden says in relation to Freeman Wills Crofts's Inspector French, 'detects for the sake of the innocent members of society' and succeeds because he has 'the help of all the innocent people in the world who are doing their duty'. After Collins and Gaboriau the professional detective, whether uniformed or in plain clothes, no longer appears in fiction as the corrupt oppressor, but as the protector of the innocent. The detective's changed character in fiction reflected a change in the nature of society, and his standing as a watchdog against evil was only seriously questioned after sixty years, in the work of Dashiell Hammett and Raymond Chandler.

· 4 ·

Interregnum

The decade in which Wilkie Collins was producing his two best books, and in which Gaboriau was creating what was later called the *roman policier*, although his crime stories were first collected together under the title *romans judiciares*, contained some notable crime novels by a writer of still unacknowledged talent, and one of the world's greatest novels, which had its origins in a crime. The notable stories were the work of Joseph Sheridan Le Fanu (1814–73) and the great novel was Fyodor Dostoevsky's *Crime and Punishment*.

I once included *Crime and Punishment* in one of those 'Hundred Best' compilations already mentioned, claiming that a crime and its effects were at the heart of the story. The phrase is accurate, and so is the further comment that Dostoevsky (1821–81) saw more deeply than any other novelist has done into the springs of violence, but I now doubt whether the book should have been included. Dostoevsky moved naturally towards mystery and sensation, both here and in *The Possessed*, and also in *The Brothers Karamazov*, but they were for him only the means through which he expressed concerns far outside the interest of the crime novelist. At their best crime writers can illuminate the condition of society and interpret psychotic states of mind, but they never move like Dostoevsky in mystical regions where spiritual truths are being considered. There are no spiritual implications to be found in Fosco's villainy, but for Dostoevsky the murder committed by Raskolnikov and the wonderful interrogation he suffers at the hands of Porfiry are no more than steps on the road to redemption through guilt. So Dostoevsky will not be considered in detail. Is this a denial of what has already been asserted, that, contrary to Auden's view, the crime story may have the character of art? No: but it does imply that even the best crime story is still a work of art of a peculiar flawed kind, since an appetite for violence and a pleasure in employing a conjurer's sleight of hand seem somehow to be adulterating the finest skills of a novelist. In a way Dostoevsky was a crime novelist, with the true taste for sensational material, but in his case the results far transcend anything the crime novelist achieves or even aims at.

Such considerations do not apply to Le Fanu. This Irish novelist and short story writer has never been popular, either in his own day or in ours, although some of his stories appear occasionally in magazines and his best-known novel, *Uncle Silas*, has been reprinted more than once. He has had no discernible influence on other writers. Yet in the last decade of his life he produced a dozen novels mostly concerned with crime, of which four are worth remembering and one is a brilliant mystery puzzle.

First one should make some qualifications. In one aspect Le Fanu was a romantic writer in the Gothic mode, working half a century after the Gothic novel had faded. His books are full of old houses and castles falling into ruin, his heroines are often at the mercy of implacable and horrifying villains, he took great pleasure in ghost stories, and was fascinated by hints of the supernatural. He was also the most notable Victorian example of a writer who seems not to have revised his original manuscripts, and certainly did not read his proofs, so that a character in his novels may appear with varying Christian names, and there are casual unexplained shifts between first and third person narrative. Le Fanu's merits are not so great that one forgets these things, but he was a writer of remarkable power in creating suspense, at his best a master of plot, and the creator of some of the most satisfying villains in Victorian literature. *Uncle Silas* (1864) is a thriller comparable to *The Woman in White*, but where Collins's literary manner was as genial as his personality, Le Fanu's is effectively chilly. His titular villain is memorable, with his marble face, black eyebrows and silver hair as fine as silk, 'like an apparition in black and white, bloodless, fiery-eyed, with [a] singular look of power, and an expression so bewildering – was it derision, or anguish, or cruelty, or patience?' *The House by the Churchyard* (1863) is in part a rambling Irish historical chronicle, full of thumping humour, but the parts about Dangerfield and his determination to dispose of anybody who knows about his criminal past is on another and higher level. The trepanning through which one of his victims dies is, as Sayers has said, one of the most horrific scenes in this kind of literature. But the book referred to as a brilliant mystery puzzle, *Wylder's Hand* (1864), is Le Fanu's chief contribution in the field of detection. It cannot compete with *The Notting Hill Mystery* for the title of the first detective novel, since there is no detective and no analysis of clues, but it poses a puzzle entirely in the manner of the detective story, and the solution of this puzzle is expertly disguised. The puzzle relates to the disappearance of the vulgar, tough, dissipated Mark Wylder, who goes first to London and then abroad. From various European cities he sends home characteristically rude and aggressive letters, and we have been prepared for his departure by a threat from the villainous Captain Stanley Lake that if necessary he will force Wylder to go abroad. At some point in the course of the story, however, the reader is bound to suspect that Wylder is dead, although the evidence of the letters is so elaborate and convincing that he cannot be sure. (Had Hammett read *Wylder's Hand*? He certainly made use of a similar device in a similar way in *The Thin Man*.) Le Fanu's supreme stroke is to show the reappearance of Wylder just at the moment when we have decided that he must be dead. The book contains two impressive and well-contrasted villains, the yellow-eyed, sleepy, menacing Lake and the snake-like, servile solicitor Larkin. It is too long, but remains a crime story markedly original for its period, and astonishingly ignored. *Checkmate* (1871) is a much weaker story, although it gives us another good villain in Walter Longcluse and introduces the theme of plastic surgery used as a device to escape the law. The operation is described in detail, with Le Fanu's characteristic cold gusto in dealing with such matters.

All this should have been enough to establish Le Fanu as one of the most important originators of the crime novel, but in this respect he has never received acknowledgement. His short stories are from the viewpoint of this study less interesting, since they are mostly supernatural shockers. One or two, however, like 'Mr Justice Harbottle' and 'Green Tea', explore the possibilities of psychotic disorder in an interesting way. Is the monkey that persecutes the pious clergyman Jennings in 'Green Tea' of supernatural origin, or is it a mental delusion? The question is left open.

With these exceptions, there was an interregnum between the time when the detective novel proper appeared, and the publication in 1887 of *A Study in Scarlet*. The explanation is simple. The history of the crime story up to the end of the nineteenth century is linked chiefly with the few writers of talent who were interested in police work, and the form itself was not yet sufficiently attractive to the public, or sufficiently well-defined, to receive much attention from hacks. There was a division still between those who in England read penny dreadfuls and in America the dime novels which began to appear in 1872, and the readers of novels which were expected to offer something a little more serious.

A few names should be recorded. Major Arthur Griffiths, an Inspector of Prisons and the author of a standard three-volume work on *Mysteries of Police and Crime*, wrote a good many crime stories and historical romances, but although a few like *Fast and Loose* (1885) and *Locked Up*

(1887) include detectives of sorts, the books are fifth-rate thrillers redeemed only by the writer's knowledge of criminal habits. Fergus Hume's *Mystery of a Hansom Cab* (1886) is a curiosity because of the enormous sale it inexplicably achieved. Writing in 1896, Hume (1859–1932) claimed that the book had sold 375,000 copies in Britain alone, with 'some few editions in the United States of America'. When it was published Hume was a New Zealand barrister in his middle twenties, and there is no reason to doubt the essential truth of his story that the book was rejected by publishers in Australia on the ground that 'no Colonial could write anything worth reading', that he then published it in that country at his own expense with some success, and that he sold the copyright for £50 to a group of speculators calling themselves 'The Hansom Cab Publishing Company' who reaped the benefit of his work. At least, this account has never been seriously contradicted. His description of the way in which the idea for the book was generated is interesting, because it shows how widespread was the influence of Gaboriau:

I enquired of a leading Melbourne bookseller what style of book he sold most of. He replied that the detective stories of Gaboriau had a large sale; and as, at this time, I had never even heard of this author, I bought all his works and ... determined to write a book of the same class; containing a mystery, a murder, and a description of low life in Melbourne. This was the origin of the 'Cab'.

It is customary to say that the book is without any kind of merit, but in fact *The Mystery of a Hansom Cab* is a reasonably good imitation of Gaboriau, containing some convincing scenes of low life. Was its success attributable to the fact that the murder took place in a hansom cab? Perhaps the setting had something to do with it. Hume wrote more than a hundred other detective stories and thrillers, none of which had any comparable success, although they earned him a comfortable enough living.

Gaboriau remained consistently popular for a long time after his death, and his chief French disciple Fortuné du Boisgobey (1824–91) paid the dead master the dubious compliment of taking over his most famous character. *La Vieillesse de Monsieur Lecoq* (1875) finds the detective calling himself in old age Lecoq de Gentilly, adding a 'de' to his name 'in view of pushing his son, whom he wished to take rank among a class of people who do not disdain the appearance of nobility'. The son, Louis, is accused of murder and about to be guillotined when Lecoq runs down the real murderer. The detective work is shaky, as might be expected from a man in his old age. Although du Boisgobey's name was coupled with that of Gaboriau, and although *The Times* praised his facility in creating incidents and unravelling plots, he is almost purely a sensational writer, lacking the analytical skill and the interest in police procedure that distinguished his master.

In America, Anna Katharine Green (1846–1935) became the first woman to write a detective novel. *The Leavenworth Case* (1878) was immensely successful, perhaps partly because of her sex, partly because of the familiarity she showed with legal and criminal matters (her father was a criminal lawyer), and partly – one is bound to think – because there were so few detective novels being written. The drearily sentimental story shifts suspicion from one lovely Leavenworth sister to another after Mr Leavenworth has been murdered, and there are passages of pious moralizing which are pulled through only with the most dogged persistence. (The book was the favourite detective story of Prime Minister Stanley Baldwin, a fact tending to confirm one's gloomy view of politicians' literary taste.) Some compensation is offered by a lively detective named Ebenezer Gryce, in the Bucket and Cuff working-man style. He is a city detective who could never, it is frankly said, pass for a gentleman. 'It is not for me to suspect but to detect,' Gryce says on an early page, and he does quite a bit of detection, although his deduction when he sees a line of smut on the cylinder of a gun after the barrel has been cleaned seems rather dubious. Gryce knew then, he says, that no woman had committed the murder. 'Did you ever know a woman who cleaned a pistol, or who knew the object of doing so? No. They can fire them and do; but after firing them they do not clean them.' There are one or two other interesting details in the book, like the use of mirror writing and the detailed medical evidence, but as a story it is extremely feeble. Green wrote many other detective stories, including some in which Gryce is a prominent character, but those I have read are on the level of *The Leavenworth Case*.

Samuel Langhorne Clemens (1835–1910), better known as Mark Twain, had less relationship to the detective story than some of his American admirers have claimed. Twain did, however, show considerable interest in the mechanics of detection. As Ellery Queen has pointed out, *Life on the Mississippi* (1883) contains a chapter about fingerprints as a means of identification, and in *Pudd'nhead Wilson* (1894) fingerprint identification is the turning point of the plot. Twain was unique among writers in appreciating the importance of fingerprints at a time when Galton's *Fingerprints* had only recently been published, and long before they were used by the police in America. *A Double-Barrelled Detective Story* (1902), Twain's last essay in detection, is a feebly humorous slap at the omniscience of Sherlock Holmes.

It seems surprising in retrospect that Robert Louis Stevenson (1850–94) made no serious attempt to write a detective story. Stevenson preferred an episodic tale to one with a tightly constructed plot, and he had no taste for the details of police work, but the creation of a mysterious atmosphere came naturally to him, and he was interested in the borderland where adventure turned into crime. But although Stevenson hovered on the brink in some books that he wrote with his stepson, Lloyd Osbourne, he never took the plunge. *The Wrong Box* (1888), with its dead body turning up in all sorts of places, is in part a lively parody of some absurdities in French detection, and one of the characters has written a detective story with the excellent title *Who Put Back the Clock?*, but it is basically a farce. The loosely linked tales in *The New Arabian Nights* (1882), in particular 'The Suicide Club' with its pattern of suicide and murder decided by the choice of a card, and the story opening with the scene praised by Henry James of the young man who enters 'an Oyster Bar in the immediate neighbourhood of Leicester Square' accompanied by two commissionaires each carrying a dish of cream tarts which he presses upon the company, certainly qualify the book for the category of thriller. *The Wrecker* is a blend of thriller and adventure story and there are elements of mystery in stories as disparate as *Treasure Island* and *The Dynamiter*. But Stevenson was attracted by the romance of mystery, not the science of detection. He put his feelings clearly in a note on *The Wrecker* rejecting the 'police novel or mystery story' because of that 'appearance of insincerity and shallowness of tone, which seems its inevitable drawback', so that the result was 'enthralling but insignificant, like a game of chess, not a work of human art'. This is a telling comment on many detective stories, not merely those of Stevenson's time.

One has a sense, in this twenty years of mostly indifferent work, of a literary form awaiting its proper medium. The form was there, the tale of detection with its apparatus of clues. The central character had arrived too, the aristocratic or workaday detective who operated by the naphtha glare of pure reason or the candlelight of common sense. In the last twenty years of the nineteenth century, through the development of printing techniques and the rise in the level of education, the perfect medium appeared: the popular periodical, selling at a low price and publishing plenty of fiction and non-fiction which, although always light and mostly trivial, was conceived on a level above that of the penny dreadful and the dime novel.

'I am the average man. I know what he wants,' said George Newnes, who founded in 1880 the weekly *Tit-Bits*, a penny paper which offered more or less informative and lively fragments gathered from other periodicals, books and newspapers, together with contributions from readers. The formula flourished, and was copied or improved on in Alfred Harmsworth's *Answers* and Cyril Pearson's *Pearson's Weekly*. In 1891 Newnes used some of the *Tit-Bits* profits for a more ambitious publication, *The Strand Magazine*. He modelled the periodical on the successful American magazines *Harper's* and *Scribner's*, asking for a picture on every page and a supply of good, exciting stories. The first issue appeared in January 1891 and sold 300,000 copies. In July the first short story about Sherlock Holmes was published in the *Strand*. It was one in a series of six for which the editor, Greenhough Smith, paid Dr A. C. Doyle of 2 Devonshire Place, London W, thirty guineas each. Asked for a second series, Doyle raised his fee to fifty guineas. He was surprised when this figure was unquestioningly accepted.

As soon as the Holmes short stories began to appear, editors, readers and writers half-consciously realized that the detective story had found its natural place in popular literature. There was to be a crime or an attempted crime, a problem, a solution reached through the skill of the detective, and all this was to be compassed within a few thousand words. Public response was immediate. *The Strand* soon reached a circulation of 500,000 which was maintained for many years. In America two of the leading periodicals of the time were *Ladies' Home Journal*, which had a circulation of nearly one million by the end of the century, and *Munsey's Magazine* with a circulation of 700,000. Neither of these much resembled the *Strand*, but both used Doyle stories, and so did *McClure's* (circulation of 370,000 in 1900), in which the author invested $5,000 made from an American lecture tour. After the immense success of the Holmes stories other editors asked for something similar, and it was quickly supplied. In this first flowering of the detective story it was seen as being essentially a short story, one which neither permitted nor demanded much in the way of characterization but allowed almost unbounded scope to ingenuity. Often an original talent like that shown by Doyle in the Holmes short stories may be submerged by the subtle grace-notes of his successors, but this has not happened in the case of Sherlock Holmes. For nearly three decades the short story remained the dominant form in crime fiction, and hundreds of complicated and clever short stories were written, but looking back on the ingenious twists and turns of Chesterton and Futrelle, Freeman and Orczy and Post, it is plain that in most of the important things the best stories about Sherlock Holmes excelled them all.

• 5 •

The Case of Sherlock Holmes

(i) The character

In 1886 Arthur Conan Doyle, an unsuccessful doctor in his middle twenties living at Southsea in Hampshire, made some notes concerning an idea for a character rather than a story, even though the notes were headed 'A Study in Scarlet'. They began 'Ormond Sacker – from Afghanistan' ('from Soudan' had been crossed out). 'Lived at 221 B Upper Baker Street with Sherrinford Holmes.' A brief outline of Holmes's characteristics followed, and a couple of fragments of dialogue. With Ormond Sacker turned into Dr John H. Watson and Sherrinford changed to Sherlock, the characters came into being. *A Study in Scarlet* was written, and rejected by several publishers before, in October 1886, Ward, Lock offered Doyle £25 for the copyright, although they said that they 'could not publish it this year as the market is flooded at present with cheap fiction'. The story appeared in *Beeton's Christmas Annual* for 1887, and attracted little attention, although it was reprinted in each of the succeeding years. In America the editor of *Lippincott's Magazine* found it interesting, and Doyle was asked to meet a Lippincott representative paying a visit to London. As the result of a dinner at which Oscar Wilde was also present, both Wilde and Doyle wrote books for the magazine. Wilde's book was *The Picture of Dorian Gray* and Doyle's was *The Sign of the Four*, which appeared in *Lippincott's* in February 1890. Later in the year it was published in London as *The Sign of Four*, which has been since then the accepted title.

It cannot be said that either of Doyle's first two Holmes books is a very original or well-devised novel. It has been suggested that he took the basic plot of *A Study in Scarlet* from an episode in *The Dynamiter*, and in *The Sign of Four* the Indian sub-plot with its theme of a treasure which is cursed owes an obvious debt to *The Moonstone*. The use of these themes is an embarrassment to Doyle because they involve passages in which detection is suspended and Holmes does not appear. After the arrest of Jefferson Hope, not much more than halfway through *A Study in Scarlet*, we are

64

concerned with a historical adventure story in Utah. *The Sign of Four* is better organized, but the tale of the treasure plays a disproportionately large part in what is after all a short novel. The prime defect of both books, indeed, is that they could have been condensed to short stories. Doyle did not think of these books in terms of novels – as Collins, for example, conceived *The Moonstone* – but as problems, each of which could have been worked out in the form of a short story.

But if the two novels, and indeed the two other long Holmes stories that Doyle wrote, cannot be counted as successes, Sherlock Holmes triumphs as a character from the moment we meet him. In appearance, manner, and in the style of his deductions, he was based on the consulting surgeon at the Edinburgh Infirmary, Dr Joseph Bell, but although Bell was the model, Holmes was the product of Doyle's own invention. In a sense Doyle was Sherlock Holmes (he showed his own skill in the analysis of more than one real-life murder case), just as one need only look at a photograph to see that he contained elements of Watson.

In his emotional reactions Doyle was a super-typical Victorian, a bluff Imperialist extrovert who congratulated himself on having 'the strongest influence over young men, especially young athletic sporting men, of any one in England (bar Kipling)', and therefore felt it a duty to volunteer for the South African War. Twenty years later he condemned the 'liquid putrescence' of the Russian Revolution and said that Post Impressionism and Futurism were part of 'a wave of artistic and intellectual insanity' sweeping across Europe. Yet Doyle was also a man of generous impulses, even when they ran counter to his own beliefs. He drew up the petition for Roger Casement's reprieve, and did not flinch when he was shown the Black Diaries, remarking with his characteristic common sense that 'as no possible sexual offence could be as bad as suborning soldiers from their duty, I was not diverted from my purpose' by the apparent revelation of Casement's homosexuality. It seems at first sight astonishing that this Victorian philistine should have created an egocentric drug-taking hero so alien from his own beliefs. The answer to this puzzle has already been suggested. The passion for absolutes of belief and behaviour, the desire to wipe the slate clean of error and impurity through some saving supernatural grace, shows constantly in Victorian life below the surface of stolid adherence to established order. The influence of Nietzsche and Wagner was widespread, and affected even those who thought like Doyle that Nietzsche's philosophy was 'openly founded in lunacy', affected indeed those who had never heard of Nietzsche. Part of Holmes's attraction was that, far more than any of his later rivals, he was so evidently a Nietzschean superior man. It was comforting to have such a man on one's side.

So much for the background. The character of the greatest of Great Detectives is in accordance with it. At first he outrages several of the period's conventions. When introduced to us he takes drugs – at the beginning of *The Sign of Four* he has been on three cocaine injections a day for months – and has fits of depression when he lies upon a sofa 'for days on end . . . hardly uttering a word or moving a muscle from morning to night'. He plays the violin extremely well, but when left to himself will merely 'scrape carelessly at the fiddle thrown across his knee'. In an age that admired above all things the acquisition of knowledge he is egotistically proud of the vast fields of his ignorance. When Watson jots down Holmes's abilities and limitations he puts 'nil' against his knowledge of literature, philosophy and astronomy, although he acknowledges the detective's 'profound' knowledge of chemistry and his limited skills in botany, geology and anatomy.

This summary comes in *A Study in Scarlet*, and later the portrait is modified. It is explained that he really only turned to cocaine 'as a protest against the monotony of existence', and the man who did not know the name of Carlyle and expressed total lack of interest in the solar system is able on other occasions to talk about Waterloo and Marengo, to quote Goethe and compare Richter to – Carlyle. A good many similar anomalies can be found in the whole saga. They reflect in part the small value attached to the stories by Doyle, and in part the need (which became increasingly insistent with each new series of stories) to make Holmes a more sympathetic figure. The very first short story, 'A Scandal in Bohemia', makes it clear that there will be no love interest. 'As a lover, he would have placed himself in a false position. He never spoke of the softer passions, save with a gibe and a sneer.' Doyle was not in the least misanthropic or misogynistic but he recognized in his readers the need for Holmes to be a man immune from ordinary human weaknesses and passions. It remains part of his attraction that he 'loathe[s] every form of society with his whole Bohemian soul', and upon occasions disregards the law. So, in 'The Abbey Grange' Holmes and Watson jointly decide that they will not reveal to the police the identity of the man who killed Sir Eustace Brackenstall; in 'Charles Augustus Milverton' they see a woman empty 'barrel after barrel' of her revolver into the blackmailer's body and then grind her heel into his face without feeling that they need to do anything about it; in 'The Blue Carbuncle' Holmes condones a felony in the hope that he is saving a soul. When the law cannot dispense justice,

Holmes does so himself. He is a final court of appeal and the idea that such a court might exist, personified by an individual, was permanently comforting to his readers.

If a man is superior to others, his superiority must be demonstrated. It is a weakness in many of Holmes's disciples that their genius is announced but not proved. Here Doyle is supreme. The claim made in *A Study in Scarlet*, that 'by a man's finger-nails, by his coat-sleeve, by his boot, by his trouser-knees, by his expression, by his shirt-cuffs – by each of these things a man's calling is plainly revealed', is justified again and again. A single instance may be allowed to serve for the dozens in the stories. Given a battered old felt hat of which Watson can make nothing, Holmes is able to deduce that the owner is highly intellectual, was fairly well-to-do but is now poor, and has been going downhill, probably under the influence of drink: 'This may account for the obvious fact that his wife has ceased to love him.' Holmes not only makes these deductions, but explains them in plausible detail. Would it be possible sometimes to reach different conclusions? No doubt, but the pleasure one gets from this opening up of a fine machine, so that every cog in it can be seen revolving, is hardly to be overestimated. Other writers try to mystify with one conclusion drawn from a fact unnoticed by the reader, where Doyle gives us a dozen, and almost always the deductions are those we might have made ourselves. This is perfectly exemplified in what is perhaps the most famous single short passage of Holmesian dialogue:

'Is there any other point to which you would wish to draw my attention?'
'To the curious incident of the dog in the night-time.'
'The dog did nothing in the night-time.'
'That was the curious incident.'

A baffling fragment? The explanation is perfect. The dog did not bark, although somebody had entered the stables where he was on watch and taken out a horse. The significance of the incident is that the intruder must have been somebody well known to the dog. The passage shows, incidentally, a sensibility to phrasing which is not often noticed as one of Doyle's characteristics. Change the words 'in the night-time' to what might superficially seem the more natural 'during the night' and the sentences run much less happily.

Holmes was very much superior to most of his fellow detectives in his mastery of disguise. In the first of the short stories he appears as a drunken-looking groom and a Nonconformist clergyman. He can be a tall, thin old man, an elderly deformed man able to take a foot off his stature for hours on end – one need not go on. Doyle no doubt took the ideas for some of these disguises from Vidocq, as he took Holmes's style of interpreting thoughts from Poe and the form of some deductions from Gaboriau. The debts were acknowledged, although Holmes himself called Dupin a very inferior fellow and Lecoq a miserable bungler, but out of the borrowings Doyle made something completely his own. Many detectives, when we look at them closely, are not much more than the bag of tricks which their creator has given them as their stock-in-trade. Like them, Holmes is conceived in outline, with attributes that are really substitutes for characterization – the eagle eye, the misanthropy, the remoteness. It is a mark again of Doyle's skill that Sherlock Holmes comes through to us as a man who genuinely had a genius for his occupation.

(ii) The stories and their author

The creator of Sherlock Holmes had other, and as he thought better, claims to consideration as a writer. Arthur Conan Doyle, later Sir Arthur (1859–1930), was one of those all-rounders whose lives blended literature and action in a way that is now very rare. He took himself most seriously as a historical novelist and when, shortly after the publication of *The Sign of Four*, he finished a book and threw the pen across the room with a cry of 'That's done it!', he was not referring to a Holmes story but to the completion of *The White Company*, the historical novel which ranks with *Micah Clarke* as his best work in this field. If his belief that *The White Company* 'would live and would illuminate our national traditions' has not come true in the sense that his historical books are not taken seriously by critics, it is because with all his virtues of lucidity and descriptive power in dealing with action, Doyle did not care to look far into character. The organizing ability shown even in ephemeral work like his history of the Boer War, the analytic skill he showed in examining the case of Oscar Slater and Edalji, were not accompanied by much depth of imagination. The people in his books and the things that happen to them are conceived on a level not far removed from that of boys' adventure stories. The supremacy of the Holmes stories in his work lies in the fact that only in these tales of the Superman who was also the Great Outsider did this intelligent bourgeois find his imagination truly set free.

Doyle was a fine story-teller, and one quality that keeps the Holmes tales alive where so much work by his immediate successors is dead, is that they are such good stories. We are hardly ever offered a mere puzzle, but a story about people briefly but vividly seen, which encompasses a problem. The skill with which Dr Grimesby Roylott is built up as an infinitely menacing figure in 'The Speckled Band' is typical. His actual appearance in the story takes up only a page and a half, yet there are few more convincing characters in this kind of fiction. When the mechanics of the story are examined, we see that an impression of Roylott is first created through Helen Stoner's unwilling description of her stepfather's strength and brutality. Then there is Roylott's visit to Holmes and the poker-bending incident, and finally the visit to Stoke Moran and the creation of a sinister atmosphere through clues like the dummy bell-rope, the saucer of milk, the ventilator, which add to our understanding of Roylott's nature. Consummately skilful writing of this kind marks the best of the stories, and many of them, like 'The Musgrave Ritual', are close to the tales of adventure in which Doyle delighted. The stories often begin with the arrival of a client in trouble, and frequently the occasion is marked by a display of Holmesian intellectual fireworks. In 'The Resident Patient' the sparking point for curiosity is the readiness of Blessington to start up Dr Percy Trevelyan in his own practice, in 'The Red-Headed League' the idea of a league of 'all red-headed men who are sound in body and mind', in 'The Missing Three-Quarter' the arrival of the telegram which says: 'Terrible misfortune. Right wing three-quarter missing.' It may seem that any professional crime writer should be able to arrest a reader's attention in this way, but anybody who has attempted it knows that this is at least as difficult as constructing a satisfactory puzzle.

Sometimes this opening passage leads on to the revelation of a crime committed or in preparation, sometimes it opens out into an adventure story, sometimes it shifts back into the past and an explanation by the visitor. Occasionally Watson apologizes for the small part played by Holmes in a story, emphasizing the fact that what concerned Doyle was the adventure as much as the detection. Some themes are repeated. The purpose of the deception in 'The Red-Headed League' is to get the pawnbroker Jabez Wilson out of his shop for a number of hours each day. Mr Hall Pycroft's curious assignment to mark off all the hardware sellers in Paris in a trade directory in 'The Stockbroker's Clerk' is similarly motivated by the need to get him out of London so that a crook may take up the job Pycroft has just been offered, and the theme is repeated again in 'The Three Garridebs' where this unusual surname is used to get Nathan Garrideb out of the room which he never leaves except to drive down to Sotheby's or Christie's. Many stories have a particular touch which is wholly Doyle's, like the task set the gull in 'The Red-Headed League' of copying out the whole of the *Encyclopaedia Britannica*, and the name invented by Holmes in 'The Three Garridebs' to prove that the man who calls himself John Garrideb is an impostor. The trap set is conventional, but the name of the invented character, Dr Lysander Starr, is peculiarly felicitous. ('"Good old Dr Starr" said our visitor. "His name is still honoured."') Such freshness of detail gives continual pleasure.

So of course does the period atmosphere which has been much and rightly praised. The London in which Holmes and Watson move, with frequent trips to a Surrey or Hampshire or Devon which proves to be no less sinister ('It is my belief, Watson, founded upon my experience, that the lowest and vilest alleys in London do not present a more dreadful record of sin than does the smiling and beautiful countryside,' Holmes says, and the events in 'The Copper Beeches' from which this comment is taken are horrible enough), has been described by other writers, but Doyle's world of four-wheelers from which intending husbands disappear, of opium dens lying between slop and gin shops, and of hotels whose expensiveness is shown by their charges of eight shillings for a bed and eightpence for a glass of sherry, remains uniquely flavoursome. We should remember, as most critics do not, that this was not 'period' material for Doyle when the first three collections of short stories and three of the four novels were written. He was writing of the world around him, a world transformed by his imagination. People think of Holmes's London as permanently dark and foggy, and one specialist in the stories has said that Holmes and Watson are 'wrapped in tobacco smoke and London fog', but the effect is largely created by the tone of Doyle's writing. It is rarely that the 'dense drizzly fog' mentioned in *The Sign of Four* or the 'opalescent London reek' of 'The Abbey Grange' appear in other stories. The weather is described only briefly in most of the tales, in phrases like 'a cold, frosty winter's evening', 'a close, rainy day in October', or 'a bleak, windy day towards the end of March'. If we try, again, to see how the magic works, it is difficult to get nearer than saying that it is somehow connected with the personalities of Holmes and Watson. The Baker Street establishment is so firmly realized, the small sitting room with chemicals about every-where, criminal relics in the butter dish, unanswered letters fixed by a jack-knife into the mantelpiece, 'VR' done in bullet marks on the wall opposite Holmes's armchair, and Mrs Hudson equally ready to provide a fresh plate of rashers and eggs or to shift the figure that Holmes has put into his window to lure Colonel Moran, that it pervades the surrounding scene. The later stories are less successful in conveying the aura of the Holmesian world, and this is because when *His Last Bow* (1917) and *The Casebook of Sherlock Holmes* (1927) appeared, Doyle was really writing of the past. A few of the stories are set in the twentieth century, but more of them go back to the nineties, and the period details in them are much less convincing.

There are weaknesses in the stories, caused by casual construction, or by contradiction of other material within the canon. The weaknesses of construction are most apparent in the novels. Only *The Hound of the Baskervilles* can be called a coherent novel, and even here the problem is not difficult to solve, and the identity of the murderer is revealed two thirds of the way through. The grip of this novel is exerted in the way in which Doyle makes us feel the terror and loneliness of the Devon moors, implied in the disturbed feelings of the sober doctor who discovers beside the body of Sir Charles Baskerville 'the footprints of a gigantic hound!' But there are flaws in the short stories too. Some have already been mentioned, but one or two may be added. In 'The Norwood Builder' the 'charred organic remains' which temporarily persuade both Holmes and Lestrade that Mr Jonas Oldacre is dead turn out to be rabbit bones, which should surely not have deceived a Great Detective. (In 'Wistaria Lodge', set in 1892, bones are examined and immediately pronounced by a doctor – not Watson – to be non-human.) Doyle himself remarked on the number of solecisms in 'Silver Blaze' that had been pointed out to him by racing men. In 'A Case of Identity' we are asked to believe that Mary Sutherland's short sight stopped her from recognizing the stepfather with whom she lived when he presented himself disguised apparently merely by tinted glasses and a moustache, and in 'The Man with the Twisted Lip' that Inspector Bradstreet did not spot the red wig, the painted face, the scar running from eye to chin that was presumably also painted, and the twisted lip created by 'a small slip of flesh-coloured plaster'. Bradstreet was admittedly unobservant, but for such negligence he should have been demoted to sergeant. The reader can make his own list of errors and improbabilities, and his own list, too, of the contradictions in the statements made by and about Holmes and Watson at different times.

Historians of the detective story have been hard upon such casualness. Sayers thought that Doyle did not always play fair with the reader, and Howard Haycraft has said that although Holmes and Watson are immortal, it is 'no disparagement' to say that the stories are 'all too frequently loose, obvious, imitative, trite, and repetitious in device and theme'. One would not like to be subject to Haycraft in a disparaging mood; but the answer to be made by those who think more highly of the stories is that Doyle 'plays fair' in his deductions more often than any other writer of short stories, in the sense that nine times out of ten we see the clue from which Holmes makes his deductions, and that some of Haycraft's objections are wrong and others of little importance. The stories are not trite, and they are obvious only in the sense that we can guess the villain, not the means by which the villainy is carried out. A few stories, and more deductions, are derived from Poe and Gaboriau, but almost always Doyle successfully turns the ideas of others to his own original uses, and the repetitiousness mostly comes in the last two volumes of short stories, which are admittedly much inferior to the first three. One is bound to agree, as Doyle agreed, with the remark that Holmes 'may not have been killed when he fell over the cliff, but he was never quite the same man afterwards'.

But to give much weight to such criticism is to fall into the error of preferring technical perfection to skill in story-telling. Many post-Holmes short stories presented better puzzles than any of Doyle's, but almost all were infinitely inferior as stories. Of the fifty-six short stories about Holmes, roughly half are tales which can be read again and again with pleasure, for the creation of a scene and an atmosphere, and for the deductions made by Holmes from evidence presented to the reader. The only other writers of crime short stories whose work can be re-read in the same way, although not for quite the same reasons, are G. K. Chesterton and Stanley Ellin.

(iii) The Holmes myth

Many creators of famous detectives would have killed them off if this had been a practical – that is, financial – possibility. Conan Doyle was perhaps the first to experience this Old Man of the Sea feeling. He worked on the first set of Holmes stories with care, although he did not take them seriously, and he thought of killing off the detective at the end of the series because 'he takes my mind from better things'. At the end of the second collection he sent Holmes and Moriarty plunging over the Reichenbach Falls, and felt a great sense of relief. As he wrote to a friend about Holmes: 'I have had such an overdose of him that I feel towards him as I do towards pâté de foie gras, of which I once ate too much, so that the name of it gives me a sickly feeling to this day.'

But it is not so easy to kill a myth. Doyle received hundreds of letters imploring him to bring Holmes back, and 'Let's Keep Holmes Alive' clubs were started in several American cities. Such moral pressures were reinforced by offers from magazines of what were at the time enormous sums of money for a new collection of short stories. In 1902, after eight years' absence, Holmes reappeared in what was said to be a pre-Reichenbach novel, *The Hound of the Baskervilles*, and in October 1903 the first story in a new series, 'The Empty House', appeared in the English *Strand Magazine* and the American *Collier's*. Doyle's postcard to his agent, which said simply, 'Very well. A.C.D.', meant that he had succumbed to the lure of an offer of $5,000 from America and a fee of £100 a thousand words from the *Strand*. 'The scenes at the railway bookstalls were worse than anything I ever saw at a bargain sale,' an eye-witness wrote, and Doyle himself remarked that everybody on the Channel boat was clutching a copy of the magazine. From this point onwards he made no attempt to abandon Holmes, but he still resented the importance with which the detective's exploits were regarded. When, a year or two before his death, he was giving a talk on spiritualism in Amsterdam and was asked to say a few preliminary words about Sherlock Holmes, his reaction was one of anger and dismay.

Sherlock Holmes became a myth so potent that even in his own lifetime Doyle was almost swamped by it, and the myth is not less potent today. Criminal and emotional problems are still addressed to Holmes for solution, and pilgrimages are made to his rooms at 221B Baker Street. In the Sherlock Holmes public house mementoes of his cases are preserved in the bar, and the sitting room at Baker Street, awaiting its occupant, may be regarded while one dines. There are Sherlock Holmes Societies or Baker Street Irregulars or Silver Blazers in almost every country in the world except those which are Communist-controlled, there are journals and meetings and dinners and visits to the Reichenbach Falls. Some of this is amusing and perhaps all of it is harmless, although I have an uneasy feeling that the members of these societies are more interested in having fun with Sherlock Holmes than in the merits of the stories

Certainly what needs to be stressed today is something that should be a cliché, and unhappily is not: that if one were choosing the best twenty short detective stories ever written, at least half a dozen of them would be about Sherlock Holmes.

· 6 ·

The Short Story:
The First Golden Age

In writing about most of Sherlock Holmes's immediate successors one has to make a change of gear. The interest of their work lies in the cleverness with which problems are propounded and solved, rather than in their ability to create credible characters or to write stories interesting as tales rather than as puzzles. The amount of talent at work in this period gives it a good claim to be called the first Golden Age of the crime story, but it should be recognized that the metal is nine-carat quality, whereas the best of the Holmes stories are almost pure gold. Yet for those prepared to accept these stories on their own level (as any addict should be) the variety of detectives and ideas offered in them gives enduring pleasure.

At the centre was always the personality of the detective, who appeared in several series of stories. A number of dichotomies mark these detectives, but the clearest division is between those in the Holmes category of Supermen, with no emotional attachments and little interest in everyday life, and the inconspicuous ordinary men who solve their cases by the application of common sense rather than by analytic deduction. The detectives in this second class are private investigators running their own agencies, because that was the fashion of the time, but they often look and sound like policemen. They are Lestrades and Gregsons, removed from the official ranks and seen with a friendly eye instead of being made the butts of genius. The Superman is almost always given his accompanying Watson, who may do a lot of the humdrum investigation. The common-sense detective often works alone.

The two most successful Supermen detectives of the period were Professor Augustus S. F. X. Van Dusen and Father Brown. Van Dusen was created by Jacques Futrelle (1875–1912), an American born in Georgia, who had a theatrical and journalistic career which was blended with the writing of novels and short stories. Van Dusen's principal appearance is in two collections of stories, *The Thinking Machine* (1907) and *The Thinking Machine on the Case* (1908).[1] He carries Holmesian omniscience to the

1. In England *The Professor on the Case.*

point of absurdity. He is introduced to us when he refers contemptuously to chess, saying that a thorough knowledge of the rules of logic is all that is necessary to become a master at the game, and that he could 'take a few hours of competent instruction and defeat a man who has devoted his life to it'. A game is arranged between the Professor and the world champion, Tschaikowsky. After a morning spent learning the moves with an American chess master, the Professor plays the game. At the fifth move Tschaikowsky stops smiling, and after the fourteenth, when Van Dusen says, 'Mate in fifteen moves', the world champion exclaims, 'Mon Dieu!' (he is not one of those Russians who knows no language but his own), and adds: 'You are not a man; you are a brain – a machine – a thinking machine.' From this time onwards Professor Van Dusen is called 'the Thinking Machine'. In appearance he is dwarfish, with a small, white clean-shaven face, long, flexible hands, and a great domed head taking a size-eight hat, under which is a heavy shock of bushy yellow hair.

The whiff of absurdity is strong, but the Thinking Machine stories are almost all ingenious. The usual story falls into two parts. In the first a mystery is shown to us, either by third-person narrative or as told to the Thinking Machine. His assistant, the reporter Hutchinson Hatch, does most of the leg-work, and the Professor then solves the case. Among the best stories are one in which poison is circulated through the application of a court plaster, another in which a man sees in a crystal ball the picture of his future murder in his own apartment some distance away (the basis of the trick is the creation of a duplicate room in the house where the victim sees the crystal ball), and a third in which a car disappears night after night in a lane which has a policeman at each end. The finest of all the Thinking Machine stories is 'The Problem of Cell 13', which begins with an assertion by the Professor that anything can be done by the power of thought. Told that nobody can think his way out of a cell, he replies that 'A man can so apply his brain and ingenuity that he can leave a cell, which is the same thing'. The story shows him doing just that, with some agreeable mystification in the course of it, and then explaining exactly how it was done. This story has became a classic anthology piece, rather at the expense of some of the others. Futrelle died when the *Titanic* went down. The evidence of his other books does not make it seem likely that his crime stories would have developed any depth of characterization, but within the limits of what he attempted he had a conspicuously original gift.

The short detective stories written by Gilbert Keith Chesterton (1874–1936) were as pungent, paradoxical and romantic as the novels, poems, literary criticism and journalism that streamed from his occasionally too-ready pen. His essential views about the detective story are set down in the first and best of the several pieces in which he discussed various aspects of the form. It was, he said, a popular realization of the poetry concealed in city life. The detective crosses a London in which 'the casual omnibus assumes the primal colours of a fairy ship', and in which the lights of the city are the guardians of a secret known to the writer but not to the reader: 'Every twist of the road is like a finger pointing to it; every fantastic skyline of chimney-pots seems wildly and derisively signalling the meaning of the mystery.' The detective story writer should be regarded as the poet of the city, and the detective as a romantic hero, the protector of civilization:

> It is the agent of social justice who is the original and poetic figure, while the burglars and footpads are merely placid old cosmic conservatives, happy in the immemorial respectability of apes and wolves. The romance of the police force is thus the whole romance of man ... It reminds us that the whole noiseless and unnoticeable police management by which we are ruled and protected is only a successful knight-errantry.

This was written in 1901, before Father Brown was thought of, and it is admirable special pleading for Chesterton's own detective stories, in which Flambeau the great criminal soon becomes a detective, like Vidocq. The stories embody also a principle that the author announced a quarter of a century later, that 'the only thrill, even of a common thriller, is concerned somehow with the conscience and the will'. This is true at least of his own very uncommon thrillers, which almost always exemplify a witty paradox about the condition of society or the nature of man. Chesterton fairly spilled over with good ideas, and they are as evident in his detective stories as in the novels that were the product of his verbal and mental dexterity, like *The Napoleon of Notting Hill* or his metaphysical thriller, *The Man Who Was Thursday*.

Chesterton wrote several other collections of what may loosely be called detective short stories outside the Father Brown series, of which *The Club of Queer Trades*, *The Man Who Knew Too Much* and *Four Faultless Felons* all contain good things, but his reputation in this field rests upon the five Father Brown collections. *The Innocence of Father Brown* (1911) was followed by the *Wisdom* (1914), the *Incredulity* (1926), the *Secret* (1927) and the *Scandal* (1935). Father Brown, the dumpy, commonplace little priest with his black hat, dingy umbrella and collection of brown paper parcels, was based upon Father John O'Connor, parish priest of St Cuthbert's, Bradford. 'The flat hat is true to life, and the large and cheap umbrella was my defence against wearing an overcoat,' Father O'Connor has written. 'Brown paper parcels! I carried them whenever I could, having no sense of style or deportment.'

It may seem odd to class a man who has difficulty in rolling his umbrella and does not know the right end of his return ticket among the Supermen of detection, but Father Brown belongs among them through the knowledge given to him by God. Logicians of the detective story complained with some bitterness that Chesterton outraged all the rules they had drawn up, that he did not tell you whether all the windows were fastened or whether a shot in the gun-room could be heard in the butler's pantry. But the very merit of Chesterton is his ability to leave out everything extraneous to the theme he wants to develop, and yet provide a clue that is blindingly obvious once we have accepted the premises of the story and the character of Father Brown. A dog whines because a stick sinks in the sea, the red light from a closed door looks like 'a splash of blood that grew vivid as it cried for vengeance', the priest of a new religion does not look round when he hears a crash and a scream, and these are genuine clues by which we may solve mysteries. And when we have accepted Father Brown, then we are bound to accept also his right to draw religious and social morals from the cases he investigates.

Often the points he is making are beautifully put. In 'The Blue Cross' Father Brown identifies a false priest because he attacks reason, which is 'bad theology'. In 'The Queer Feet', the trick of which rests on the fact that a man in evening dress is indistinguishable from the waiter who is serving him, the criticism is social. 'Reverend Sir, your friend must have been very smart to act the gentleman,' Colonel Pound says at the end of the story, and the priest replies: 'Yes, it must be very hard work to be a gentleman, but, do you know, I have sometimes thought that it must be almost as laborious to be a waiter.' The paradoxes at their best are perfect. Why does a man wear a startling purple wig? Because by drawing attention to it he diverts any possible curiosity from his presumedly deformed but in fact normal ear. How can a black man conceal himself in a white country? Why, by posing as a soot-masked nigger minstrel.

The Chesterton short stories are a diet too rich for everyday consumption. Two or three, not six or seven, should be read at a sitting. And they have their faults, which spring from the fact that he was never able to take anything that he wrote quite seriously. Sometimes the detective stories, like his novels, topple into absurdity because the premises of the tale are too fantastic, but this does not happen very often. The first two books are on a higher level than the others, but, reading them all again before writing about them, it seemed to me still that the best of these tales are among the finest short crime stories ever written. A personal choice would include 'The Queer Feet', which has already been mentioned, 'The Secret Garden' with its puzzle of two heads and only one body, 'The Man in the Passage', in which a superb comic trick is pulled off with a mirror, the logical exercise in 'The Paradise of Thieves', and 'The Dagger with Wings', in which a legend is fulfilled when the body of a man looking like an enormous bat is found spreadeagled among unspotted snow. This last story has some loose ends hanging that will not please purists, but after a dozen readings I feel fresh admiration for the cleverness with which the trick is embodied in the legend, and the brilliance of the central picture.

A reading of Chesterton reinforces the truth that the best detective stories have been written by artists and not by artisans. In considering other Supermen detectives of the period we are dealing with journeymen of letters who do not pretend to art. Some had good ideas and some could construct a good story, but they had no ideas as clever as Futrelle's and no poetic inspiration like that which often touched Chesterton. Sir Hugh Greene's selections from tales about the detectives he calls 'the rivals of Sherlock Holmes' show convincingly the superiority of the absent Sherlock.

Originality, certainly, must be granted to the Old Man in the Corner invented by Baroness Orczy (1865–1947). He preceded her better-known Scarlet Pimpernel and appeared in three collections, *The Case of Miss Elliott* (1905), *The Old Man in the Corner* (1909)[2] and *Unravelled Knots* (1926). The Old Man sits in the corner of an ABC teashop consuming glasses of milk and pieces of cheesecake, endlessly tying and untying knots in a piece of string, and giving his solutions of cases that have baffled the police to a girl reporter named Polly Burton, who seems never to have read the newspapers, since the Old Man has to describe the background of every case to her in detail. He is never seen to move from his seat, although he mentions attending court hearings in several cases. The misanthropic Old Man is concerned only with demonstrating his own cleverness. He does not care at all about justice, and it is a peculiarity of the stories that in many of them the criminal goes free. 'Hang such a man! Fie!' he cries about one murderer, and of another he reflects only that 'There goes a frightful scoundrel unhung'. In the last story of *The Old Man in the Corner* it is a presumption that he has himself committed murder.

Such a character could be a springboard for all sorts of social comments,

2. In America *The Man in the Corner*.

but these seem never to have been in Baroness Orczy's mind, and apparently she wrote the stories in this way because it absolved her from any need to turn theory into practical proof of guilt. The writing is lively, and some of the stories contain ideas put to use by better writers, like that of two men planning a murder so that the man with an obvious motive has an alibi, while his apparently uninvolved companion commits the crime. Too often, however, they depend upon police work so inefficient as to make Lestrade look like a genius. Baroness Orczy was also responsible for a woman detective more disastrously silly than most of her kind, *Lady Molly of Scotland Yard* (1910), and for a legal investigator, Patrick Mulligan, who appears in *Skin o' My Tooth* (1928). Lady Molly, really Lady Molly Robertson-Kirk, is 'head of the Female Department', and has a husband who is in Dartmoor convicted of murder. She ends up clearing him of the crime after an unexplained five-year delay, and presumably settles down again to domesticity.

Ernest Bramah Smith (1868–1942), who dropped his commonplace surname for his writings, showed also a stroke of distinct originality in creating the blind detective Max Carrados. The Carrados stories were perhaps a diversion from the mock-Chinese tales about Kai-Lung which had at one time an unaccountably large number of admirers. The blind detective appears in *Max Carrados* (1914), *The Eyes of Max Carrados* (1923) and *Max Carrados Mysteries* (1927). His Watson is an inquiry agent named Louis Carlyle, who changed his name when wrongly struck off the solicitorial rolls for falsifying a trust account. Carrados (whose name is really Max Wynn) suffers from a disease called amaurosis, which causes blindness while leaving the external appearance of the eye unchanged. In a radio talk about Carrados in 1935, Bramah said that the idea of a blind detective came to him while watching a crime play in which the detective behaved very stupidly. 'Why not have a blind detective?' he thought. 'A really blind one.' The flippantly conceived idea was successful. Carrados and Carlyle make an agreeable variation on the Holmes–Watson relationship, with Carlyle more sophisticated and more distinctively characterized than most assistants, and Carrados insistent on the value of having 'no blundering, self-confident eyes to be hoodwinked'. His super-sensitive auditory nerve enables him to hear the cry of a newsboy in the street which is inaudible to other people in a room, and he knows that a man is wearing a false moustache because he carries 'a five-yard aura of spirit gum, emphasized by a warm perspiring skin'.

It is a defect of such discoveries that the reader cannot make them himself, as he can often make them in the Holmes stories, but the tales about Carrados are well constructed and interesting. Unlike most crime writers, Bramah sometimes linked his stories to actual social events of the period. In 'The Knight's Cross Signal Problem' the young Indian Drishna responds to Carlyle's indignation about his terrorist act in causing a rail crash by asking: 'Do you realize, Mr Carlyle, that you and your Government and your soldiers are responsible for the death of thousands of innocent men and women in my country every day?' A later story, 'The Missing Witness Sensation', deals with the kidnapping of a man by Sinn Fein so that he cannot give evidence against them. Carrados handles an unusually wide variety of cases, including in the first volume alone stories about a jewel theft, the railway crash already mentioned, attempted murder, fraud, and the burglary of a safe deposit. Bramah ignored the limiting idea, which had almost become established by the time of his first Carrados book, that every investigation must concern a murder, and the stories are the more interesting for it. Like other Superman detectives Carrados feels no hesitation about amending the processes of law, in one case to the point of ordering a murderer to commit suicide.

Holmes never concerned himself with fingerprints as he did with tobacco ash, newsprint and secret writing. Many detectives of this period mention the use of science in solving crimes, but few are seen in the act of using it. The distinction of R. Austin Freeman (1862–1943) is that his Dr Thorndyke is actually seen to be a forensic scientist. His square green box covered with Willesden canvas contains a great variety of materials for the detection of crime. When he says, 'Will you give me the Vitogen powder, Jervis', or goes to work on footprints with his plaster tin, water bottle, spoon and little rubber bowl, we are conscious of watching actual processes of detection. Freeman had a firm basis of medical knowledge, and he put this and the admiration he felt for one of his instructors, the great Victorian expert in medical jurisprudence, Dr Alfred Swayne Taylor, to good use.

For a man who began his literary career late, Freeman produced a great many books. The first of them, *The Adventures of Romney Pringle* (1902), published under the pseudonym of Clifford Ashdown and written by Freeman together with a medical colleague who was also a prison officer, is said to be the rarest book of crime short stories. His debut under his own name came with *The Red Thumb Mark* (1907) when he was forty-five years old, and he produced an average of rather more than a book a year up to a short time before his death. Many of them were novels, but it is safe to say that with the exception of one or two, like *Mr Pottermack's Oversight* (1930), these are markedly inferior to the short stories. With Freeman we confront for the first time the crime writer who produced work of no other kind, and whose talents as a writer were negligible. Reading a Freeman story is very much like chewing dry straw. This is how Thorndyke talks as late as the middle twenties:

A philosophic conclusion, Jervis, and worthy of my learned friend. It happens that the most intimate contact of Law and Medicine is in crimes against the person and consequently the proper study of the Medical Jurist is crime of that type.

Was ever reader in this manner wooed? If readers were won (and they were), if some remain (and they do), it is because of his accuracy in detail, and because of the originality shown in one collection of short stories. In *The Singing Bone* (1912) Freeman invented what has been called the inverted story. In these stories we see a crime committed, and then watch Thorndyke discover and follow clues that lead to the criminal. There is no mystery, and not much surprise, but the interest of watching Thorndyke at work is enhanced by our own prior knowledge. Freeman never repeated this experiment, which was developed, much later and with more skill, by Roy Vickers.

It is rather dubiously that one includes Thorndyke among the Supermen, but although he is in character almost anonymous, he has the proper passionless approach to ordinary human affairs. There is less doubt about Uncle Abner, the hero of *Uncle Abner, Master of Mysteries* (1918) by Melville Davisson Post (1871–1930). The stories are set in pre-Civil War Virginia, and Uncle Abner is 'one of those austere, deeply religious men who were the product of the Reformation ... the right hand of the land'. He is compared more than once with Cromwell, he carries a Bible in his pocket, he exemplifies the spirit of righteousness in his disorderly society.

The Uncle Abner stories are very highly regarded in America, but comparatively little known elsewhere. This is no doubt because their settings and themes are often distinctively American – 'The Edge of the Shadow' contains an argument about the validity of slavery and concerns the murder of an abolitionist, and in the course of 'A Twilight Adventure' Uncle Abner stops a lynching for cattle-stealing and gives a lecture on the dangers of circumstantial evidence. To English readers Uncle Abner is likely to seem a distant and implausible figure, and if one judges in terms of plot the stories have surely been overpraised. They include an ingenious but far-fetched locked-room mystery in which the solution is provided by the sun's rays focusing through a bottle of raw liquor and exploding a percussion cap on a fowling-piece, and a cunning story based on phonetic misspelling, but Uncle Abner's deductions are often of dubious validity, like his conclusion that a man followed the left side of a wall 'because his controlling side was on the left – because he was left-handed'.

If Post has been overrated, however, the stories by Frederick Irving Anderson (1877–1947) about the *Adventures of the Infallible Godahl* (1914) deserve to be better known. Godahl, a criminal who always succeeds, is the creation of a writer named Oliver Armiston. In one of the best stories the two become confused in a Borgesian manner, as Armiston is duped into using Godahl's talents to provide the means of committing an actual crime. Anderson also created the engaging Sophie Lang, a kind of feminine counterpart of Godahl. The Godahl stories have appeared in volume form only in the United States, *The Notorious Sophie Lang* (1925) only in Britain.

The detective as ordinary man is embodied in the Martin Hewitt stories written by Arthur Morrison (1863–1945). The first series of them ran in the *Strand* during 1894, and they were illustrated by Sidney Paget, who had also interpreted the appearance of Holmes. In looks and behaviour Hewitt represents a conscious reaction – and almost the first reaction, as the date shows – from the Superman detective. He is a 'stoutish clean-shaven man, of middle height and of a cheerful, round countenance', who 'maintains that he has no system beyond a judicious use of ordinary faculties'. The first and best of the Hewitt collections contains cases with unusual ideas in them, like 'The Stanway Cameo Mystery', in which a dealer discovers that the cameo he has sold is a forgery and steals it back again to save his reputation. There is another story about jewels stolen by a carefully trained parrot, and 'The Loss of Sammy Throckett', which deals with the kidnapping of a runner expected to win a handicap race in the North of England, contains socially interesting details. But Morrison, a journalist and short story writer concerned with actual poverty and crime (he wrote an excellent book about London slum life, *Tales of Mean Streets*), seems always to have been disturbed by the idea of treating crime light-heartedly, and the later collections are rather humdrum.

The stories about Paul Beck and his son, by M. McDonnell Bodkin (1850–1933), do not deserve the total neglect into which they have fallen. Bodkin was an exuberant Irish barrister, and for a short time a Nationalist MP, who became a judge in County Clare. His first detectival creation, Paul Beck, is described as a 'stout party in grey' who 'don't seem particular bright'. He has a ruddy face, curling light-brown hair, a chronic look of mild surprise in his light blue eyes and the appearance of a milkman rather than a detective. Beck does not profess great intelligence: 'I just go by the rule of thumb, and muddle and puzzle out my cases as best I can.' In saying this he hardly does himself justice, for *Paul Beck, the Rule of Thumb Detective*

(1898) shows him exercising a good deal of native wit, even though the famous detective Murdock Rose is scornful about him. The book had a very good press, and Beck was favourably compared with 'the late lamented Sherlock Holmes'. *Dora Myrl, the Lady Detective* (1900) was no less absurd than other stories of the time about women detectives, who retained an impossible gentility of speech and personality while dealing with crime. In *The Capture of Paul Beck* (1909) Dora and Beck end up married after being on opposite sides in a case, and *Young Beck, a Chip off the Old Block* (1911) introduces their son, also Paul. These stories are unusual in that they are mostly based on young Paul's life at university and just after leaving it, in company with his friend Lord Kirwood, son of the Secretary of State for Foreign Affairs, who is among the sillier Watsons. The cases of Paul Junior have great freshness. They include one of the finest card-cheating stories ever written, and one in which Bodkin made good use of his knowledge of the House of Commons. The Becks, senior and junior, are possibly the best Plain Man detectives of their era.

Other Supermen and Plain Men, although not very many of the latter, were at work in the field of the short story during this period, but there seems no need to particularize any of them, except perhaps the prolific Dick Donovan, the pseudonym of J. E. Preston Muddock (1843–1934), who spanned in a curious way the gap between the detective proper and the great flood of penny dreadful figures, headed by Sexton Blake and including Nelson Lee, Dixon Hawke and Falcon Swift, which began in imitation of Holmes – but of course an active non-analytical Holmes, always chasing or being chased by a super-villain – in the nineties. In America a similar development was taking place, as Joan M. Mooney has shown in a valuable detailed discussion of the Nick Carter and Old Cap Collier stories. The crudity of the few penny dreadfuls I have read precludes them from consideration, but Donovan is a different matter. His plots are often absurdly melodramatic, but the level of his writing is sometimes reminiscent of rather inferior Trollope.

The most nearly acceptable Donovan is in the novels told in the third person, some of them recounting the exploits of other detectives like Calvin Sugg, a typical post-Holmes figure, who speaks at least six languages fluently and has been given innumerable medals by various governments, but the most popular Donovan works were the short stories in which he boastfully recounted his own exploits. Like Holmes he was thought to be a real person and received many letters, including one from a woman in Brighton who asked him to shadow her husband. In his autobiography Muddock notes regretfully the preference for his detective stories over his other writings and says: 'I have never been in full sympathy with my Donovan work.'

There are two writers still unmentioned whose work should be included in relation to the short story of the time, although what they wrote was nearer to the thriller than to detection. The Arsène Lupin stories of Maurice Leblanc (1864–1941) and the Raffles tales of E. W. Hornung (1866–1921) represent the last flicker for a long time of the criminal hero tradition. *Arsène Lupin, Gentleman-Cambrioleur* (1907) introduced him as the leader of a gang of thieves who masquerades in various disguises and outwits the police of every country, impersonating an English detective at Scotland Yard, making a fool of Holmlock Shears (Herlock Sholmès in the original) and, in the Vidocq manner, taking charge of the search for Lupin while posing as the chief of the Sûreté. Lupin is a rogue rather than a villain, and in the later stories he is often on the side of law and order. The short stories about him come off better than the novels. There is something irritatingly slapdash about them all, but the absurdities have at times a certain grandeur. In the novel 813 (1910) Lupin poses as the Chef de la Sûreté for four years, and arrests himself during the investigation. The ghost of Vidocq still lingers.

A. J. Raffles is a more interesting character, although the interest is partly sociological. Raffles is on the surface the image of a perfect English gentleman. He is captain of the school cricket team and later the finest slow bowler of his decade (an amateur, naturally). Apart from playing cricket all the summer he leads a life of apparent idleness. Apparent: for he really makes a living as a burglar, and *Raffles, the Amateur Cracksman* (1899) records his adventures in collaboration with Bunny, who has worshipped Raffles since fagging for him at school. In one curious story Bunny dresses as a woman, and there are suggestions of a platonic homosexual relationship between them.

The series, which includes the later *Raffles* (1901) and *A Thief in the Night* (1905) shows the public school ethos turned round, with the traditional virtues of sticking to your chums and doing the decent thing used in the service of theft. Raffles sometimes does the decent thing by conventional standards, as on the occasion when he sends a gold cup stolen from the British Museum back to the Queen. On another occasion he explains to Bunny that it is not a betrayal of hospitality to steal the jewels at Lord Amersteth's house, because he has been 'asked for my cricket, as though I were a pro'. It is less easy to excuse his conduct in jumping overboard when his situation becomes desperate, leaving Bunny to face a long prison sentence, or when he burgles the house in which Bunny's girl lives.

Bunny's own ethical code is also distinctly odd. After a little initial reluctance he enters wholeheartedly into burglary, but refuses to stoop to 'personal paragraphs and the baser journalism'.

Hornung, who also wrote some indifferent detective and adventure stories, had no satirical intentions. He was Conan Doyle's brother-in-law, and Doyle strongly disapproved of Raffles, saying, 'You must not make the criminal a hero.' Since Raffles is seen through the worshipping Bunny's eyes, he undoubtedly is a hero, although Bunny often says things like 'Raffles was a villain, when all is written', and promises to 'paint in every wart'. The stories are always lively, although occasionally absurd, and both Raffles and Bunny come through very clearly. They are also often intentionally funny. Hornung was a dexterous punster, as is shown by his remark that 'Though he might be more humble, there's no police like Holmes', and the Raffles stories contain one superb pun. When Raffles and Bunny pay a visit to the 'Raffles Relics' in Scotland Yard's Black Museum, they see the spectacles and jemmy of Charles Peace, and the master murmurs: 'The greatest of the pre-Raffleites.' Hornung never sees Raffles as an enemy of the class in which he had been brought up, as an earlier writer would have done, but as a man who adheres to the standards of this class even though he is a crook. For him, as for Bunny, Raffles's sins are cancelled out by his heroic death in the Boer War.

The Golden Age of the short story, which began with Holmes, ended with the Second World War. The Holmes stories are the best things in the period, but they are not the only things worth remembering. Most of the short story's better practitioners in these years turned to detection as a relief from other work, and partly for this reason much of what they wrote retains its freshness. They enjoyed using a form which, still in its infancy, offered infinite opportunities for variation, and there is a gaiety in the often unsophisticated capers they cut which was slowly lost by the writers who followed them.

The Rise of the Novel

(i) Changes in reading habits

One has to be careful to discover, and not to impose, a pattern in the shape of any sort of literature. Although the short story was the dominant form in crime fiction for roughly thirty years, novels were of course being written during this period. The decline of the short story's popularity, which became sharply noticeable after the First World War, corresponded to the novel's rise, and both of these were linked with social, technical and economic changes. The emancipation of women which took place during the War played a large part in the creation of a new structure in domestic life, particularly in Europe, through which women had more leisure, and many of them used it to read books. The rise of the large circulating libraries, associated in Britain particularly with the names of Boots the Chemists and W. H. Smith the book and newspaper wholesalers, greatly changed middle-class reading habits.

There was a branch of Boots or Smiths in most towns of any size, and every branch had its library from which books could be borrowed either on annual subscription or by paying a few pennies a book. Newsagents and stationers started their own little libraries, often obtaining stock from a central wholesaler and charging twopence a week for all except the most recent books, so that these became known as 'twopenny libraries'. Some of the twopenny libraries stocked chiefly the thrillers and Westerns that remained staple reading for the male working class, but many others were used overwhelmingly by women. Supply again followed their demand for books that would reinforce their own view of the world and society – long, untroubling 'library novels', light romances, detective stories. Many of the detective stories were written by women, and essentially also *for* women.

At the same time changes in the style of urban living and in the nature of travel greatly affected magazine sales. More and more people travelled by car and read nothing at all on the journey. Railway journeys became shorter and men no longer queued at railway bookstalls to buy the latest issue of the *Strand* or any other magazine. They were more likely to be reading a newspaper on their way home from city to suburb, or a book from the circulating library on a journey from town to town.

(ii) Up to Rinehart and Christie

The basic problem for authors writing novels during the era of the short story's supremacy was that if a mystery could be stated and solved in a few thousand words, there seemed no reason for expanding it to a novel ten times as long. Often they made a slightly uneasy attempt to guy the whole form. *The Big Bow Mystery* (1892) by Israel Zangwill (1864–1926) is much more nearly a parody than has been acknowledged. This novelette, written in a fortnight to meet a sudden demand from the London *Star*, is a mystery in which a man is found with his throat cut in a room locked, bolted and 'as firmly barred as if besieged'. The detective is the murderer, and committed the crime after the opening of the door, dashing across the room while another man was present and cutting the sleeping victim's throat without leaving more than a trace of blood. The solution of the locked-room mystery in *Lè Mystère de la chambre jaune* (1907), by Gaston Leroux (1864–1941), is no less preposterous, although this was called by John Dickson Carr's Dr Fell 'the best detective tale ever written'. Here the explanation involves a nightmare, the accidental firing of a revolver, and a whole concatenation of coincidences. Leroux's book, which appeared as *The Mystery of the Yellow Room* in America in 1908 and in Britain a year later, contains a number of clever touches, but it shows the French abandonment of the last traces of Gaboriau's realism in dealing with the police. The hero, Rouletabille, appears in several other novels marked even more strongly by the sensationalism that separates the French crime story from its British and American counterparts.

That the line between the comic and the serious in the detective story is a fine one is shown by the most famous novel of these years, *Trent's Last Case* (1913). Its author, Edmund Clerihew Bentley (1875–1956), made his living as a journalist, and was for more than twenty years chief leader writer on the *Daily Telegraph*. Bentley had a talent for light humorous writing, and invented the tart little four-line verse known as the clerihew. In 1910 he thought that 'it would be a good idea to write a detective story of a new sort'. The book would be light-hearted, because Bentley disliked both the egotism and the seriousness of Holmes. The detective also was to be treated lightly, and perhaps for this reason was originally called Philip Gasket. In tune with this was the 'most pleasing notion of making the hero's hard-won and obviously correct solution of the mystery turn out to be completely wrong', so that the whole thing would be 'not so much a detective story as an exposure of detective stories'. Bentley started with the last chapter in which Gasket is staggered by the revelation of what really happened, and worked backwards from this, revising the plot several times while walking from his Hampstead home to his Fleet Street office. The final result seemed to him poor, and when John Buchan, who was at that time reader for Nelson's, accepted the book, Bentley thought that he was offering far too much money. With Gasket changed to Trent it was published in England, and in America under the title *The Lady in Black*. Its success was immediate, not as an 'exposure' of detective stories, but as light entertainment.

Writing elsewhere about *Trent's Last Case*, I said that it is difficult to understand the high regard in which the book was held, and that 'the writing seems stiff and characterless, the movement from one surprise to another, and the final shock of revelation, rather artificial'. Perhaps this judgement was too severe. I think it remains true, though, that the book falls into two parts which are not very well connected. The opening treats the death of the millionaire Sigsbee Manderson with an almost savage irony, stressing that 'to all mankind save a million or two of half-crazed gamblers, blind to all reality, the death of Manderson meant nothing'. His epitaph is provided by the editor of the newspaper who looks at the large broadsheet announcing 'Murder of Sigsbee Manderson' and says: 'It makes a good bill.'

This ironic note recurs occasionally but is not maintained, and Manderson, after being introduced with such a flourish, becomes more shadowy as the story proceeds. The major part of the book deals with Trent's investigation, and his (as it proves erroneous) discovery of what really happened. Much of this is ingenious, although it depends upon some actions that seem very unlikely, like an innocent man's removal of a denture from the dead Manderson's mouth. Of more importance is the fact that the detection wavers uneasily between a desire to treat the whole thing as a joke and Bentley's impulse to write seriously about the fact that Trent falls in love with the woman whom he supposes to be involved in the murder. There is a similar uncertainty in the treatment of Trent, who, as Bentley said, 'is apt to give way to frivolity and the throwing about of absurd quotations from the poets at almost any moment', and yet since he is the hero cannot be regarded as a figure of fun. But perhaps this is still pressing too hard on a book that was acclaimed everywhere as something new in detective stories. The other works in which Trent appears, published more than twenty years later, showed only that Bentley was not able to adapt himself to the further development of the form.

The difficulties that confronted the writer of detective novels at this time are shown also in the construction of *At The Villa Rose* (1910), the first detective story by A. E. W. Mason (1865–1948). Mason, like Doyle, was an extrovert personality who found in the detective novel an outlet for dark imaginings that had no place in dashing historical romances like *The Four Feathers*. In characterization *At The Villa Rose* is greatly superior to Bentley's book, and it has an ingenious plot with a firm though distant basis in two actual murder cases. Mason was determined, however, to 'make the story of what actually happened more intriguing and dramatic than the unravelling of the mystery and the detection of the criminal'. Accordingly the criminal is revealed not much more than halfway through, and the essential element of suspense is largely lost. Yet *At The Villa Rose* can still be re-read with pleasure. Both the detective, Inspector Hanaud of the Sûreté, and his Watson, Mr Ricardo, are original creations. The stout, broad-shouldered Hanaud, who looks like 'a prosperous comedian', carries out quite a lot of closely argued detection, and the lazy wine-loving Ricardo is one of the few Watsons to emerge as a distinct personality.

A book that must be mentioned at this point, although it is outside the detective canon, is *The Three Impostors* by Arthur Machen (1863–1947). Neglected at the time of its publication in 1895, but recently available in Britain, this is the finest of Machen's tales of terror, a sort of *New Arabian Nights* with the diabolism of the nineties replacing Stevensonian cheerfulness. The opening line: 'And Mr Joseph Waters is going to stay the night?' (and there are few crime novels with a more tantalizing and disturbing opening line) leads into a series of cunningly interwoven tales, each extremely ingenious, the whole ending with the appalling discovery made by Machen's amateur investigators in a decayed suburban house. It cannot be denied that the book is imitative of Stevenson, but this artificial flower of the nineties has a genuine poisonous scent. By its side such a book as *The Lodger* (1913), the attempt made by Mrs Belloc Lowndes (1868–1947) to convey the terror of the Jack the Ripper murders, looks forced and meretricious. Machen's horrific imaginings were real to him, Mrs Lowndes's are designed to give the reader an entirely comfortable shiver.

It is this kind of shiver one gets, certainly, from the books of Mary Roberts Rinehart (1876–1958). These were stories written to a pattern. All of them deal with crime, and the crime is almost always murder. There is a detective, but his activities are often less important than those of the staunch middle-aged spinster, plucky young widow or marriageable girl who finds herself hearing strange noises in the night, being shut up in cupboards, overhearing odd and apparently sinister conversations, and eventually stumbling upon some clue that solves the mystery. Much of what happens in these stories occurs by chance, and the mystery is prolonged only by the obstinate refusal of the characters to reveal essential facts. Mrs Rinehart's books belonged to the 'Had I But Known' school, the absurdities of which were wittily summed up by Ogden Nash:

Sometimes it is the Had I But Known what grim secret lurked behind the smiling exterior, I would never have set foot within the door;

Sometimes the Had I But Known then what I know now, I could have saved at least three lives by revealing to the Inspector the conversation I heard through that fortuitous hole in the floor . . .

And when the killer is finally trapped into a confession by some elaborate device of the Had I But Known-ers some hundred pages later than if they hadn't held their knowledge aloof,

Why, they say, Why, Inspector, I knew all along it was he, but I couldn't tell you, you would have laughed at me unless I had absolute proof.

These are the first crime stories which have the air of being written specifically for maiden aunts, and they exploited a market which, with the spread of library borrowing, proved very profitable. From Rinehart's second book and first success, *The Circular Staircase* (1908), at the climax of which spinster Rachel Innes finds herself shut up with the murderer in a small secret room behind the great old chimneypiece ('I knew he was creeping on me, inch by inch'), the formula of needless confusion and mock-terror did not change. The settings became more varied, yet also more enclosed. As one commentator has said, 'It does not really matter much to the world view which emerges whether the backdrop is New York City or Connecticut, a town or a country house, the stability and balance most usually associated, sentimentally at least, with an agrarian order are assumed.' People in the books die but this is not important, because in relation to the real world none of them was ever alive. Nobody is ever doing any work, although suspects may be labelled solicitor, doctor, chauffeur.

Sometimes the confinement of the society in which violence takes place is carried to fantastic lengths. Rinehart went on writing until a year or two before her death, and *The Album* (1933) is typical of her later novels. It deals with five families living in Crescent Place, 'a collection of fine old semi-country houses, each set in its own grounds', insulated from the city outside by an entrance gate marked Private 'so that we resemble nothing so much as five green-embattled fortresses'. The action literally never moves outside the Crescent. Reporters and photographers cause no trouble after an initial visit, and make no attempt to gain access to the houses although four murders are committed, the first with an axe and the last involving a headless trunk. Within this totally closed circle none of the characters works, although one apparently did, since we are told that 'he had given up even the pretence of business since the depression, and spent a good bit of time tinkering with his car in the garage'. Even such tinkering is unusual, for there are cooks, a gardener, a chauffeur, various helpers. These people really have nothing to do, apart from being suspected of murder. The murderer, naturally, is one of them. Her actions, when her identity is revealed, are outrageously unlikely.

Rinehart's work was naive, but in some ways her world was that of the detective novel after the First World War, as it is discussed in the next chapter. The main line of development, however, was marked clearly by the appearance in 1920 of Agatha Christie's first novel, *The Mysterious Affair at Styles*.

Agatha Christie (1890–1976) was brought up by her widowed mother and had no formal education, either at school or at home. After writing two or three novels which she says were 'long and confused' and were rejected by publishers, she decided to try her hand at a detective story. The influences working on her were 'the pattern of the clue' and 'the idiot friend', as developed in the Holmes stories. She worked during the First World War in a hospital and so obtained some knowledge of poisons, which she put to use in the story written in odds and ends of leisure time over a period of eighteen months. It was turned down by three publishers and kept by the Bodley Head for nine months. John Lane then agreed to publish the book, which sold about 2,000 copies. She made £25 out of the British publication and had to wait for ten years before it appeared in the United States.

The Mysterious Affair at Styles is not one of Agatha Christie's best detective stories, although it is based upon a characteristically cunning idea and contains some of those equally characteristic sleights of hand by which the reader is deceived into making what prove to be unjustifiable assumptions. It ushered in a very distinctive detective, the Belgian Hercule Poirot, whose appearance impresses one as being rather like that of Humpty Dumpty with a moustache, and a Watson of extreme stupidity in Captain Hastings. It revealed a gift for writing light, agreeable and convincing dialogue, and the plot was constructed with firmness and coherence. Yet these things had been done before. Agatha Christie's book is original in the sense that it is a puzzle story which is solely that, which permits no emotional engagement with the characters. Bentley wavered into seriousness against his original intentions; it is possible to be disturbed about the fate of Mason's Celia Harland; the reader's identification with the principal character is a prerequisite of enjoying Mrs Rinehart. Christie's first book is notable because it ushered in the era during which the detective story came to be regarded as a puzzle pure and complex, and interest in the fates of its characters was increasingly felt to be not only unnecessary but also undesirable. It was the beginning of what came to be known as the Golden Age.

· 8 ·

The Golden Age:
The Twenties

(i) Laying down the rules

Up to the middle twenties there had been little serious consideration of crime stories as a particular kind of literature, and no attempt had been made to assess the detective story as something having rules which could be strictly formulated and which it was important to observe. By the end of the decade, however, a body of criticism had been produced which tried to lay down the limits within which writers of detective stories ought to operate.

Some of this work has already been mentioned, but to understand what happened to crime fiction between the Wars, it is necessary to consider the rules in more detail. The attitude from which they sprang was that the detective story was a kind of game played, as Knox put it, between 'the author of the one part and the reader of the other part'. When one talked about rules, he went on, it was not 'in the sense in which poetry has rules ... but in the sense in which cricket has rules – a far more impressive consideration to the ordinary Englishman'. (Knox was writing for his countrymen, but one supposes that he expected foreigners also to obey the rules, even though they did not understand cricket.) To infringe the rules was, to say the least, extremely bad form.

Starting from the assumption that the detective story was a game, the rules had two purposes, first to describe the nature of the game and then to show how it should be played. What made a detective story distinct from other superficially similar forms of literature? Well, clues had to be provided, and it was necessary that the detective should draw from them rational and inevitable conclusions. Any conclusions reached purely by instinct, through accident or through coincidence showed a failure on the part of the author and were unfair to the reader. Wright regarded an author who deceived the reader in this way as no better than a practical joker, and said that 'if the detective does not reach his conclusions through an analysis of clues, he has no more solved his problem than the schoolboy who gets his answer out of the back of the arithmetic'.

The detective was the vitally important figure. What sort of person should he be? Freeman, deprecating the 'vast amount of rushing to and fro of detectives or unofficial investigators in motor cars, aeroplanes or motor boats', stressed that the connoisseur looked for 'an exhibition of mental gymnastics', which was obviously best provided by an intellectual or scientific detective like his own Thorndyke. S. S. Van Dine, writing in his own person as Willard Huntington Wright, agreed that the chief interest of the story should be mental analysis and was equally scornful of detectives continually in physical danger, although he regarded Thorndyke as 'an elderly, plodding, painstaking, humourless and amazingly dry sleuth'. (Sayers thought him probably the handsomest detective in fiction.) Wright said that the detective must be 'a character of high and fascinating attainments – a man at once human and unusual, colourful and gifted', by implication resembling his own Philo Vance. Although most detectives during the twenties continued to be eccentric amateurs they were less anti-social than Holmes, and Sayers noted in 1928 a tendency to produce detectives remarkable only for their ordinariness, like Freeman Wills Crofts's Inspector French.

And then, what kind of crime should the detective investigate? There was a great shift here from the short stories that were frequently concerned with some sort of fraud. Wright, often the most extreme of these theorists, said that the crime simply must be murder, because 'three hundred pages is far too much pother' for interest to be maintained in any mere fraud or deception. The other legislators tacitly agreed, without expressing themselves so definitely. Nobody, rather curiously, expressed a preference for murder on the ground that its punishment when detected was in many countries the irrevocable one of death.

The legislators turned to the criminal. It was agreed that he must be introduced early in the story and must not turn up three quarters of the way through, as sometimes happened in early detective stories. He must not be the detective, or at least not the official detective. This rule was often infringed, most notably in Leroux's *Mystery of the Yellow Room* and in Bernard Capes's neglected *tour de force The Skeleton Key* (1919). He must not be a servant because this was 'a too easy solution' and 'the culprit must be a decidedly worth-while person' (Wright). Servants, except as servants, were really not worthwhile. It was taken as a matter of course in Golden Age detection that murder most often took place where servants were around, but no servant could ever be guilty of more than petty theft or attempted blackmail. There were a few exceptions to this rule, in which somebody might pretend to be a servant, but they were rare. Nor could the murderer be a professional criminal. It was necessary, in fact, that he should be part of the same social group that contained the other suspects. He might be socially linked with them in the capacity of doctor or solicitor, or he might have the ambiguous position of a secretary. John Dickson Carr, writing in 1935, thought that statistics would show the secretary to be still the most common murderer in crime fiction, although no doubt members of the murderee's family would have come first if they had been admitted as a category. And it was accepted that the motives for all crimes should be personal, and within that context rational. They should not be committed for reasons of state or on behalf of theoretical principles or by somebody merely insane. It was permissible that the people in a story should think that a crime was irrational, or had been carried out by an international spy who was selling secrets, but the reader knew that there would always turn out to be a personal motive.

There were rules about the story itself rather than the characters, some flippant and others serious. If scientific devices were used, the reader must be given a hint of their nature. Some deprecated Thorndyke's investigations, on the ground that you would be no wiser after he had shown you his discoveries, unless you happened to know the effect of belladonna on rabbits or had 'an intimate acquaintance with the fauna of local ponds'. Undiscovered poisons were ruled out, and so were supernatural solutions. Insistence that the writer must play fair with the reader was universal, and Knox, in deploring the use of secret passages, virtuously pointed out that when he had introduced one, he had been 'careful to point out beforehand that the house had belonged to Catholics in penal times'. Knox, never one to resist facetiousness, thought that no Chinaman should appear in a story, a remark unintelligible except on the basis that he would not be a likely member of any English murder group. In America Earl Derr Biggers's Charlie Chan offered not merely a Chinese character, but a Chinese detective.

Other rules were more seriously conceived. The importance of unity of mood was stressed, and Wright was the first to lay down firmly the rule that there must be no love interest, because through it such unity was damaged. This rule was often broken, but in relation to sex the Golden Age detective story was strikingly inhibited. Money and sex are two main motives for murder, but although this was acknowledged in theory, in very few of these stories are the characters seen as anything other than puppets in a game of murder. To see them in depth would have been against the rules. As Sayers said, these people lived 'more or less on the *Punch* level of emotion', and if they were to be considered more seriously their emotions would 'make hay of the detective interest' which was the truly important thing.

Sexual feeling was not the only aspect of life ignored in these stories. The period in which they were written was one in which the number of unemployed in Britain rose to three million and remained near that mark for a decade, in which boom in America was succeeded by slump and slump by depression, in which dictatorships rose to power. It was a period that ended in a long-expected war. These things were ignored in almost all the detective stories of the Golden Age. In the British stories the General Strike of 1926 never took place, trade unions did not exist, and when sympathy was expressed for the poor it was not for the unemployed but for those struggling along on a fixed inherited income. In the American stories there were no bread-lines and no Radicals, no Southern demagogues or home-grown Fascists. The fairy-tale land of the Golden Age was one in which murder was committed over and over again without anybody getting hurt.

And why not? one of the ghosts of those past Golden Age critics might say: *Don't we always escape in fairy tales from what is disagreeable in life, isn't that their very purpose? Must we always be worrying about the state of society?* But these were very special fairy tales. Social and even political attitudes were implied in them. It is safe to say that almost all the British writers in the twenties and thirties, and most of the Americans, were unquestionably right-wing. This is not to say that they were openly anti-Semitic or anti-Radical, but that they were overwhelmingly conservative in feeling. It would have been unthinkable for them to create a Jewish detective, or a working-class one aggressively conscious of his origins, for such figures would have seemed to them quite incongruous. It would have been equally impossible for them to have created a policeman who beat up suspects, although this was the time when American newspapers wrote about the Third Degree. Acknowledging that such things happened, they would have thought it undesirable to write about them, because the police were the representatives of established society, and so ought not to be shown behaving badly. And although an unemployed man might be seen sympathetically if he was trying to be helpful to his social betters, he was usually regarded as somebody who just refused to work. The social order in these stories was as fixed and mechanical as that of the Incas. We are very far in these books from the radicalism of Chesterton, and a long way even from passages like Bentley's denunciation of Sigsbee Manderson.

Golden Age writers would not have held it against Manderson that he had become rich by speculation, although they might have regretted his brashness and vulgarity. The social mores of British detective and thriller writers during the inter-war years are amusingly analysed in Colin Watson's *Snobbery With Violence* (1971).

Our approach to the crime story is so different from that of the most characteristic Golden Age writers that it is hard now to believe that all this ever happened. The Detection Club still exists, but it is no longer confined strictly to writers of pure detective stories as it once was, and members no longer 'solemnly swear never to conceal a vital clue from the reader' at their initiation. As many of them write thrillers rather than detective stories, such an oath would be meaningless. There is no limit to folly, but it seems surprising that the intelligent men and women who devised the rules did not see that they were limiting the scope and interest of their work. The puzzle of Who and Why and How remains a vital element in most crime fiction, but to abjure voluntarily the interplay of character and the force of passion was eventually to reduce this kind of detective story to the level of a crossword puzzle, which can be solved but not read, to cause satiety in the writers themselves, and to breed a rebellion which came sooner than has been acknowledged.

Nevertheless, for several years the rules received at least lip-service, and it was discovered that detective stories were extremely easy to write. If none of the skills of a novelist was needed, if all one had to do was to construct a puzzle and then set down the events relating to it in a bald, featureless narrative, why then almost anybody with time to spare and paper available might try his hand. In the great flood of British and American detective stories that began after the First World War, as H. R. F. Keating has recently said, 'dullness in everything except the riddles was the rule'. In these years the detective story reached peaks of ingenuity that have never since been attained and are now rarely attempted; and, sometimes in the same book, it dropped into abysms of absurdity and dullness that have never again been plumbed.

(ii) Mistresses and masters

In retrospect, four names stand out in the twenties, those of Agatha Christie, Dorothy Sayers and Anthony Berkeley in Britain, that of S. S. Van Dine in America. Ellery Queen and John Dickson Carr belong properly to the thirties, although both published their first books before the end of the decade.

Agatha Christie's career moved in a steady but unspectacular way until 1926, when *The Murder of Roger Ackroyd* appeared. A second impression was called for within a few weeks, and the book was already a success when, seven months after its publication, she disappeared. This happened at a critical emotional period in her life, and after a nation-wide search she was discovered in a famous spa suffering from amnesia. The affair undoubtedly helped the sale of her books, but the important point is that *Roger Ackroyd* was already a success. A work so notably original in its field could not have failed to find a wide audience.

In an obvious sense, the book fits comfortably within the conventions that have been outlined. The setting is a village deep in the English countryside, Roger Ackroyd dies in his study, there is a butler who behaves suspiciously but whom we never really suspect, and for good servant measure a housekeeper, parlourmaid, two housemaids, kitchen-maid and cook. We are offered two of the maps that had by now become obligatory, one of the house and grounds, the other of the study. So far so conventional, but we notice at once the amused observant eye which makes something interesting out of the standard material. It is a mark of the best Golden Age writers that they were unable to stick to those injunctions about subduing the characters. The narrator's sister, Caroline, good-natured but intensely inquisitive, a retailer of one ridiculous rumour after another, is a genuine comic character done with affectionate ridicule. The detective is Poirot, who in the best Holmesian style asks obscure questions that turn out to be meaningful, like his concern here with the colour of a suspect's boots.

Every successful detective story in this period involved a deceit practised upon the reader, and here the trick is the original one of making the murderer the local doctor, who tells the story and acts as Poirot's Watson. (Original with Christie, that is, for in an earlier book she had made a gesture towards the same device.) Once the trick has been accepted the use of it is exquisitely fair, but should it be accepted? It certainly outraged one of the commandments in Knox's Detective Decalogue which said that the thoughts of the Watson must not be concealed, and Wright thought it 'hardly legitimate', although it was defended by Sayers. Christie's best books, apart from this one, came in the thirties and later, but *Roger Ackroyd* is the first book to show her finest skills at full stretch, together with her characteristic zest.

Similar zest and gaiety, erring at times in the direction of flippancy, marked also the early work of Anthony Berkeley Cox (1893–1971), who wrote first as Anthony Berkeley and later as Francis Iles. His full achievement as Francis Iles is discussed in the next chapter, but as Anthony Berkeley he was responsible in the twenties for one of the most stunning trick stories in the history of detective fiction. *The Poisoned Chocolates Case* (1929), which began as a short story and was then enlarged into a novel, is at once cunning and irreverent – irreverent, that is, in the way it cocked a snook at the pedantic solemnity which had by then invaded not merely writing about the detective story, but the actual books. The novel offers six separate solutions to the question: who sent the poisoned chocolates that killed Joan Bendix? One of these solutions is proposed by Roger Sheringham, the amateur detective who appears in most of Berkeley's early books. Like Trent, Sheringham was conceived almost as a joke, a caricature of an offensive acquaintance. He was taken seriously by readers, however, so that Berkeley had 'to tone his offensiveness down'. None of the other early novels is equal to *The Poisoned Chocolates Case*, but all have a liveliness that keeps them fresh even today.

Of Dorothy (Leigh) Sayers (1893–1957) it is not easy to write fairly. For her whole-hearted admirers she is the finest detective story writer of the twentieth century, to those less enthusiastic her work is long-winded and ludicrously snobbish. The early books are as ingenious as the later ones, and differ from them chiefly in her attitude to Lord Peter Wimsey. It is from a point of view a long way short of idolatry that they are discussed here.

Her merits were rare among the crime writers between the Wars. Her mind was clear and incisive, and she had read very widely in crime literature. Her introductions to the first two volumes of *Detection, Mystery and Horror*, published in 1928 and 1931,[1] show an acute intelligence at work. She was the first writer to place five of Poe's stories rather than three within the canon, the first to acclaim the merits of Le Fanu in this field. Everything she says calls for respect, even though some of it may prompt disagreement. And in reading her novels and short stories it is impossible not to admire the careful craftsmanship with which they have been made. Her plots are organized with care, the details she produces about a means of murder are often original and always carefully researched. In the best of her early novels, *Unnatural Death* (1927),[2] murders are committed by the injection of an air bubble into an artery, which stops the circulation and so causes an apparently natural death. The book is a compendium of clever touches (who else has thought of making not one set of false footprints, but three, as the villain does here?), and the method was at least

1. In America these short story collections were called *The Omnibus of Crime*.
2. In America *The Dawson Pedigree*.

possible, although its validity has been questioned. *The Unpleasantness at the Bellona Club* (1928) is partly concerned with the decision about an inheritance involved by the question of whether General Fentiman or Lady Dormer was the first to die, and similarly cunning strokes can be found in most Sayers books.

The case against Sayers rests chiefly upon the same evidence that admirers would cite in her favour. It is based upon the way she wrote, and upon the character of her detective. Edmund Wilson called a later novel, *The Nine Tailors*, 'one of the dullest books I have ever encountered in any field', and there can be no doubt that by any reasonable standards applied to writing, as distinct from plotting, she was pompous and boring. Every book contains an enormous amount of padding, in the form of conversations which, although they may have a distant connection with the plot, are spread over a dozen pages where the point could be covered in as many lines. This might be forgivable if what was said had some intrinsic interest, but these dialogues are carried on between stereotyped figures (her English yokels are particularly to be deplored, with facetious professional men running them close) who have nothing at all to say, but only a veiled clue to communicate. These people, like the clubmen in the Bellona Club or the minor upper-class characters in *Clouds of Witness* are indeed conceived in the terms of a sketch for *Punch*, and *Unnatural Death* shows her flinching away from anything more serious.

It would be charitable to think that Wimsey, like Sheringham, was conceived as a joke but, unhappily, there is every indication that Sayers regarded him with an adoring eye. Lord Peter, the second son of the Duke of Denver, is a caricature of an English aristocrat conceived with an immensely snobbish, loving seriousness. His speech strongly resembles that of Bertie Wooster, slightly affected by Arthur Augustus d'Arcy of the *Magnet*. He sometimes wears a monocle, and it would seem that it may have been either a real monocle or a powerful magnifying lens. He drops the last letters of words, says things like 'I'll drop in on you later and we'll have a jolly old pow-wow, what?', and asks of a man following him, 'Is the fellow a sahib?' At times his self-conscious humour is excruciating, as in passages like this one where he addresses himself to Detective Inspector Parker:

'Even I am baffled. But not for long!' he cried, with a magnificent burst of self-confidence. 'My Honour (capital H) is concerned to track this Human Fiend (capitals) to its hidden source, and nail the whited sepulchre to the mast even though it crush me in the attempt!' Loud applause. His chin sank broodingly upon his dressing-gown, and he breathed a few guttural notes into the bass saxophone which was the cherished companion of his solitary hours in the bathroom.

One is not surprised that the family motto is 'As my Whimsy takes me'. The Wodehouse note is repeated in the Jeeves-like Bunter, Wimsey's 'confidential man and assistant sleuth', whose conversational style is made clear on the first page of *Clouds of Witness*: '"Good morning, my lord. Fine morning, my lord. Your lordship's bath-water is ready."'

All this might be more endurable if Wimsey ever appeared to have the knowledge of history, antiques, music, gastronomy and other matters that he is said to possess, but these qualities are asserted rather than demonstrated, and when demonstration is attempted it is sometimes wrong. When Wimsey tells Parker that he should ask Bunter 'to give you a bottle of the Château Yquem — it's rather decent', he does so in apparent ignorance of the fact that this sweet dessert wine is not an all-purpose tipple. (In the same spirit Thorndyke orders a bottle of Barsac before considering what he is going to eat.) Add to this the casual anti-Semitism which allows Wimsey to say things like 'Olga Kohn — who sounds like a Russian Jewess — is not precisely out of the top drawer, as my mother would say', and you have a portrait of what might be thought an unattractive character. It should be added that many women readers adore him, and have complained that this view of Wimsey is unjust.

In America, during the same decade, S. S. Van Dine produced a similar monster of snobbish affectation in Philo Vance. Willard Huntington Wright (1889–1939), who used the name of S. S. Van Dine for his crime stories, was a journalist and art critic who wrote under his own name a number of books, including a study of Nietzsche and an interesting but commercially unsuccessful novel called *The Man of Promise* (1916). He turned to serious reading of crime stories during a long period of illness, and used a pseudonym for his first crime story, *The Benson Murder Case* (1926), because he thought that although British novelists could write detective stories as a sideline without damaging their reputations, 'Being an American, I rather feared ostracism if I boldly switched from esthetics and philologic research to fictional sleuthing.' He hid, therefore, behind 'an old family name and the Steam-Ship initials'. Van Dine plotted his criminal career carefully, beginning with the submission of three very long synopses which were immediately accepted, and planning to abandon crime stories after writing six of them in as many years. In the event the books were so overwhelmingly successful, and together with the films made from them brought in so much money, that Wright–Van Dine wrote nothing else. Howard Haycraft says that his second book, *The Canary Murder Case* (1927), 'broke all modern publishing records for detective fiction' at the time.

It is difficult now to grasp the extent of Van Dine's success in America, and to a much lesser extent in Britain. Van Dine's second book was in the American best-seller lists for months, and the third was even more successful. It was said that he had lifted the detective story on to the plane of a fine art, and by his own account he was the favourite crime writer of two Presidents. Wright, a self-conscious aesthete with an admiration for the Nietzschean superior man, was delighted, but the pleasure was not unalloyed. His fate is curiously foreshadowed in that of Stanford West, the hero of his novel, who sells out by abandoning the unpopular work in which he searches for 'a sound foundation of culture and aristocracy' and becoming a successful novelist. The title of an article Van Dine wrote at the height of his fame, 'I used to be a Highbrow and Look at Me Now', reflects both his pleasure, and his regret that he was no longer regarded seriously as a writer.

Philo Vance, who might be called Wimsey's American cousin, was Wright's wish-fulfilment projection. He is 'a young social aristocrat' who spent some time at Oxford and later 'transferred his residence to a villa outside Florence', although all his cases take place in urban America. Just under six feet tall, slender, sinewy and graceful, he has what was even at the time a slightly outdated Byronic charm. 'His chiselled regular features gave his face the attraction of strength and uniform modelling', although 'a sardonic coldness of expression precluded the designation of handsome'. Like Wimsey he wears a monocle and drops the 'g' at the end of words like *amazin'* and *distressin'*, and he has a ludicrous manner of speech, represented by remarks like: '"I note that our upliftin' Press bedecked its front pages this morning with head-lines about a pogrom at the old Greene mansion last night. Wherefore?"' He has an encyclopedic knowledge about absolutely everything, or at least about everything related to the cases in which he is concerned, a knowledge supported by a tremendous apparatus of footnotes. This learning is continually and unnecessarily obtruded, so that he answers a question from the wooden-headed Sergeant Heath about what he has been doing by saying: '"I've been immersed in the terra-cotta ornamentation of Renaissance façades, and other such trivialities, since I saw you last."' He expresses always a languid world-weary superiority to the crimes he investigates and solves.

All this may sound intolerable, but there is something more to be said. Van Dine's erudition, at least in matters connected with art, painting, music and comparative religion, was real where Sayers's was defective. Partly in consequence of this, and partly because he took such pains with the idealized self-portrait, Vance does come through as a personality of real intellectual attainment in a way that Wimsey does not. In the early books his knowledge is directly related to the cases in which he is involved, and information is given which enables the intelligent reader to follow the deductions. And the best of the Van Dine stories are models of construction. Utterly remote from real life, they remain fascinating by strict adherence to the rules of their own dotty logic, and through their creator's self-absorbed immersion in his own work. There is a sort of grand imaginative folly about the best books, *The Greene Murder Case* (1928) and *The Bishop Murder Case* (1929), which carries us along once the premises of the story are accepted. In the first of these stories a whole series of murders is carried out which prove to have been copied from material in a great crime library. Do the crimes seem impossible? Van Dine is able to show that every one of them can be paralleled in Hans Gross's great handbook on criminal investigation. *The Bishop Murder Case* is an even more astonishing performance. Again there is a series of murders, apparently the work of a maniac who bases himself on nursery rhymes, so that Johnny Sprig is shot through the middle of his wig and Cock Robin is killed by an arrow. Are the crimes meaningless? Obscure intellectual clues are remarked by or planted on Vance, connected with chess, Ibsen's plays, mathematical theories. In the end the murderer dies when Vance swaps the drink he has poisoned after distracting attention by exclaiming in admiration at sight of a Cellini plaque, '"Berenson told me it was destroyed in the seventeenth century."' When District Attorney Markham says that this death was murder, the detective's reply is characteristic. '"Oh, doubtless. Yes – of course. Most reprehensible ... I say, am I by any chance under arrest?"'

Ogden Nash summed up later feelings about Vance in two lines:

> Philo Vance
> Needs a kick in the pance.

No doubt. Yet admiration should not be withheld, from these two books at least. In their outrageous cleverness, their disdainful disregard of everything except the detective and the puzzle, they are among the finest fruits of the Golden Age.

(iii) Humdrums, farceurs and others

The plan of the house indicating where the body was found, the map of the grounds showing the garden and the summerhouse, were standard accessories to the story of the period, and in many British books a timetable appeared too. This timetable, often of a railway or bus journey, was offered in preparation for the breaking of an alibi, and it was used in greatest detail and most often by Freeman Wills Crofts (1879–1957), who put his knowledge as a railway engineer to frequent although hardly varied use. In a Crofts story the murderer can often be identified at an early point by his apparently unbreakable alibi, which is duly broken by dogged Inspector (later Superintendent) French. Crofts's first book, *The Cask* (1920), which traces back in elaborate detail the way in which a cask came to contain gold coins and a woman's hand instead of a piece of statuary, has a grip and cleverness that he never quite repeated. His plotting became increasingly mechanical, particularly after the appearance in his fifth book of the plodding French. Crofts knew nothing about Scotland Yard, and did not feel it important that he should learn the details of police procedure, perhaps thinking that a detailed knowledge of railway time-tables was enough. He succeeded so well in making his detective common-place (in fact police detectives are markedly colourful characters) that he became uninteresting. *The Loss of the Jane Vosper* (1936) is one of the best French stories, showing Crofts's care in getting a background right, and his surprising ability to write scenes of action. *Inspector French's Greatest Case* (1925) can also be recommended.

Crofts was not just a typical, but also the best, representative of what may be called the Humdrum school of detective novelists, whose work poured from the presses during the decade, and indeed for long afterwards. Most of them came late to writing fiction, and few had much talent for it. They had some skill in constructing puzzles, nothing more, and ironically they fulfilled much better than Van Dine his dictum that the detective story properly belonged in the category of riddles and cross-word puzzles. Most of the Humdrums were British, and among the best known were Major Cecil Street, (who used the name of John Rhode), R. A. J. Walling, J. S. Fletcher, and Sir Henry Lancelot Aubrey-Fletcher, who wrote as Henry Wade. All were much praised in their time. The collaborative Humdrum of G. D. H. and Margaret Cole should be mentioned, because the Coles were both deeply involved in the Labour Movement, and G. D. H. Cole was a famous figure within it, yet their books never treated seriously the social realities with which in life they were so much concerned. American Humdrums were fewer, and less alkaline, than their British counterparts.

More lively than the Humdrums were the Farceurs, those writers for whom the business of fictional murder was endlessly amusing. These were almost wholly British, partly because the writing of such stories called for a degree of sophistication that American writers did not possess during this decade, and partly because Britain between the wars was such a safe country in which to live. If you lived in Chicago, or even in Paris, during the twenties you were much less likely to treat murder light-heartedly than if you lived in London.

One of the most talented Farceurs was Philip MacDonald (1900?–1981), who introduced Colonel Anthony Gethryn in *The Rasp* (1924). MacDonald was one of those writers who find it easy to think of an idea, but hardly ever manage to carry through a fully coherent plot. A restless but careless experimenter, he belongs in spirit to the twenties, although two of his best stories, *Rynox* (1930)[3] and *X v Rex* (1933),[4] were written in the following decade. *Rynox* begins with an epilogue in which nearly £300,000 is delivered in used pound notes to the Naval, Military and Cosmos Assurance Company, and then traces the means by which this has happened, with occasional asides from author to reader. In *X v Rex*, written under the pseudonym of Martin Porlock, there is a very elaborate description of the police measures taken in an attempt to trap an 'invisible man' mass murderer, and the way in which he evades them. (One murder is carried out by a sandwich man, firing under cover of his board.) The build-up in this story is most tantalizingly done, although the climax, as often with MacDonald, is rather a let-down.

Monsignor Ronald Knox (1888–1957) is the super-typical Farceur of the decade, one who never allowed into his his half-dozen detective stories the faintest breath of seriousness to disturb the desperate facetiousness of his style. *The Viaduct Murder* (1925), with its amateur investigator who gets everything wrong, owes a good deal to Bentley, but a more characteristic book is *Footsteps at the Lock* (1927), one of those stories in which a man who is presumed dead turns out to have staged his own disappearance. Knox was fascinated by the Holmesian apparatus of clues and deductions, as MacDonald was fascinated by methods of murder, and neither of them bothered much about concealing the identity of the easily spotted villain.

Probably the most entertaining book of this kind written during the twenties is *The Red House Mystery*, the only detective story of A. A. Milne (1882–1956). More than twenty years after the book's publication in 1922 Raymond Chandler made an attack on it which successfully convicted Milne of characteristic Farceur-like carelessness in plotting, and of condoning some outstanding improbabilities. Chandler's attack is devastating

3. In America *The Rynox Murder Mystery*.
4. In America *Mystery of the Dead Police*.

– although the sort of analysis he makes would be damaging to many Golden Age detective stories – yet I was able to re-read the story without much loss of pleasure, and even with admiration of Milne's skill in skating over thin ice. Rex Stout seems to be right in pinning the word 'charming' to the book's light, easy way with murder, its dexterous shifts of suspicion and emphasis. There are improbabilities that have to be ignored as Milne ignores them, but the charm remains potent.

Improbabilities were not confined to Farceurs. The crime stories written by Eden Philpotts (1862–1960), under his own name and that of Harrington Hext, were among the most ridiculous of the time. Two examples will be sufficient. In *The Grey Room* (1922) people who sleep in this room die because the heat of the mattress releases a Borgia poison contained in fifty miles of wire put between the flock mattress and its satin casing. There is no need even for the victim to sleep on the mattress, for in one case a hot-water bottle placed in the bed does the trick. In a Harrington Hext book, *The Thing at Their Heels* (1923), a Radical clergyman (any Radical is automatically to be suspected in this era) kills four people so that the family estate can descend to him and become a home for outcasts.

Among the principal achievements of the decade were A. E. W. Mason's second and third detective stories, *The House of the Arrow* (1924) and *The Prisoner in the Opal* (1928). Mason was a member of the Detection Club, but he had little patience with the attempt to draw up a set of rules, and little liking for the way in which he saw the detective story going. He put his position clearly a few years later in a radio interview, when he said that the question was whether the detective novel should consist 'simply of a conundrum and its answer', or whether, as he preferred, it should 'present one facet of a story which shall seek to enchant the interest of its readers on the different ground of the clash of its characters and the diversity of their interests'. These two books fulfil such requirements. They are both good detective stories and they are also among the best of his novels, containing a genuine *frisson* of terror, given through use of the detective form. With our present degree of sophistication, the puzzle in *The House of the Arrow* is rather easy to solve, but this fact affects very little the pleasure one has in reading the book, and *The Prisoner in the Opal* is one of the few crime stories to make successful use of devil worship and the Black Mass. Hanaud and Ricardo reappear, skilfully interwoven into the pattern of the stories, and the quality of the detection in both books is of high quality. Mason's last two crime stories, *They Wouldn't be Chessmen* and *The House in Lordship Lane*, show his powers in decline.

Before the end of the twenties a certain weariness with mechanical ingenuity was beginning to be apparent. Van Dine, appearing in his own person as Wright, declared in 1927 that only the 'inept and uninformed author' would any longer use such 'fashions and inventions of yesterday' as the cipher message containing the solution, the murder committed by an animal, the phonograph alibi, the discovery of a totally distinctive cigarette, the forged fingerprints, the dummy figure, the dagger or other sharp instrument shot from a machine, the locked-room murder committed after somebody had entered the room. A rebellious note was struck, too, as well as a weary one. In 1930 Anthony Berkeley said in the preface to what was actually a disappointingly conventional book called *The Second Shot* that:

I am personally convinced that the days of the old crime-puzzle, pure and simple, relying entirely upon the plot and without any added attractions of character, style, or even humour, are in the hands of the auditor; and that the detective story is in the process of developing into the novel with a detective or crime interest, holding its readers less by mathematical than by psychological ties.

Both Wright and Berkeley were to be proved truthful prophets, although both underestimated the tolerance of readers, the skill of new writers in burnishing up dingy devices so that they shone freshly, and the ability of established ones to adapt their techniques.

· 9 ·

The Golden Age:
The Thirties

(i) New blood

When one looks at the Golden Age in retrospect the developing rebellion against its ideas and standards is clearly visible, but this is the wisdom of hindsight, for during the thirties the classical detective story burgeoned with new and considerable talents almost every year. Just before the decade began Ellery Queen and John Dickson Carr published their first books, and in the middle of it Michael Innes and Nicholas Blake brought a fresh style and approach to the form. Margery Allingham and Ngaio Marsh used the standard formula in a way rather different from that of Christie and Sayers, and in America a fleet of women writers played their own variations on the theme. The French detective story, which had been quiescent for years, was triumphantly revived by a Belgian, Georges Simenon. In numbers also the detective story grew enormously during the thirties. Haycraft has some interesting figures about the number of crime stories mentioned in the American *Book Review Digest*. No more than a dozen were reviewed in 1914, a figure which had grown to 97 in 1925 and to 217 in 1939. These figures say nothing about the number of books actually published, of which there are no details available, but as he says the increase is probably 'relative and representative'. In Britain as in America no details are available in actual figures, but it is safe to say that if 1914 is taken as a basis, the number of crime stories published had multiplied by five in 1926 and by ten in 1939.

In dealing with the mass of stories published in the thirties, and the greater number appearing with every year up to the present time, I have by wish and necessity been selective rather than comprehensive. It should be understood that in the thirties, and later still, many Humdrums continued to write and some new ones to appear. One was Arthur William Upfield (1888–1964), who created the half-caste detective Napoleon Bonaparte. The 'Bony' books have the advantage of an original detective, whose tracking skills are again slightly reminiscent of Fenimore Cooper,

108

and of the unusual Australian setting. The earlier ones are well told in a straightforward way, the later are marked by some curious stylistic affectations, but the characters apart from Bony are uniformly wooden, and none of the books really moves out of well-worn Humdrum tracks.

Urged on by friends and less friendly critics, I tackled again the work of Gladys Mitchell (1901–83), but emerged after half a dozen books defeated by what appeared an average Humdrum. What seem typical Mitchell stories, like *My Father Sleeps* (1944) and *Here Comes a Chopper* (1946), are full of travelogue details. 'Modest but satisfactory kit' is forever being packed in and taken out of rucksacks, and young men and women are never happier than when arguing about whether they have taken the wrong footpath. Many tediously fanciful aspects of English life, morris dancing, witchcraft, amateur archaeology, get lengthy examination in the Mitchell *oeuvre*. *Tom Brown's Body* (1949) is reasonably entertaining in its account of public-school life – although less amusing than R. C. Woodthorpe's neglected *The Public School Murder* (1932) – but like many books of the period fades away after the murder. I reached the end of this book, and of *Laurels are Poison* (1942), but found the later Mitchell impenetrable.

Apart from Upfield and Mitchell, there were in the thirties many reasonably competent writers who produced work echoing that of the major practitioners, but the history of the crime story is that of its principal talents. Of these the two most notable newcomers in the first half of the thirties were John Dickson Carr and Ellery Queen.

John Dickson Carr (1906–77), who used also the pseudonym of Carter Dickson, was unique among crime writers in his devotion to one form or another of the locked-room mystery. In his first crime story, *It Walks by Night* (1929), the essential elements of the Carr puzzle are laid out by the French detective Bencolin:

> 'The murderer was not hiding ... There is no possibility of false walls, for you can stand in any door and test the entire partition of the next room. Tear open floor or ceiling, and you will find only floor or ceiling of the next room ... In short, there are no secret entrances; the murderer was not hiding anywhere in the room; he did not go out by the window; he did not go out by the salon door ... Yet a murderer *had* beheaded his victim there; we know in this case above all others that the dead man did not kill himself.'

In *The Hollow Man* (1935),[1] Carr offers in one chapter, through his detective, Dr Gideon Fell, a lively and learned discussion of locked-room murders and their possible solutions under seven different classifications,

---

1. In America *The Three Coffins*.

with some sub-divisions relating to methods of tampering with doors. In dozens of books Carr–Dickson rang the changes on the possibilities with astonishing skill. Often his postulates are improbable, but the reader rarely feels them to be impossible, and the deception is built up, sustained with teasing hints that can be interpreted in half a dozen different ways, and at last revealed with staggering skill. The best Carr–Dickson is the most ingenious, and my vote goes to *The Hollow Man* itself, one of the books which, as Dr Fell says, 'derives its problem from illusion and impersonation'. (The kind of improbable postulate I mean, which doesn't affect enjoyment at the time but may raise doubts afterwards, is shown here by the evidence of three witnesses, all of whom accept the inaccurate time shown by a street clock. Did none of them possess a wrist watch?) The conjurer's illusion here is marvellously clever.

A panel of writers, editors, critics and fans were asked in 1980 to name the best locked-room stories. Four of the best ten were by Carr, and *The Hollow Man* got almost double the votes of any other book. The three other Carr–Dickson novels in the first ten were *The Crooked Hinge* (1938), *The Judas Window* (1938) and *The Ten Teacups* (1937).[2] To these I would add a further favourite of my own, *The Emperor's Snuff Box* (1942). The dates are significant. For almost twenty years Carr's fertility and inventive power seemed limitless. He wrote two or more books a year, all of them playing variations on the locked-room theme. In 1950, however, *The Bride of Newgate* ushered in a series of inferior detective stories that were also historical romances of a disastrously slapdash and extravagant kind.

The trouble with exploiting a formula like that of the locked room is that everything else becomes subservient to it, or at least that is what happened with Carr. He was strongly influenced by Poe and Chesterton (Dr Fell with his great bulk, his cane, his eye-glasses on a black ribbon, flowing cloak and rumpled hair, is a very Chestertonian figure). His books are full of macabre events and possibilities, and of Chestertonian paradox, but in the later work especially these are only stage trappings. There is genuine feeling in many of Chesterton's short stories, but very little in any of Carr's writing after his first half-dozen books. Since the whole story is built around the puzzle there is no room for characterization, and the limitation of these clever stories is clearly expressed in the fact that what one remembers about them is never the people, but only the puzzle.

Carr is an American writer who is often regarded as British, partly because of his rumbustiously Anglo-Saxon tone and partly because many

---

2. In America *The Peacock Feather Murders*.

of his best books have an English setting. There is no doubt about the American origins and manners of Frederic Dannay (1905–82) and Manfred B. Lee (1905–71), two cousins born Daniel Nathan and Manford Lepofsky, who under the name of Ellery Queen combined in one of the most successful and lengthy collaborations in literary history. Like Carr they were unusual in coming to crime writing as young men, and like him they showed for many years an agreeable zest. The early Queen stories, and also those written under the name of Drury Lane, showed some debt to Van Dine. In Wright's stories 'S. S. Van Dine' appears as the recorder of Vance's cases, and 'Ellery Queen' added a grace-note of a similar kind by making the author identical with the detective. It was my impression that in the early books Ellery Queen himself had many of Vance's characteristics, but although he speaks with a drawl, calls his father 'pater' and is given to airing bits of out-of-the-way knowledge, a re-reading showed that the resemblances are superficial. Ellery is an amateur investigator – and in fact a detective story writer – always at hand when his father, Inspector Richard Queen, is confronted by a difficult case.

The word 'ingenuity' gets a good deal of work in writing about the Golden Age, and certainly one would not wish to avoid it in relation to the early Queen novels. The ingenuity is of a kind quite different from Carr's, resting in a relentlessly analytical treatment of every possible clue and argument. In the early books a 'Challenge To The Reader' appears some three quarters of the way through, in the form of a statement saying that the reader has now been presented with all the clues needed to solve the case, and that only one solution is possible. The rare distinction of the books is that this claim is accurate. These are problems in deduction that do really permit of only one answer, and there are few crime stories indeed of which this can be said.

Again, which of the Queen novels containing this challenge is the best must be largely a matter of individual taste. My own favourite is *The Greek Coffin Mystery* (1932) with its brilliant surprise ending, but almost equally good are *The Dutch Shoe Mystery* (1931) which has a perfect piece of extended reasoning about the shoes left by the murderer, *The French Powder Mystery* (1930), in which you have to wait until the last line for the solution, and *The Chinese Orange Mystery* (1934) with its turned-round clues. Judged as exercises in rational deduction, these are certainly among the best detective stories ever written.

More sensitive than Carr, or less persistently adherent to a formula, Dannay and Lee gave up the Challenge and the close analysis of clues, and made Ellery a less omniscient and more human figure, in search of a wider significance and more interesting characterization. Perhaps their immense reading in the field of crime stories made them dissatisfied with what they were doing, perhaps they felt that they had worked out this particular vein. In any case, their first ten books represent a peak point in the history of the detective story between the wars.

Among the most extraordinary performances of these years were the three 'Obelist' stories (an obelist is 'one who harbours suspicion') of C. Daly King (1895–1963). King was a psychologist who wrote a book called *Beyond Behaviourism*, and another on *The Psychology of Consciousness*. Psychologists enter most of his stories, and in *Obelists at Sea* (1934) four of them, all belonging to different schools, investigate a murder at sea. At the end of each book King provided a 'clue finder', showing by page references that 'the arch-criminal hereinbefore has been suggested by sundry indications', as he coyly put it. The most remarkable of his books, one with a gloss of slightly meretricious cleverness, is *Obelists Fly High* (1935), in which a famous surgeon flying to operate on his brother, the American Secretary of State, receives a death threat which is carried out on the plane. The book begins with a shooting-it-out epilogue between the police guard of the surgeon and an unnamed villain, and ends with a prologue which reveals a wholly unsuspected murderer. The glitter is meretricious because the solution outrages our capacity for belief. Nobody, however, could deny the originality of the obelist stories. King's other work was much inferior to them, and with the coming of the War he gave up writing crime stories.

It looked at one time as though the work of Rex (Todhunter) Stout (1886–1975) might similarly represent a peak, in the creation of the most original and plausible Holmes-and-Watson pair. He began to write crime stories late in life, after the production of some interesting but commercially unsuccessful novels, and *Fer de Lance* (1934) introduced his puffing, grunting, Montenegrin-born heavyweight detective Nero Wolfe, and Wolfe's tough, sometimes aggressive assistant Archie Goodwin. Stout may have begun with the intention of gently guying the whole detective form. Wolfe sits in his oversized chair, unable to cross his legs because his thighs are so fat, taking trips in the elevator up to his collection of ten thousand orchids in the plant-room under the roof, and solving crimes without moving from the house. Goodwin, a man of action ('I do read books, but I never yet got any real satisfaction out of one') is Wolfe's eyes and legs for anything that takes place outside the old brownstone on West Thirty-fifth Street.

Plotting was not Stout's strong suit, and Wolfe's solutions were sometimes arbitrary or instinctive, but in *Fer de Lance*, *The League of Frightened Men* (1935) and other early books, notably *The Red Box* (1937), the dialogue crackles, Archie dashes around and almost falls in love, and Wolfe is built up into a slightly comic but always impressive figure. But time went on and books piled up, Wolfe had sometimes to be taken away from home, and the problems involved in all series characters who appear in many stories became evident. These are, of course, all the greater when the characters are built up from a few superficial attributes, like love of beer and orchids and a gourmet's appreciation of food. Slowly, slowly, the Wolfe stories declined. The decline became steep after the end of the forties, which produced some books very near to Stout's best work, like *The Silent Speaker* (1946), *Second Confession* (1949) and *Even in the Best Families* (1950),³ the last of Wolfe's encounters with the super-criminal Arnold Zeck. There are good things to be found in the later novels, of which *The Doorbell Rang* (1965) is one of the freshest, but most convey a sense of effort, of a man going through the motions of creating one more story about characters who have ceased to mean much to him. Nero and Archie have a place in American mythology relating to the detective story, and the American view of Stout's merits would place him much higher than is suggested here. In person Rex Stout was an astonishingly energetic man with multifold interests. He was indefatigable in support of many causes relating to authors, and remained to his death a committed radical of a distinctively American kind.

During the thirties the style of the detective, and particularly of the amateur detective, changed. The habit of disguise finished with the Second World War. Very few detectives who emerged after that time attempted to change their appearance. The tradition of omniscience was maintained in Dr Fell, the barely distinguishable Sir Henry Merrivale who is Carter Dickson's investigator, and Ellery Queen, but the detectives springing from the new talents of Margery Allingham, Ngaio Marsh, Nicholas Blake and Michael Innes behaved more like normal human beings, and were capable of making mistakes. This change was accompanied by a cautious drawing of the blinds that are kept permanently down in the house of classical detection, so that a little light from the outside world peeped in. The work of Margery Allingham (1904–66) and the New Zealander Ngaio Marsh (1899–1982) often viewed the social scene with a gently ironic eye. The first novel in which Allingham's talents are really on display, *Death of a Ghost* (1934), contains a lively picture of the hangers-on feeding on

3. In America *In the Best Families*.

the posthumous fame of a great Victorian and Edwardian artist, and Ngaio Marsh's *Death in Ecstasy* (1936) goes into considerable detail about one of those semi-dotty, semi-erotic mystical cults that are commonplace today. Other early Allinghams used a publishing house and smart Mayfair as backgrounds, and Marsh put her knowledge of the theatre into *Vintage Murder* (1937). Of course all crime stories have some background setting, but whereas in a wholly classical novel like the first Queen, *The Roman Hat Mystery*, the theatre where the crime takes place is devised as a puzzle box, Allingham and Marsh comment upon the affectations of near-artists or the pretensions of theatricals.

They found it difficult, however, to combine this sort of thing with writing a detective story. The first forty-odd pages of *Death of a Ghost* have amusing things to say about artists and critics. Then comes the murder, and all this is forgotten in the need to discover clues and investigate suspects. In Marsh's work of this period there are often long and tedious post-murder examinations of suspects. Both writers were to refine their technical skills in later books. In the meantime they were known chiefly for their detectives, whose characters testified to that Anglo-American snobbery upon which Sayers played so successfully. Margery Allingham's Albert Campion is lank, pale, fair-haired, spectacled, and 'the general impression one received of him was that he was well-bred and a trifle absent-minded'. He is indeed well-bred, having close connections with the upper reaches of the peerage, and perhaps distant ones with royalty. His servant, Magersfontein Lugg, is a comic Cockney described in an early book as 'a Vulgarian in the service of Mr Campion'. Ngaio Marsh's Inspector (later Superintendent) Roderick Alleyn, although a professional detective, is by no means of humble birth. His mother is Lady Alleyn, a breeder of Alsatians, and Alleyn is very much at home in places where most professional detectives would feel uneasy. Both Allingham and Marsh were intending to draw naturalistic portraits, but the result is simply that their detectives are less distinctive and interesting than Vance and Queen, although it is true that they may be regarded as less objectionable.

Cecil Day-Lewis (1904–72), the only detective story writer to have been Poet Laureate, began in 1935 to write detective stories under the name of Nicholas Blake. He brought to the Golden Age a distinct literary tone, and in his early books a left-wing political attitude. Both were unusual at the time. I can remember still the shock I felt when on the first page of Blake's first book, *A Question of Proof* (1935), T. S. Eliot's name was mentioned. Most of the new writers, like the old ones, had at least implicit right-wing sympathies. Their policemen were all good, their Radicals bad or silly, they took the existing social order for granted. None would have produced a book like Blake's second, *Thou Shell of Death* (1936),[4] in which a national hero based distantly on T. E. Lawrence is the murderer, nor would the solution to the mystery have been produced by Nigel Strangeways's recognition of a quotation from the Jacobean dramatist Tourneur. Strangeways was a real innovation, a genuine literary detective rather than one of those given quotations to spout. The best of the pre-war novels, and perhaps Blake's most successful book, is *The Beast Must Die* (1938), a clever variation on a trick used by Agatha Christie.

Blake's first book was written to pay for the leaking roof of his cottage, and Strangeways was originally based on W. H. Auden in his appearance and some of his habits. The truly engaging thing about these early books is their bubbling high spirits, the obvious pleasure the author got from playing with detection. One should not exaggerate the political concern or the literary character of the books, for these things were apparent chiefly in contrast to the attitudes of his colleagues. The enthusiasm slowly faded and Nigel Strangeways became a more conventional figure. The later Blakes were less good than the early ones, but there are good things to be found in them, when his sympathies and emotions were involved. Particularly interesting are *A Tangled Web* (1956)[5] and *A Private Wound* (1968). Strangeways does not appear in either of these books.

Michael Innes (the pseudonym of John Innes Mackintosh Stewart, 1906–) gave his books a very thick coating of urbane literary conversation, rather in the manner of Peacock strained through or distorted by Aldous Huxley. The Innes novels were instantly acclaimed as something new in detective fiction, from the publication in 1935 of *Death at the President's Lodging*, a title with misleading implications for the United States, where it was lamely renamed *Seven Suspects*. The *Times Literary Supplement* said that he was a newcomer who at once took his place in the front rank, and on the publication of *Hamlet, Revenge!* (1936) called him 'in a class by himself among writers of detective fiction'.

There was actually nothing very new about Innes's approach. J. C. Masterman in *An Oxford Tragedy* (1933) had produced very much the same kind of 'don's delight' book, marked by the same sort of urbanity. But Innes is the finest of the Farceurs, a writer who turns the detective story into an over-civilized joke with a frivolity which makes it a literary conversation piece with detection taking place on the side. There is no greater

4. In America *Shell of Death*.
5. In America *Death and Daisy Bland*.

quotation spotter or capper in crime literature than Inspector (later Sir John) Appleby, and few Innes characters of this period will flinch at playing a parlour game which involves remembering quotations about bells in Shakespeare. Appleby, when confronted by the 'fourteen bulky volumes of the Argentorati Athenaeus', murmurs: 'The Deipnosophists ... Schweighauser's edition ... takes up a lot of room ... Dindorf's compacter ... and there he is.' Appleby shows off, not out of sheer pretentiousness like Wimsey or Vance, but from genuine high spirits. The Innes stories cannot compare as puzzles with the work of Van Dine or Queen. Their strength is in their flippant gaiety, and perhaps the best of them all is *Stop Press* (1939),[6] in which he dispenses with the almost obligatory murder, and keeps the story balanced on little jets of unfailingly amusing talk. Innes's achievement as a writer of spy stories and thrillers is discussed separately.

The crime stories of C. H. B. Kitchin (1896–1967), in particular *Death of My Aunt* (1929), have attracted a small band of fervent admirers. Perhaps the best of them is the last, *Death of His Uncle* (1939), in which, although we are likely to discover the truth before his stockbroker investigator, there is a good deal of pleasure to be obtained from the always urbane and at times elegant writing. Kitchin did not bring anything new to the crime story although he has his place as a minor, amiable Farceur.

Just before the War John Strachey wrote an article for the *Saturday Review of Literature* in which he picked out Innes, Blake and Allingham as the 'white hopes' of the British detective story. It was an intelligent choice, but in fact only Allingham was able to develop her talent further in the post-war world. Innes's later orthodox crime stories are no longer conversation pieces fizzing with wit, but over-complicated and often extremely improbable tales. Appleby is more likely to discuss the weather than to expand on Schweighauser and Dindorf. Among the later books *A Private View* (1952),[7] the best of several novels about painters and the art world, and *The New Sonia Wayward* (1960)[8] can be recommended, but they are minor achievements compared with his first four novels. Neither Innes nor Blake really represented a new departure, as they seemed to do at the time. Their innovations, compared with those of Francis Iles, were superficial rather than radical.

6. In America (regrettably) *The Spider Strikes.*
7. In America *One-Man Show.*
8. In America *The Case of Sonia Wayward.*

(ii) The end of Van Dine, Sayers, Christie

The detective, then, was still there and still very often an amateur, but even in the work of long-established practitioners like Sayers and Christie he was changing. Against all her previously stated principles about love affairs in detective stories, Dorothy Sayers gave Lord Peter a wife, and built a whole book around his falling in love with her. Agatha Christie got rid of Poirot's Idiot Friend, Captain Hastings, and modified the little Belgian a great deal because she felt him to be increasingly absurd. She also refused after the thirties to allow him to appear on the stage, and actually wrote him out of a story in which he had been the central character, when she turned if from a book into a play.

Philo Vance, however, could not change. Wright had laid down the laws that relate to detective stories and their investigators, and Vance adhered to them. He became not less but more erudite, talking often about subjects that had little to do with the case in hand. His affectations and eccentricities were not softened like those of other Great Detectives, but became more pronounced. With this went an increasingly bizarre choice of subject, an increasing strain in the treatment. The decline in the Vance books is so steep that the critic who called the ninth of them one more stitch in his literary shroud was not overstating the case. Wright died of a thrombosis in 1939, rich, but, as he bitterly recognized, no longer much respected. The last line of his single straight novel, after the hero has settled for easy fame instead of hard integrity, is: 'Behind his smile was a sense of unutterable and tragic irony.' Willard Huntington Wright must have recognized that irony.

The development of Sayers can be charted best from an essay she wrote in 1937, in which she said that she had always wanted her books to be 'novel[s] of manners instead of pure crossword puzzle[s]', so moving back to the tradition of Collins and Le Fanu. She had 'indulged in a little "good writing" here and there' and had been encouraged by its reception. With this encouragement she had introduced a love element into *Strong Poison* (1930), produced a 'criticism of life' in *Murder Must Advertise* (1933) and at last in *Gaudy Night* (1935) had, as she thought, succeeded in 'choosing a plot that should exhibit intellectual integrity as the one great permanent value in an emotionally unstable world' and so managed to say 'the things that, in a confused way, I had been wanting to say all my life'.

There is a breathtaking gap here between intention and achievement. Wimsey remains essentially unchanged. He still says things like 'What-ho! that absolutely whangs the nail over the crumpet', and a snobbishness outrageous even for Sayers has provided him with a pedigree and a family history which, together with a long biographical note, act as preface to the new editions of each book. The books themselves, with the exception of the lively *Murder Must Advertise*, show an increasing pretentiousness, a dismal sentimentality, and a slackening of the close plotting that had been her chief virtue. *Gaudy Night* is essentially a 'woman's novel' full of the most tedious pseudo-serious chat between the characters that goes on for page after page. Mrs Q. D. Leavis seems perfectly right in placing this later Sayers beside Marie Corelli and Ouida, and in saying that she performed the function of 'giving the impression of intellectual activity to readers who would very much dislike that kind of exercise if it was actually presented to them'. Sayers is hardly likely to have agreed with this attack, but after *Busman's Honeymoon* (1937), which was frankly subtitled 'A Love Story with Detective Interruptions', she turned away from the hero of whom she had said, 'I can see no end to Peter this side of the grave.' In the last twenty years of her life she wrote no more detective novels. When, a few years before she died, her American publishers asked for a new introduction to accompany an omnibus volume, she refused it, saying that she had written the books only to make money and had no further interest in them.

One moves with pleasure from these records of disillusionment to one of success. During the thirties Agatha Christie produced, year after year, puzzle stories of varied ingenuity and constant liveliness. Her skill was not in the tight construction of plot, nor in the locked-room mystery, nor did she often make assumptions about the scientific and medical knowledge of readers. The deception in these Christie stories is much more like the conjurer's sleight-of-hand. She shows us the ace of spades face up. Then she turns it over, but we still know where it is, so how has it been transformed into the five of diamonds? It is on her work during this decade, plus a dozen of her earlier and later books, that her reputation chiefly rests, perhaps most specifically upon *Peril at End House* (1932), *Lord Edgware Dies* (1933),[9] *The ABC Murders* (1936)[10] and *Ten Little Niggers* (1939).[11] Her work stayed at its peak until roughly the end of the Second World War. Then there was a slow decline, but several of the books written in the fifties and sixties find her almost on top form. Particularly recommended are *Mrs McGinty's Dead* (1952), *The Pale Horse* (1961), which contains a murder method imitated in real life, and *Endless Night* (1967), one of her

9. In America *Thirteen at Dinner*.
10. In America *The Alphabet Murders*.
11. In America *And Then There Were None*, later *Ten Little Indians*.

few excursions into the psychological crime story. She was not a good writer, but she was a supreme mistress in the construction of puzzles and had a skill in writing light, lively and readable dialogue that has been consistently underrated by critics. There was also a darker side to her imagination, something that has been little recognized. Her concern with poisoning as a method of murder was almost obsessive. There are 83 cases of poisoning in her stories, some by means as exotic as coniine, gelsemium and ricin. Her death left a gap that will never be filled, because her exact combination of qualities is unimaginable in the world of the eighties.

(iii) Achievements and limitations

Many Golden Age writers whose work was highly regarded remain undiscussed, including Josephine Bell and E. R. Punshon in Britain, Mignon G. Eberhart, Conyth Little, Mabel Seeley, Helen Reilly and Elizabeth Daly in America. The list could easily be lengthened. But the most notable practitioners have already been examined in detail, and the period can properly be judged by them.

The Golden Age achievement can be seen at its best in the close plotting of the early Queen, Van Dine and Sayers stories, the cunning tricks of Christie, the locked-room deceptions of Carr, the literary ease of Innes and Blake. If we consider the crime story only as a puzzle, nothing written during the last thirty years comes within trailing distance of the Golden Age work, although it should be said that little attempts to do so. If we consider it as a frivolous entertainment, nothing has been produced that is the equal of early Innes. There are no trick stories nowadays as good as those of Christie and Carr.

In constructing the detective story as a perfect mechanism, however, the Golden Age writers sacrificed almost everything else. Their work pandered to the taste of readers who wanted every character de-gutted so that there should be nothing even faintly disturbing about the fate of victims or murderers. To insulate your writing totally from life is also to make it trivial. Although crime stories are fairy tales, in the end they must inevitably be 'about' life more than most other fiction. We can enjoy a certain degree of make-believe, but if the effect is wholly artificial, in the end we dissent from what is being offered us. The Golden Age was not the main highway of crime fiction that it looked at the time, but a minor road full of interesting twists and views which petered out in a dead end.

A curious experiment by the thriller writer Dennis Wheatley with the planning co-operation of J. G. Links, which began in 1936 with the publication of the 'murder dossier' *Murder Off Miami*,[12] blew the gaff on the artificial nature of the Golden Age story, although this was not the authors' intention. These 'murder dossiers' were artefacts rather than books. They contained 'real' clues in the shapes of such things as hair, matches, poison pills, in transparent envelopes, along with photographs of the characters and the scene of the crime. The text came in the form of telegrams, letters, memoranda, police documents and reports, all reproduced in facsimile. In Britain the dossiers were produced in loose-leaf form with ribbon bindings, in America at first between stiff covers. The solution of the problem depended on the illustrations. In the first dossier the presence of the wrong kind of toothbrush on the washstand and the fact that one character's coat did not fit very well had to be spotted, and in *The Malinsay Massacre* a close study of the family tree which is reproduced at the beginning reveals that the storyteller himself is the logical murderer.

The first dossier sold 80,000 copies in Britain at the very low price of 3s 6d. The second and third were less successful, but still sold well. The fourth, *Herewith the Clues*, was an almost complete failure. In America and in other countries they had less success than in Britain. The sudden end of the dossiers, which are now collectors' items (some have been reprinted), reflected partly the coming of the War and partly increased costs, but principally the fact that it was very nearly impossible actually to read them. There was in the nature of things no characterization of any kind, and interest rested solely in the comparison of the texts with the visible clues in an attempt to discover discrepancies. Once the gimmick of the visual clues and the letter facsimiles lost its impact, the stories could be recognized as frankly dull, and nobody would be inclined to 'read' one of these dossiers a second time. But then the orthodox detective puzzles of the time were only similarly bloodless and characterless games of a more sophisticated kind, after all.

Something of this was understood by the late thirties. When Sayers said that 'after a time ... the writer gets tired of a literature without bowels' she was perfectly right, although she mistook an aristocratic pedigree for bowels. Allingham, Queen, Stout, Blake, Innes, all recognized that the old order had to change and tried to change with it, but they carried with them the ball-and-chain of detective heroes who could not be sacrificed because of their popularity. There was also a groundswell of conscious objection to the rules and to the game, which has already been mentioned.

12. In America *File on Bolitho Blane*.

The promise of 'a novel with a detective or crime interest' made by Anthony Berkeley (Cox) was fulfilled by his alter ego, Francis Iles. In *Malice Aforethought* (1931) and its successor *Before the Fact* (1932) there is no puzzle of the classical kind. From the start the villain is plain to us, and his intentions are known. The problem is whether he will be able to carry them out successfully. What was new about the books may be expressed in the first sentences of *Malice Aforethought*: 'It was not until several weeks after he had decided to murder his wife that Dr Bickleigh took any active steps in the matter. Murder is a serious business.'

Everything is laid out, the doctor's plans, their fulfilment, the police investigation. Some critics have said that a similar approach was made earlier, by Mrs Belloc Lowndes and by Austin Freeman in his 'inverted' stories, but Iles's method is so much more subtle that his work is really not comparable. The fascination of these two books lies in the interplay of character, the gaps between plot and execution, and the air of suburban or small-town normality with which Iles invests the whole thing. The slow revelation of the villain's character in *Before the Fact* is beautifully done, and the books show very clearly that the naming of the criminal in the last chapter is not the only way of surprising the reader. Iles was a very clever writer, and the only criticism that might be made of these outstandingly original books is that they have just occasionally an air of contrivance out of keeping with their generally realistic tone.

The third Iles book, *As for the Woman* (1939), was interesting but less successful than the first two. Announced as the first volume of a trilogy, it had no successor. During the thirties Cox also wrote several Anthony Berkeley books. One of them, *Trial and Error* (1937), exploits a variation of the Iles theme in the sense that we see Mr Todhunter, who has only a few months to live, deliberately planning and apparently carrying out a murder. Too flippantly conceived to be on the same level as the Iles stories, this is still a highly enjoyable book with several characteristically clever twists and turns.

The Iles books were admired, although the masterly way in which they broke away from the conventions of the detective story was not fully appreciated. Iles had several followers, who faithfully copied his avoidance of the classical puzzle and tried hard to catch his particular blend of cynicism and realism, but for the most part succeeded only in being casual about murder. Among them were Richard Hull, the pseudonym of Richard Henry Sampson (1896–1973), and Anthony Rolls, the name under which the historian and belle-lettrist Colwyn Edward Vulliamy (1886–1971) wrote crime stories. In *Murder of My Aunt* (1934), the best of Hull's books, an epicene young man tries to kill his aunt, first through an apparent car accident, then by arson and finally with poison. The joke has become laboured long before the end, in which she foreseeably murders him. Rolls's *The Vicar's Experiments* (1932)[13] is about a clergyman who suddenly begins to suffer from homicidal delusions, believing that he has 'been chosen by the Inscrutable Purpose to be the destroyer of Colonel Cargoy'. A good deal of what follows is very amusing, but the story falters sadly once suspicion of the clergyman has been aroused. The weakness of Iles's followers was that they found it almost impossible to resist being facetious, whereas the master himself wrote about murder in a manner blending the detached interest of a recording angel and the impersonality of a court reporter. Rolls's later books, published twenty years and more after *The Vicar's Experiments*, did not repeat its success, and Hull had declined into a comparatively conventional writer by the fifties, when his last book appeared.

Something of Iles's realism, although not his humour, is present in *A Pin to See the Peep-Show* (1934) by F. Tennyson Jesse (1889–1958). Taking the famous Thompson–Bywaters murder case as a basis, she produced a soundly realistic crime novel which is especially good in showing the romantic Edith Thompson, renamed Julia Almond, as she becomes more and more completely caught in a web of fantasy.

The best book written under the influence of Iles – the influence was less direct and so the story more original – was *Verdict of Twelve* (1940) by Raymond Postgate (1896–1971). Stories about juries tend to have a dismal similarity (the favourite plot finds jurymen who tried some ancient murder case being killed off one by one), but Postgate's puzzle, set in terms of the characters of the jury members and their reactions, remains fresh on a second or third reading. A certain diffusion of interest between the jury and the case they are trying is the only weakness of a highly accomplished first crime story, which had two slightly disappointing successors.

Altogether the Iles school, including its founder, showed a certain lack of staying power. Iles's own long-term effect upon the crime story was permanent and important, but for the time being his influence faded.

13. In America called *Clerical Error*, and later reissued under this title in Britain with Vulliamy acknowledged as the author.

· 10 ·

The American Revolution

Almost from the beginning the American crime story was deeply in debt to its British counterpart. (Poe was an exception.) Writers like Van Dine, and Queen in the first stage of his career, put an American gloss on what was essentially a British central figure, and there was nothing peculiarly native about the Rinehart formula. Stories in the Rinehart manner, involving heroines who ventured into situations where they found themselves in close proximity to a murderer with nobody else around, were produced by several other writers, some of whom were more skilful than Rinehart, although none quite equalled her success. Eberhart's Nurse Keate and Susan Dare had a good many narrow escapes.

A truly American crime story, making full use of the manners, habits and language of the United States, and breaking completely with European tradition, appeared in the twenties. It emerged through the pulp magazines, so named because they were printed on cheap, grainy wood-pulp paper. The early crime pulps, which appeared during the First World War, were fairly tame magazines using orthodox detectives and a good deal of British material, but they changed rapidly so that by the mid-twenties the dominating figure in them was the American private eye. The pulps catered for a large audience, literate but not literary, eager at one extreme for stories about fantasy figures with names like The Shadow and The Spider, and at another for tales of realistic violence set in recognizable surroundings. They were the blue-collar workers' version of the crime story, and their popularity reflected the rise of the gangster in American society with the coming of Prohibition in 1920 and its accompanying civic and police corruption.

The writers for these pulp magazines had no literary intentions. Their hardboiled dicks did not inhabit the same world as the Great Detective. Where the Great Detective avoided and often scorned violence, to the hardboiled dick it was as natural as drinking. 'Many people have their little peculiarities. Mine was holding a loaded gun in my hand while I slept,' says Carroll John Daly's Race Williams, said to be the first hardboiled dick.

Williams used his gun very often, mostly against other gunmen, explaining that 'You can't make hamburger without grinding up a little meat'. The Great Detective's language was affected or colourless, that of the hard-boiled dick pungent as cigar smoke or garlic. The Great Detective was omniscient, and believed in the supreme power of reason. The hardboiled dick moved instinctively, was as fallible as the next man, and put faith in his gun.

There were a great many pulp magazines, but much the most notable was *Black Mask* during the reign of Captain Joseph T. Shaw, from 1926 to 1936. When he took over, Shaw had little knowledge of pulp fiction and was determined to make it less crude, although not less violent. He encouraged the best writers by using them consistently and more often, and increased the rate of pay, which was a miserable cent a word. As Shaw told his authors, he wanted stories of violent action directly told, and he eliminated everything unconnected with the physical excitement he demanded as rigorously as Ezra Pound blue-pencilled the adjectives in the early work of Hemingway. Shaw believed also, in contrast to Golden Age writers, that 'action is meaningless unless it involves recognizable human characters in three-dimensional form'. The stories in *Black Mask* had a corporate style, whether they were written by Daly, Erle Stanley Gardner under his early pseudonym of Charles M. Green, George Harmon Coxe, Raoul Whitfield, Lester Dent, or even by Raymond Chandler, whose first story 'Blackmailers Don't Shoot' was published by the magazine in 1933. Shaw was intelligent enough to recognize in Dashiell Hammett one writer of exceptional natural talent, a talent that was first trimmed to fit the requirements of the magazine and then expanded in at least two of the century's finest crime novels.

Samuel Dashiell Hammett (1894–1961) was one of those independent free-wheeling hard-living Radicals who seem to Europeans typical of one kind of American. He left school at thirteen and had all kinds of jobs, including that of a Pinkerton detective. In his witty notes 'From the Memoirs of a Private Detective' he says that he was once falsely accused of perjury and had to perjure himself to escape arrest, that he knew a detective who attempted to disguise himself and was taken into custody by the first policeman he met, that a chief of police gave him a complete description of a man down to a mole on his neck but forgot to mention that he had only one arm, and commented: 'That the law-breaker is invariably soon or late apprehended is probably the least challenged of extant myths. And yet the files of every detective bureau bulge with the records of unsolved mysteries and uncaught criminals.'

Raymond Chandler, writing in 1944, said that Hammett 'gave murder back to the kind of people that commit it for reasons, not just to provide a corpse; and with the means at hand, not with hand-wrought duelling pistols, curare, and tropical fish'. This is only half-true, or is not true in its implication that Hammett wrote realistically in a documentary sense. What his stories have, even the earliest and least of them, is a flavour wholly individual. This flavour comes partly from the bareness of a style in which everything superficial in the way of description has been removed, partly from his knowledge of actual criminal investigation, and partly from the wistful cynicism with which he wrote. The early short stories about a fat middle-aged detective called the Continental Op are remarkable in the way they are written, but not in the things they say. Their tersely casual characterization is attractive in a gritty way, but they are rarely memorable. Hammett's achievement rests upon his five full-length stories, *Red Harvest* and *The Dain Curse* (both 1929), *The Maltese Falcon* (1930), *The Glass Key* (1931) and *The Thin Man* (1934).

The first lines of *Red Harvest* show how far removed the story was in tone and feeling from any contemporary detective story, British or American: 'I first heard Personville called Poisonville by a red-haired mucker named Hickey Dewey in the Big Ship in Butte. He also called his shirt a shoit. I didn't think anything of what he had done to the city's name.' The corruption of the city is conveyed on the same page in a view of its policemen which would not have appealed to Sayers or to Queen:

> The first policeman I saw needed a shave. The second had a couple of buttons off his shabby uniform. The third stood in the centre of the city's main intersection – Broadway and Union Street – directing traffic, with a cigar in one corner of his mouth. After that I stopped checking them up.

The narrator in this story is the Continental Op, who within hours of his arrival is plunged into a blood-bath of battles between rival gangsters. The police are crooked almost to a man, and in one comic sequence a gang boss whose house is under siege gets away by sending a couple of men out with bribes and then driving off in a Police Department car. The Continental Op plays off one gang boss against another, does his share of killing, destroys them all, and leaves Poisonville a clean town, although one which, as the Op knows, will revert to violence and corruption within a few years. This world of total violence was not far removed from life in some parts of urban America, and Hammett does not make the gang bosses glamorous or the Continental Op a crusader. The bosses are scum on top of the stew, the detective observes certain elemental decencies and loyalties, that is all. Sam Spade in *The Maltese Falcon*, Ned Beaumont in *The Glass Key*, are nearly but not quite dishonest. In the end they answer to the demands of some kind of justice, rather than those of love or friendship.

With all his innovations of form and language, Hammett kept the puzzle element from the orthodox detective story. Who gunned down Spade's partner Miles Archer in an alley, killed Taylor Henry in China Street, caused the disappearance of the thin man, Clyde Wynant? The problems are composed just as skilfully as those in an orthodox detective story, but in the best of Hammett they are the beginning and not the end of the book's interest. *The Maltese Falcon* and *The Glass Key* offer a gallery of characters and scenes unexcelled in the crime story, all of them seen with a Dickensian sense of the truth in caricature. One portrait must stand for twenty, that of Caspar Gutman in *The Maltese Falcon*:

The fat man was flabbily fat with bulbous pink cheeks and lips and chins and neck, with a great soft egg of a belly that was all his torso, and pendant cones for arms and legs. As he advanced to meet Spade all his bulbs rose and shook and fell separately with each step, in the manner of clustered soap-bubbles not yet released from the pipe through which they had been blown. His eyes, made small by fat puffs around them, were dark and sleek. Dark ringlets thinly covered his broad scalp. He wore a black cutaway coat, black vest, black satin Ascot tie holding a pinkish pearl, striped grey worsted trousers and patent-leather shoes.

In *The Glass Key* the theme is again that of the gangster-ruled town, seen this time not in terms of pure violence but of personal integrity. Paul Madvig is a half-honest gang boss, a back-slapper not very quick in the uptake. Ned Beaumont, his much more intelligent sidekick, is devoted to him. As James Sandoe has said, the book is not only a detective story but 'an exceptionally delicate scrutiny of friendship under curious conditions'. The women in the book are painfully real, where Miss Wonderly in *The Maltese Falcon* is still a bit of a pipe-dream. Some of the tricks and strategies, like those in the chapter where Beaumont destroys the feeble editor of the *Observer*, are memorable. The prose is more subtle and complex than that of the short stories or of *Red Harvest*, which was thought by André Gide to have given pointers to Hemingway and Faulkner.

The Glass Key is the peak of Hammett's achievement, which is to say the peak of the crime writer's art in the twentieth century. Constant re-reading of it offers fresh revelations of the way in which a crime writer with sufficient skill and tact can use violent events to comment by indirection on life, art, society, and at the same time compose a novel admirable in the carpentry of its structure and delicately intelligent in its suggestions of truths about human relationships. As a novel *The Glass Key* is remarkable, as a crime novel unique. It was succeeded by *The Thin Man*, a continuously charming and sparkling performance, which was still for Hammett a slight decline. And that was the end. The books were filmed, the production of 'Thin Man' comedy thrillers with William Powell and Myrna Loy became for a time a minor industry. Hammett went to Hollywood and wrote no more books. His whole writing career, outside screen work in Hollywood, covered only eleven years and the novels only five.

The brevity of his career as a writer springs from the fact that for Hammett, much more than for most men, his books were a minor offshoot of a hard, reckless life. His drinking from the twenties onwards, one of his friends told me, was explicable 'only by an assumption that he had no expectation of being alive much beyond Thursday'. He regarded *The Glass Key* as his best book, but thought little of any of them, and refused to allow the short stories to be reprinted. He went to prison during the witch-hunt of the fifties because he refused to reveal the names of contributors to the funds of a Communist front organization. He was probably, but not certainly, a card-carrying Communist. His friend and lover Lillian Hellman said that although he was 'often witty and bitingly sharp about the American Communist Party ... he was, in the end, loyal to them'. By his own standards Hammett was perhaps a failure, but they are standards far removed from those we use in dealing with most crime writers. *The Glass Key* can stand comparison with any American novel of its decade.

It can stand comparison, for example, with *Sanctuary* (1931), by his friend William Faulkner. The principal contribution made to the crime story by Faulkner (1897–1962) was perhaps his short stories about Gavin Stevens, but the novels are always hovering on the edge of crime fiction, although only *Sanctuary* and possibly *Intruder in the Dust* can really be classed as crime novels. *Intruder in the Dust* (1948) has the apparatus of an orthodox detective story – a murder, a substitute body, an empty coffin, Gavin Stevens as investigator – but the true interest for Faulkner lies in the relationship between the town's whites and the Negro accused of murder. *Sanctuary* is another matter. Before writing it, Faulkner said much later, he asked himself what would sell ten thousand copies, and then 'invented the most horrific tale I could imagine and wrote it in about three weeks'. That 'about three weeks' was not accurate, and he need not have been so deprecatory, for the book is not merely a potboiler. With its terrified heroine-victim and its voyeuristic villain it is a shocker, which probably provided the germ of *No Orchids for Miss Blandish*, but unlike most shockers it is a book really *written*, and the theme gives Faulkner's curdled prose a distinct air of menace. With its romanticism about sexual violence, *Sanctuary* looks forward to much that has been disagreeably developed by later crime writers, but what a French critic has called Faulkner's 'technique of hallucination' makes the book memorable, and suffuses it with a queer sort of poetry.

Few of Hammett's contemporaries – that is, of those whose approach to crime writing resembled his – had a distinctive talent. Two of them, however, made considerable contributions to the American revolution in the crime story. *Little Caesar* (1929), the first novel by W. R. Burnett (1899–1982), has a good claim to be called also the first gangster novel. It tells the story of the rise of an Italian petty mobster, Cesare Rico Bandello, from his beginnings as 'just a lonely yegg, stitching up chain-stores and filling-stations', to brief eminence as leader of a Chicago gang. The book is written mostly in dialogue, and a three-page glossary was thought necessary in the English edition. Yet the language, accurate but dry, lacks the richness of Hammett's slang, and Burnett's deliberate restraint in characterizing Rico makes him in the end curiously blank. Edward G. Robinson's excellent playing of the part in a fairly faithful adaptation gave the figure style and colour lacking in the novel. The pedestrian quality of Burnett's writing was shown also in his other considerable contribution to the *genre*, *The Asphalt Jungle* (1949). This had the benefit of what was at the time an original idea, the criminal caper that demands participation from several men, each with a vital part to play, but the figures are all stereotypes, the smooth crooked lawyer, the planning 'genius' who dislikes violence, the safe-breaker who is doing the job for wife and family, the hooligan who wants to revisit scenes of childhood innocence. Burnett was never less than a skilful plotter, never more than an efficient writer. A comparison of *Little Caesar* with *Red Harvest* helps to show why Hammett was supreme in this field.

James M. Cain (1892–1977) produced in *The Postman Always Rings Twice* (1934) a tart, taut tale of sex and money, told with concentration on the bare, relevant material of crime. Cain once said that he had read a little of *The Glass Key* and then 'said forget this goddamn book'. If he had persevered he might have gone beyond the homespun wisdom of saying about his own books: 'How you write 'em is write 'em.' The sexual passages of *Postman*, which now seem commonplace, were shocking at the time, but what vitiates Cain's writing is a coarseness of feeling allied to a weakness for melodrama. His tastes were those of American cinema in the thirties and forties, which helps to explain why *Postman* and the cunningly plotted long short story 'Double Indemnity' made excellent films.

The gap between Burnett and Cain and most of the *Black Mask* or *Dime Detective* writers was wide. Burnett and Cain considered themselves novelists, not mere penny-a-liners, and were treated as such by many critics who would have regarded pulp writers as beneath notice. And it is true that, in spite of recent attempts to take seriously the now-forgotten pulp writers of the period, like Paul Cain (unrelated to James M.), Lester Dent, Norbert Davis and Raoul Whitfield, few of them had more than the elementary writing skill of describing violent action with some conviction. One or two of their successors, whose work has appeared in paperback originals, have also been praised. Jim Thompson (1906–76), probably the best of them, is no more than an efficient imitator of other writers in the genre, particularly James M. Cain, on the evidence of four novels recently reissued. Some of Thompson's books have been filmed, and he strikes one as a writer whose talent was for the cinema rather than for the novel – he worked on the scripts of two excellent Kubrick films, *The Killing* and *Paths of Glory*. What these writers lack is individuality, so that it is difficult to tell the work of one from another.

Cornell George Hopley-Woolrich (1903–68), who wrote as Cornell Woolrich, William Irish and George Hopley, is at present a cult figure in America, 'one of the greatest suspense writers in the history of crime fiction', as one enthusiast mistakenly puts it. Woolrich wrote for *Black Mask* and many other magazines, but his work was only loosely associated with that of more typical pulp writers. His best writing is in the novels he produced at great speed in the early forties, including *The Bride Wore Black* (1940) and one of the Irish books, *Phantom Lady* (1942), but the melodramatic silliness and sensationalism of many of his plots, and the continuous high-pitched whine of his prose – seen at its worst in the collection of stories *Nightwebs* (1971) – preclude him from serious consideration.

The distinctive mark of Jonathan Latimer (1906–83) is an irresponsible gaiety that marks out his work from the ordinary competent hard-boiled novel. The best Latimers, *Headed for a Hearse* (1935) and *The Lady in the Morgue* (1936), two of the first books about his cynical, humorous, womanizing detective Bill Crane, are almost super-typical books of the period. *Solomon's Vineyard* (1941), in which Crane does not appear, is a savage and for its time sexually outspoken book. Latimer's post-war work, unhappily, is no more than a faint carbon copy of the Crane novels.

The American revolution made the hard-boiled crime story respectable. *Red Harvest* and *The Maltese Falcon* were recognized as new, remarkable, and American. 'The writing is better than Hemingway, since it conceals not softness but hardness,' said one typical comment. With the groundwork thus laid, the crime story could be treated as literature. Raymond Chandler (1888–1959) was highly conscious of the fact that he was working in what he called a mediocre form and trying to 'make something like literature out of it'. Such an implicit contempt for what you are doing is not a good receipt for any kind of writing, yet Chandler succeeded.

Chandler came late to the writing of crime stories. In youth in England he had written whimsical reviews and sentimental poems for magazines, but these activities were submerged when after the First World War he became an American executive working in an oil syndicate. He was forty-four when, after being fired from his job, he began to read the pulps and 'decided that this might be a good way to try to learn to write fiction and get paid a small amount of money at the same time'. His early short stories are almost indistinguishable from much of the other material in *Black Mask*, although a good deal is made of them now. His reputation, like Hammett's, rests on his novels. There were seven, beginning with *The Big Sleep* (1939), published when he was fifty years old.

Chandler had a fine feeling for the sound and value of words, and added to it a very sharp eye for places, things, people, and the wisecracks that in their tone and timing are almost always perfect. 'Did I hurt your head much?' Philip Marlowe asks a blonde in *The Big Sleep* after he has hit her with his gun. She replies: 'You and every other man I ever met.' It is impossible to convey in a single quotation Chandler's almost perfect ear for dialogue, but it comes through in all the later books, whether the people talking are film stars or publicity agents, rich men, gangsters or policemen. To this is joined a generous indignation roused in him by meanness and corruption, and a basic seriousness about his violent entertainments. The actual plotting of the books improved greatly as he became more sure of himself. In the first two or three stories the joke he made about solving plot problems by having a man come in the door with a gun is not too far away from the truth, but the plots of *The Little Sister* (1949) and *The Long Goodbye* (1953) are as smoothly dovetailed as a piece of Chippendale. Yet plotting was never something he really enjoyed. Nothing could better indicate the difference between Chandler and a typical Golden Age writer than the fact that for the Golden Age writer the plot is everything and the writing might often be done by computer, whereas Chandler thought that 'plotting may be a bore even if you are good at it' but 'a writer who hates the actual writing to me is simply not a writer at all'. And we do read Chandler first of all for the writing, and afterwards for the Californian background, the jokes, the social observation, the character of Marlowe. The plots are firm and adequate, but they are not what we take away from the books.

It must be said that in the inevitable comparison between Hammett and Chandler, Chandler comes off second best. There was a toughness in Hammett that Chandler lacked, and did not appreciate. It comes through in his remark that the Hammett style could 'say things he did not know how to say or feel the need of saying' but that 'in his hands it had no overtones, left no echo, evoked no image beyond a distant hill'. Chandler set himself to remedy this, and to create in the private detective Philip Marlowe a man who should be 'a complete man and a common man and yet an unusual man ... to use a rather weathered phrase, a man of honour'. Yet the detachment in Hammett that seemed to Chandler inadequate was really a mark of strength. Chandler's famous rhetorical invocation to his dream detective hero which begins 'down these mean streets a man must go who is not himself mean, who is neither tarnished nor afraid', is too long to quote in full, but after reading it one can hardly be surprised that Marlowe was originally called Mallory. Sam Spade and the Continental Op have their crude code of ethics, but they are rough people doing dirty work. We can believe that private detectives were something like this. Philip Marlowe becomes with each book more a piece of wish-fulfilment, an idealized expression of Chandler himself, a strictly literary conception.

All this has to be said, yet Chandler was a very good writer, a good critic of the work he liked, and a sensitive, intelligent man. He wrote his own epitaph as a writer in one of his witty letters: 'To accept a mediocre form and make something like literature out of it is in itself rather an accomplishment ... Any decent writer who thinks of himself occasionally as an artist would far rather be forgotten so that someone better might be remembered.' Chandler's best work runs no risk of being forgotten.

Hammett wrote a scathing review of Van Dine's first novel, but had no real interest in the form of the crime story. Chandler had. 'It is the ladies and gentlemen of what Mr Howard Haycraft calls the Golden Age of detective fiction that really get me down,' he said in 'The Simple Art of Murder', the most powerful attack ever made on the classical detective story. By this time, it is true, he was knocking at an open door, for the limitations of the Golden Age's arbitrary conventions had been realized by several critics. Three years before Chandler's article appeared in 1944,

Philip Van Doren Stern had made many of the same points more gently in an article called 'The Case of the Corpse in the Blind Alley':

The great need of the mystery today is not novelty of apparatus but novelty of approach. The whole genre needs overhauling, a return to first principles, a realization that murder has to do with human emotion and deserves serious treatment. Mystery story writers need to know more about life and less about death – more about the way people think and feel and act, and less about how they die.

· 11 ·

Simenon and Maigret

The case of Georges Simenon (1903–   ) requires a separate chapter. He is one of the very few European crime writers (if we regard Britain as an offshore island) to have become famous outside his own country. Simenon is certainly much more than the author of the Maigret books, and it is among the 'hard' novels, as he calls them, that his best work is to be found, among them the universally praised *The Stain on the Snow* (1950; the dates given are those of French publication), *Monsieur Monde Vanishes* (1967), *Sunday* (1960) and *In Case of Emergency* (1958). These books are very various, but one theme often repeated is that of the emotional or financial power exerted by one person over another, and of a central figure moved by desperate need to break free of the bonds imposed by family, sex or money. The hard novels are often concerned with crime, yet they do not seem quite to come within the canon of the crime story. A book like *The Man Who Watched the Trains Go By* (1942), is very much a study in character first, a crime story second, even though Sergeant Lucas from the Maigret stories has strayed into it and become a Superintendent.

The first thing an English reader is likely to notice about the Maigret saga is the contrast between the realism of the characterization and background and the sensationalism of the plot. In *The Madman of Bergerac* (1932) Maigret dives out of a train in pursuit of a man who has occupied the upper bunk in his sleeping berth, is shot by him, taken to the little town of Bergerac, and spends the rest of the story recuperating in a hotel room and trying to discover the apparent madman who has killed two women by use of a long needle stuck through the heart, and has attacked a third. Maigret knows that the murderer is one of the people who visited his hotel room, because he has carelessly dropped a railway ticket in the passage outside. The origins of the crime prove to lie far back in the past, in an extraordinary tale, revealed casually at the end of the book, about a doctor working in an Algiers hospital who discovers that his villainous father, condemned to death for his crimes, is also there. The doctor saves his father by burning down part of the hospital and substituting another body for that of his father. This doctor later establishes himself as a respectable figure in Bergerac. The 'madman' is in fact the father, now a psychopath, who has paid unwelcome visits to his son, murdering a woman each time. After the second of these murders the doctor kills his own father and empties his pockets of identificatory material, but carelessly drops the railway ticket outside Maigret's door.

Why should a plot of Simenon's be singled out for its improbability, it may be asked? What is a touch of arson, a body-substitution, a psychopath who stabs with needles, compared to a locked room? One is disconcerted by things in Simenon that can be taken for granted in John Dickson Carr, just because Simenon's characters are convincing as real men and women. If they were cardboard cut-outs one would mind much less what sort of conduct was attributed to them. The art of Simenon lies in making the implausible acceptable. Consider the opening of another early story, *Maigret and the Hundred Gibbets* (1931), in which Maigret follows a man over France and to the Dutch–German border simply because he sees him stuffing a large sum of money into an envelope and posting it. The man is shabby, and carries a cheap fibre suitcase, so what is he doing with so much money? Maigret manages to buy an identical case which he stuffs with newspaper, exchanges the cases at a railway station, and is in the next hotel room when the man shoots himself after discovering the exchange. Looked at in any reasonable light the detective's behaviour is highly improbable. The astonishing thing is that when one reads the books all this is made acceptable, and both these novels are extremely interesting and convincing stories. In the latter, there are bits of characteristic deadpan humour in the original police belief that Maigret is himself the man they are looking for, the relationship between the doctor who has something to hide, his wife and his mistress is sketched with easy mastery, and the feeling of a French provincial town as sensed, although not seen, by Maigret while he fidgets in bed is perfectly done. This early Maigret is a typical story, similar in its merits and weakness to others. The settings never fail, giving always an impression of personal involvement with Paris or Antibes, a shop by the Belgian frontier or a Guinguette by the Seine. The weather is described with such vigour and pleasure that it is, again, as though the writer were actually soaking up the rain or sun that he is writing about. Simenon's susceptibility to physical experience of this kind is greater than that of any other contemporary novelist. And the characters grow in this thick soil of sensuous experience, they fit perfectly into sleazy or criminal city life, a small town's close provincialism or the uneasy potential violence of a port. They take colour and conviction from their surroundings, and there seems almost no limit to the kinds of people Simenon knows.

If a single story had to be chosen to represent the finest qualities of the Maigret novels without any of their defects, it might be *My Friend Maigret* (1949). Here Maigret takes the chance to get away from rainy Paris to the heat-soaked island of Porquerolles in the Midi. An old crook has been murdered, it is thought because he boasted that Maigret was his friend. Accompanied by a Scotland Yard detective who has come to study Maigret's methods (but as Maigret says, he has no methods), the detective goes to Porquerolles and there shows his gift for absorbing like a sponge the nature of the people who live on the island, and concealing behind his apparently sluggish enjoyment of the local food and drink the capacity for interpreting behaviour which is his greatest detectival asset. The crime proves to be a product of that total nihilistic rejection of any standard of behaviour by some of the young which Simenon was contemplating long before the days of student revolt, and there is some fine characterization. The crook's former girlfriend, who was once helped by Maigret and is now the madame of a brothel, is particularly good. The Scotland Yard man is merely touched in, but Maigret's uneasiness in his presence provides some passages of unstrained comedy. There are no coincidences, no improbabilities. This is certainly one of the best half-dozen Maigret stories.

Although the finest stories are among the hard novels, the creation of Maigret is Simenon's greatest achievement. We know him as well as we know Sherlock Holmes, certainly better than any other modern detective, through his screen, radio and TV interpretations. For me the British Rupert Davies is the nearest thing to a perfect Maigret, but there have been French, German, Dutch and other actors playing the part. On the screen he has been played by Charles Laughton and Harry Baur. A recent radio Maigret series used the ingenious device of a discussion between Maigret and his creator at the start of each story.

Maigret defies the law that makes all other fictional detectives two-dimensional. Holmes is a deerstalker, a magnifying glass and a capacity for reasoning, not a human being. Wimsey is Bertie Wooster endowed with intelligence but still ridiculous, Poirot a stock version of the comic foreigner, Nero Wolfe exists only in relation to food, beer and orchids. They all come out of fairy tales of classical detection.

Maigret is different. He is more than a pipe, a trilby and a liking for aperitifs, although such things help to fix our understanding of his appearance and style. Maigret, seen all the way round, emerges as the ideal French bourgeois, married to a solid, reliable woman who is also a good cook, sometimes pedantic and fussy, humane and decent but limited in his views like any other member of his class. We know that Maigret would think modern art incomprehensible, distrust liberal education, be uneasy in the presence of the aristocracy and resent his own feeling of discomfort. He is much affected by weather, capable of doing distinctly scatty things on a fine spring morning, made gloomy or irritable by persistent rain. We know how he talks to his wife in unbuttoned moments (although we never see him literally unbuttoned in bed), and that he is sexually susceptible to other women. He has no obvious politics, but we are pretty sure how he would vote.

And Simenon has created for him a background just right for his class and personality. His father was bailiff at a château in the Auvergne. He met Louise, who became Madame Maigret, when taken by a former student friend to a party at which she provided the reassurance which the awkward young man needed. He gave up his medical studies and became a policeman almost by accident, but perhaps basically because he felt himself to be a man 'who would at first glance understand the destinies of others'. Only in this important respect is Maigret a superior version of the Average French Bourgeois Man — or perhaps in this and in the occasional flashes of intuitive understanding about motives and action that make him a great detective.

A witty and delightful view of him is provided in *Maigret's Memoirs* (1950), which shows us this background, and also describes Maigret's relationship with his creator. The detective complains that Simenon put a bowler hat on his head when he never wears one, and said that he habitually wears an overcoat with a velvet collar, when in fact this is an old coat which almost always hangs in the wardrobe.

The Maigret stories stand quite on their own in crime fiction, bearing little relation to most of the work done in the field. It has been said more than once, and truly, that they are not orthodox detective stories. The bases of the tales are often slight, almost anecdotal. There are no great feats of ratiocination in them, and the problems they present are human as much as criminal. The ambience of the stories is wonderfully real, the characters are often memorable, yet we are rarely emotionally moved by them. How nearly correct is Simenon in feeling that he is unjustly treated by readers' concentration on Maigret, and how good a writer is he? There is no doubt about the immense variety of his characterization and settings. The range of his male characters is extraordinary, and his women are less limited than has been suggested — suggested even by Simenon himself. Maigret, that repairer of destinies, is a wholly convincing figure. And yet —

And yet there is something lacking on the highest level. The coolness and detachment that serve so well in creating atmosphere are also limiting factors. No doubt it is true that Simenon lived his characters while writing about them, as he has claimed more than once, but still it appears that he dissects his people rather than entering their personalities. And the brevity of the novels suggests his unwillingness to explore the details of a section of society, or even of a character. The best books are fine small works of art, but they are *small* works of art. To read them and then to look at Balzac's novels is to move from miniatures to frescoes. The books, hard novels and Maigret stories alike, can be more easily admired than loved. Their creator is in some ways the most extraordinary literary phenomenon of the century: but his talents have been those of a literary surgeon rather than a great creator.

'Mr Queen, will you be good enough to explain your famous character's sex life, if any?'

Looking back at the decade that began with the Second World War, it can be seen as one of desperate struggle by established crime writers to adapt to new conditions and ways of feeling. The War was a watershed in the history of the crime story, separating not only the world of housemaids and nurses from that of daily helps and *au pair* girls, but also the world of reason from that of force. The assumption of the classical detective story was that human affairs are ruled by reason. Crimes were committed by individuals, small holes torn in the fabric of society. The individuals were discovered, the holes mended, by the detective who represented the force of order, and he did this through a process of reasoning. Such beliefs were buttressed by the existence of the League of Nations, and most Golden Age writers adhered, consciously or unconsciously, to the often expressed view that there would be no war in Europe, this year or next year either. The War forced upon them the acknowledgement that quite a different world existed, one in which force was supreme and in which irrational doctrines ruled more than one nation. It was a world much more like that of *Red Harvest* than that of *Gaudy Night* or *The Greek Coffin Mystery*. Naturally the writers did not think of it in those terms, but with the end of the War efforts to adapt to the world of the atomic bomb marked the nature of crime writing. Later other adaptations were made: to the Pill, the loosening of verbal and ethical standards, the use of torture as an interrogation procedure; but the Second World War marked the decisive change. After it, the crime story was never quite the same.

The immediate question for established writers was what could be done with the Great Detective, who in a symbolic sense had failed to prevent the War and in a realistic one appeared more absurd as scientific and forensic aids to detection became more refined and more important. The idea of the British Superintendent or the American Chief of Police pleading with the languid investigator to spare a little time from his research into Transylvanian folksongs and solve a problem that had baffled the best police brains of Scotland Yard or New York looked increasingly ridiculous, yet how could 'Ellery Queen' sacrifice Ellery Queen or Margery Alling-ham give up Albert Campion? And there were other incongruities, equally painful to face. Hammett, when introducing Ellery Queen to a lecture audience, began by asking: 'Mr Queen, will you be good enough to explain your famous character's sex life, if any?' Such a question could not have been asked before the Second World War. Holmes could then be accepted as a misogynist, Poirot as an ageing bachelor, Queen as a figure susceptible to feminine beauty but above or outside emotional entangle-ment, but with the acceptance during the fifties and sixties of the fact that everybody has some kind of real and/or fantasy sex life, such easy answers would no longer do. It now appeared suggestive of impotence to fall in love with lovely ladies in a purely platonic way like Ellery; there seemed something sexually ambiguous about the household of Nero Wolfe and Archie Goodwin ... Without going into more details, it is clear that Hammett's question showed up sharply the totally mythical nature of the Great Detective. Queen's response was to say that a wife, mistress or even physical love affair planted on Ellery after all these years would upset readers. That was no doubt true, but the difficulty remained, and was recognized.

The solutions attempted varied with individual writers. Some ignored the problem altogether. John Dickson Carr's Gideon Fell and H. M. came puffing and wheezing into the post-war world creaking like antique engines on a grass-grown track. Dannay and Lee, however, made a determined attempt to give up the formula they had used so brilliantly. From Calamity Town (1942) onwards, the Ellery Queen books were often set in the small town of Wrightsville, with its 'complacent elms, wandering cobbles, and crooked side-streets nestled in the lap of a farmer's valley and leaning against the motherly abdomen of one of New England's most matriarchal mountain ranges'. There is a rejection of artificiality, an approach to naturalism, in Calamity Town, There Was An Old Woman (1943) and The Murderer is a Fox (1945). These stories have much that is admirable about them, and a real effort is made in them to find a new approach to the mystery story.

But Dannay and Lee could not bring themselves to give up Ellery. His pince-nez have gone, occasionally he loses his father, but Ellery himself remains, a Golden Age figure out of place in the kind of stories that the cousins were trying to write, tales in which the characterization was detailed and perceptive. Ellery is excluded from *The Glass Village* (1954), but this attempt to comment critically on McCarthyism, then at its height, loses much of its intended impact through the melodramatic way in which the material is treated. (The inhabitants of a small New England village capture a murder suspect, beat and almost lynch him, and then try him for murder themselves.) *The Glass Village* might have been more successful if the approach had been naturalistic, but by this time Dannay and Lee had abandoned naturalism and Wrightsville. In *Ten Days' Wonder* (1948) and *Double, Double* (1950) fantastic ingenuity took over at the expense of characterization, and although one may admire the cleverness of the later books, there is still something preposterous about them. The postulates of *The Player on the Other Side* (1963), in which four cousins, each living in his own 'castle', are being killed off one by one, outdo Van Dine in absurdity, and acceptance of the story is not helped by the presence of the religious symbolism that touches much of the later Queen. The best of Ellery Queen, which was very good, is in the marvellously clever early books and the tales of Wrightsville which promised something Dannay and Lee were not quite able to perform.

Poirot was intelligently modified. His moustaches and his language were trimmed and he became, as Christie put it, 'more and more of a private investigator and less of an engaged enquiry agent'. With that her public rested content, and if the author herself was dissatisfied, so that she removed Poirot from books turned into plays, she found solace in the activities of her second string, Miss Marple, who has placidly knitted her way through a good many cases since her first appearance in 1930. To an outside eye Miss Marple seems more unreal than Poirot, but in spite of an inevitable faltering of invention, Agatha Christie managed the problem of adaptation better than most of her contemporaries.

Some writers went no further than smoothing down the rough edges of their detectives and making them nearer to ordinary humanity. Patrick Quentin's theatrical producer, Peter Duluth, and Edmund Crispin's Professor Gervase Fen, are not detectives, but people to whom things happen. Agreeable characters and perceptive men, they were still only shadows of the Great Detectives of the past, just as Nigel Strangeways and Nero Wolfe in their later incarnations were only a faint echo of the men they had been before the War. But what was the point of having an amateur detective at all, if he was not to be in some way exceptional? The thought must have occurred to Margery Allingham, who used considerable skill in changing Campion from the near-Wimsey or near-Wooster figure of the early books into a character altogether more serious and mature. In *Coroner's Pidgin* (1945)[1] the intelligence behind his apparent vacuity is stressed:

There were new lines in his over-thin face and with their appearance some of his old misleading vacancy of expression had vanished. But nothing had altered the upward drift of his thin mouth nor the engaging astonishment which so often and so falsely appeared in his pale eyes.

Campion played a smaller part in these later books, where her Stevensonian feeling for adventurous romance with a hint of horror in the background were given full play. *More Work for the Undertaker* (1948) shows her moving away from the orthodox crime story while retaining its puzzle element, and in the best of all her books, *The Tiger in the Smoke* (1952), she broke away completely from the old conventions to produce a thriller of the highest quality about a hunted man and his hunters. Yet one feels in these books, as in the best of the later Queens, that good as they are they would have been better still without the presence of the detective who belonged to an earlier time and a different tradition.

Ngaio Marsh never went so far as Allingham in attempting to write novels with a detective element, rather than detective stories. Her capacity for amused observation of the undercurrents beneath ordinary social interchanges was so good that one hoped for more than she ever tried to do. The first half of *Opening Night* (1951)[2] gives a brilliant picture of the intrigues taking place before the opening of a new play. All this is, as it should be, preparation for the murder that takes place, and we hope that after the murder the book will remain in the same key and that the problems will be resolved as they began, in terms of character. To our disappointment, however, Marsh takes refuge from real emotional problems in the official investigation and interrogation of suspects. The temperature is lowered, the mood has been lost.

In later books like *When in Rome* (1971) and *Black as He's Painted* (1974) she similarly evaded the problems in terms of character suggested early in the books. Dame Ngaio defended her practice with modesty and charm, saying that she always began with two or three people about whom she wanted to write, and involved them in a crime of violence, but that 'the more deeply and honestly [a novelist] examines her characters, the more disquieting becomes the skulduggery that [she] is obliged to practise in respect to the guilty party'. To the suggestion that she avoided emotional problems she replied that this was 'almost a definition of one of the major

1. In America *Pearls Before Swine*.
2. In America *Night at the Vulcan*.

limitations of the genre'. Well, not quite. Other writers managed to square this circle, and engaging though the books are, one is bound to regret that Ngaio Marsh did not take her fine talent more seriously.

Patrick Quentin and Edmund Crispin have already been mentioned. Quentin's story shows an interesting and typical development. Richard Wilson Webb and Hugh Callingham Wheeler (1912–   ) collaborated in books written under the names of Q. Patrick and Jonathan Stagge. These were competent, but in no way exceptional, Golden Age crime stories. Patrick Quentin seems to have been a name invented to provide another pseudonym, but almost from the first the Quentin books were better than those of Patrick or Stagge. All of them had 'Puzzle' in the title, and *Puzzle for Fools ... Players ... Puppets ... Wantons ... Fiends ... Pilgrims*, appeared in the space of ten years. Then in the late forties the Puzzle stories and Peter Duluth, their appropriately lighthearted central character, were abandoned, together with the other pseudonyms. The later Quentin books, some of them written by Wheeler alone after Webb left the collaboration, are more serious in tone and more subtle in approach. There is no investigator. The books don't dig quite deep enough to be called serious crime novels, but all are alert studies of people who commit crimes for plausible reasons. On their own level these stories are credible, where a book like *Ten Days' Wonder* is not. The level of these later Quentins is very even, but *The Man with Two Wives* and *The Wife of Ronald Sheldon*[3] are two of the best. The last Quentin book appeared in 1965. In recent years Wheeler has turned to writing for the theatre and cinema.

The Crispin story shows the difficulties of a writer emerging at the end of the War who adhered by sympathy to Golden Age standards. Robert Bruce Montgomery (1921–78), who used the name of Edmund Crispin, was the last and most charming of the Farceurs. His first book, *The Case of the Gilded Fly* (1944),[4] was written when he was still an undergraduate. Crispin's master was, and remained, Michael Innes in the eight novels and one collection of short stories he produced at the rate of one a year until 1953. In the quarter-century that followed he published only one disappointing novel, *The Glimpses of the Moon*, which appeared in the year before his death. Crispin's work is marked by a highly individual sense of light comedy, and by a flair for verbal deception rather in the Christie manner. If he never gives the impression of solid learning that can be sensed behind Innes's frivolity, he is also never tiresomely literary. At his weakest he is flippant, at his best witty, but all his work

3. In America *My Son the Murderer*.
4.   In America *Obsequies at Oxford*.

had a high-spiritedness rare and welcome in the crime story. His third book, *The Moving Toyshop* (1946), about a toyshop that really does seem to move mysteriously from one part of Oxford to another, is probably his best, although the Shakespearian excursion *Love Lies Bleeding* (1948) is delightfully funny.

Nothing is more indicative of the changed atmosphere in which the new writers worked – writers, that is, who produced their first books near the end of the Golden Age or later – than the abandonment by most of them of the series character who appeared in a succession of books, and gave readers the comfortable pleasure of asking for a book not by the author's name but by that of his hero or detective. Of course the series character continued and continues to exist, but he is no longer an almost essential ingredient of a crime writer's success. The reaction against the pre-War Superman detective was partly political, prompted by distrust of all Supermen, and partly based upon the writers' feeling that they had something of interest to say which would be hampered rather than helped by the development of a single character. As the American critic Anthony Boucher said: 'It is all but impossible for any writer above the hack level to write about people and problems without implying some set of values, some ethical standard.' It has already been said that an ethical standard was implicit in the social values taken for granted by Sayers, Christie, Rinehart. (And it should perhaps be emphasized again that such names stand for dozens of their epigones, like Anthony Gilbert and Georgette Heyer in one country, Mignon G. Eberhart, Elizabeth Daly and Helen Reilly in another.) Such social values demanded the solution of problems by a detective, either amateur or professional. The attitudes of the new writers were different. They wanted to combine popular entertainment with a study of 'people and problems', and often they felt that an investigator was out of place.

There disappeared with the Great Detective much other impedimenta of the Golden Age, the accessories that had enhanced his feats. By 1950 there were few drawings of the grounds and the house, with the body shown in copse or library, stories based on the elucidation of alibis through timetables had vanished, nobody was dealing in unknown poisons, and methods of murder had become noticeably less bizarre. This happened gradually and some books like Ngaio Marsh's *Scales of Justice* offered a map, but nowadays you might read a hundred crime stories without finding a drawing of the manse or the manor house, and without discovering any murder weapon more arcane than knife or revolver. The new writers were inclined to ask Why rather than How, and their Why was often concerned with the psychological make-up and social background of killer and killed.

This was true even of a writer like Cyril Hare, whose work would have fitted comfortably into the Golden Age pattern if he had begun to write a few years earlier. Cyril Hare was the pseudonym used by Alfred Alexander Gordon Clark (1900–1958), a barrister who was on the staff of the Director of Public Prosecutions during the Second World War and later became a County Court Judge. Hare showed from the first an agreeable liveliness in writing dialogue, and an unusual capacity for using his legal knowledge. In his fourth book, *Tragedy at Law* (1942), his gifts coalesced, and the account of the life of a Judge on circuit is done with a sense of comedy and a feeling for character that keep one totally absorbed in the misadventures of the Honourable Sir William Hereward Barber, Justice of the King's Bench Division of the High Court of Justice. The mystery is interesting too, but what holds us from the start is the account of the legal world that Hare was able to see with detachment and intimate affection. He never equalled this book, the first half of which is outstanding among portraits of legal life in crime fiction, but all his work is marked by careful plotting and a nice ear for conversation.

In the late fifties I produced the dubiously useful list of the Hundred Best Crime Stories already mentioned, for an English Sunday paper. They were dismayed when many of the selections proved to be out of print, and although I insisted upon some of my unobtainable selections (what was the good of choosing books which readers couldn't buy, the paper not unreasonably asked), I agreed after prolonged arguments to make some substitutions which seemed harmless at the time but look regrettable now. The list was also partly co-operative, in the sense that I approached several critics and asked them to select their favourite recent crime stories. Among them was Howard Haycraft, historian and devotee of the classical detective story. It is a striking confirmation of the decay in the classical form that the only post-war writer thought by Haycraft worthy to enter the canon was Elizabeth Mackintosh (1897–1952), who wrote plays under the name of Gordon Daviot and crime stories as Josephine Tey. Her first crime story, *The Man in the Queue* (1929),[5] introduced the slight, dapper Inspector Grant, and for its time and of its kind was an unusually interesting performance, although it depends upon the supposition that a man stabbed in a theatre queue will not cry out, or even know what has happened, before he collapses a minute or two later. Other Teys were

5. In America *Killer in the Crowd.*

published intermittently, and all have something original about them, in particular *The Franchise Affair* (1948), which translates the eighteenth-century disappearance of Elizabeth Canning into modern terms, and then offers an explanation which really applies to the modern rather than the eighteenth-century case. The opening, which sets out the mystery, is wonderfully good. The solution is a little disappointing, not only because it is foreseeable, but because the central figures are no more than conventionally sketched.

The book selected by Haycraft as her best, with the agreement of several other critics, was an unquestionably original but also freakish performance called *The Daughter of Time* (1951). In this, Grant, immobilized after falling thorugh a trap-door, provides with help from an American student a solution to the mystery of the Princes in the Tower, on the lines that they were murdered at the instance not of Richard III but of Henry VII. There is nothing new about the theory, as the student discovers at the end of their research, and Grant's almost total ignorance of history is the most remarkable thing about the book. The pleasure taken by critics in the slow unfolding of a thesis already well known suggests a similar ignorance on their part. Still more to the point is the fact that this amateur rehashing of a well-known argument, interspersed with visits from friends to the detective's bedside is, as one might expect, really rather dull.

Many rate Josephine Tey more highly than I do: but whatever one thinks about her merits, her most praised work was not only preoccupied by the past but also belonged to it. The anticipatory notes of the coming themes were struck in four books published during the forties. The themes they announce are those of the realistic and even brutal novel about real-life crime, the story based upon a setting conceived in such detail and with such firmness that the ambience seems to dictate the crime, and the novel which uses a criminal theme as a means of investigating human psychology. One of the books was English, the other three American, and none would have been written before the War.

A Case To Answer (1947)[6] was much the best of the three crime novels written by Edgar Lustgarten (1907–78). Like Hare, Lustgarten had a professional knowledge of the law, which he used to emphasize the sordidness of his theme. Hare would never have contemplated as a possible subject the murder and mutilation of a prostitute in Soho and the trial of the respectable young businessman accused of her death, but if he

6. In America *One More Unfortunate.*

had done so one may be sure that the detective puzzle would have been at the heart of the story. Lustgarten gives us instead an account of the evidence at the trial. Such concentration on a single theme can become wearisome, and this difficulty is evaded rather than solved by some lively but largely irrelevant sketches of Judge and counsel. The book is no masterpiece, but at the time it had the jarring impact of something unpleasant but real, in contrast to the mild, fading pleasures offered by most current detective stories. The ending, which implies that the wrong verdict has been reached, also seemed shocking. In this suggestion that the operations of justice are fallible, *A Case to Answer* was an original book, one giving notice of things to come.

In the Depression years Kenneth Fearing (1902–61) was a poet whose rolling lines of despair, protest and Whitmanesque optimism remain underrated. Among his few crime stories *Dagger of the Mind* (1941) was much admired by Chandler, but *The Big Clock* (1946) is his principal contribution to crime fiction. Like many American writers before and since, Fearing had worked on *Time* magazine, and an organization very similar to that of Henry Luce is really the book's chief character. The various periodicals run by the organization are invented with a lot of felicitous detail, and the device is perfectly worked into the plot by which George Stroud of *Crimeways* is given an assignment to find the missing witness he knows to be himself. We are never in any doubt that the megalomaniac proprietor, Earl Janoth, is the murderer of his bisexual mistress. The excitement of the story springs from the way in which Stroud manages to mislead his own investigators, although as point after point involving him is discovered the net moves in always more closely. *The Big Clock* has an air of conviction which comes from Fearing's close observation of the background. The film made from the story, with Charles Laughton as Janoth and Ray Milland as the technically innocent but morally null hero, was for once not a travesty of the book.

'Like an athlete who runs her first mile in 3.59 and then retires, Helen Eustis asserts that her first mystery novel was also her last,' Anthony Boucher wrote in 1958, adding that the 'one and only Eustis whodunit is a highpoint in modern murder'. The title of *The Horizontal Man* (1946) comes from Auden – we are a long way in feeling, although not in years, from the time when it was a surprise to find Eliot's name mentioned in a crime story. The book begins with the murder of Kevin Boyle, a full-time professor of English and part-time poet on an American campus, by a woman who loves him. The puzzle is: find the lady. Helen Eustis (1916–) offered in this remarkable crime story a murder mystery which

Boucher called 'the trickiest bit of strict "fair play" since Dr Shepherd told of the murder of Roger Ackroyd', but she gave a good deal more than that. *The Horizontal Man* is a very intelligent novel, and also (this is what the story depends on) a successful dive into the waters of abnormal psychology. If Lustgarten's book gave us murder as it often sordidly is, and Fearing's showed the kind of surroundings nurturing a tension that can lead to violence, Eustis investigated the personality patterns that can lead to crime. All of these books use the sexual motive in a way from which Golden Age writers would have flinched. The writers were implicitly asking, as earlier crime novelists would not have cared to do, for a freedom of comment equal to that of any other novelist.

The same can be said of John Franklin Bardin (1916–81), an American writer for years little known in his own country. The first Bardin crime story, *The Deadly Percheron* (1946), is a sort of exercise in surrealistic logic. *The Last of Philip Banter* (1947) is equally remarkable in the way it creates and maintains a mood of menace. His third and finest book, *Devil Take the Blue Tail Fly* (1948), is a psychological study. At first sight it may seem to go no further than Helen Eustis, but its treatment of a similar theme has a greater depth of understanding. The book is, so far as I know, unique in modern crime fiction in showing a world seen solely from a schizoid's point of view. From the opening, when Ellen Purcell wakes on the morning of her discharge from hospital and finds the friendly nurses strangely reluctant to turn their backs, to the last terrifying pages, the vision of the world and what happens in it is wholly hers. This memorable novel was a failure in England, where the earlier books had been much praised, and it did not find an American publisher until the late sixties. With its failure, Bardin began to publish a series of crime novels under the name of Gregory Tree, but these slickly sophisticated books lack altogether the imaginative intensity of the earlier work. A paperback omnibus volume containing the three early novels was issued in 1976, and brought Bardin the attention he deserved, but the only novel published after its appearance, *Purloining Tiny*, was a sad disappointment.

With work of this kind the crime novel had become something different, in form as well as content. It is true that the detective story was not dead. Edmund Crispin observed with gentle mockery in 1959 that although people had been pronouncing 'the doom of the detective story' for a long time, the writers survived: 'Mrs Christie still has butter to put on her bread. Mr Carr seems confident of being able to continue supporting his wife and family. There is happily no hint from America that Mr Queen is feeling the pinch.' He went on to suggest that 'the drifting, opportunist variety of writer' had now abandoned the detective story in favour of 'the thriller, or the so-called psychological crime tale, or the *soi-disant* "naturalistic" murder story', and that the detective story would be all the better for this detachment of 'its catchpenny hangers-on'.

No doubt Crispin would not have written in quite the same terms a few years later. Today all three of the writers he mentioned are dead, and Carr and Queen had lost a large part of their audience with their later books. But nobody would deny that detective stories continue to be produced by new writers in Britain, and to a lesser degree in America. The point is that in plotting and execution almost all are feeble things compared with the older ones. From a time that one could roughly put as the end of the forties, writers shied away from the conventions of the Golden Age story, and today the crime story has returned to its origins. Its variety of approach and style is very great, embracing at one end the police novel and at the other the more or less fantastic spy story. Somewhere in between are stories about crime of a more or less naturalistic kind.

The new approach has involved the cutting of the bonds by which detective story writers had confined themselves – or to put it in another way, the abandonment of everything that had been regarded by the Golden Age writers as good taste. It could no longer be assumed that policemen were by definition honest, or that they would never work over a suspect. They were shown as human beings like others, embodying a justice that was itself much flawed. There is a passage in Chandler's *The Lady in the Lake* which is both an excellent piece of writing and a summary of what many writers felt about policemen as a group:

> They had the calm weathered faces of healthy men in hard condition. They had the eyes they always have, cloudy and grey like freezing water. The firm set mouth, the hard little wrinkles at the corners of the eyes, the hard cruel and meaningless stare, not quite cruel and a thousand miles from kind. The dull ready-made clothes, worn without style, with a sort of contempt; the look of men who are poor and yet proud of their power, watching always for ways to make it felt, to shove it into you and twist it and grin and watch you squirm, ruthless without malice, cruel and yet not always unkind. What would you expect them to be? Civilization had no meaning for them. All they saw of it was the failure, the dirt, the dregs, the aberrations and the disgust.

By contrast with the policemen, the behaviour of the private detective may be tough, but is based on ethical standards. As Spade says to Brigid O'Shaughnessy, alias Miss Wonderly, when she asks if he would have given her up to the police if the falcon had been real and not a fake: 'Don't be too sure I'm as crooked as I'm supposed to be. That kind of reputation might be good business – bringing in high-priced jobs and making it easier to deal with the enemy.' And as he says to her a little earlier about the killing of his partner, Miles Archer: 'It happens we were in the detective business. Well, when one of your organization gets killed it's bad business to let the killer get away with it. It's bad all round – bad for that one organization, bad for every detective everywhere.' Such are the modest standards by which the Hammett detective lives.

By the sixties American writers had gone far beyond Hammett and Chandler in their readiness to draw crooked or sadistic cops. Samples of both appear even in work so tied by the conventions of a series as Ed McBain's 87th Precinct stories. British writers were slower to treat the police in this way, and in 1960 the American publisher of Julian Symons's *The Progress of a Crime* expressed a certain amount of shocked surprise at the police treatment of suspects. Nowadays it might almost be said that a policeman in a crime story may be considered suspect of violence or corruption until proved innocent. A detective now may be a Jew or a black or a homosexual. He also can be, and often is, a womanizer who sleeps with his more attractive suspects. It is a long way from Marlowe, who rejected all sexual temptation until he met Linda Loring.

The treatment of sex has changed as much as the treatment of the police. Murder might have been associated with rape before the War, but the rape would have been mentioned delicately. 'Any sign of – interference?' the police investigator occasionally asked, and if the surgeon shook his head he might well 'sigh with relief'. Today all this has changed. Rape is now perhaps more frequently encountered in books than even in life, and semen tests on clothing or in vagina are often given in detail. Transvestism, lesbianism or homosexuality may be made the basis of stories, and blackmail by means of pornographic films or photographs is commonplace, with the pictures sometimes described. (Even such an old-fashioned writer, in this sense, as Carr, once made use of sex photographs of a girl taken at her lover's request as a plot feature.) Detailed accounts of sex acts are less frequent in the crime story than in ordinary novels, and four-letter words are less used, but the situation is wholly different from that prevailing a few years ago when several English publishers turned down Nicolas Freeling's first book, *Love in Amsterdam*,[7] because it was thought to be too sexually outspoken, and it was commonplace for words and passages to be queried on the ground that they would be disliked by many readers. Very few words or phrases would be thought objectionable today.

7. In America *Death in Amsterdam*.

In dealing with violence crime writers were always allowed more freedom, even though such violence has obvious associations with sex. The pleasure found by Mickey Spillane's Mike Hammer in crunching his heel into the faces of men and occasionally beating up women who are on the 'wrong' side has often been remarked on and reproved, but it is nothing new. 'Sapper's' *Bulldog Drummond* (1920) finds Drummond forcing the villainous Lakington into a bath of acid from which he emerges with his clothes burned off and 'mad with agony'. In *The Black Gang* (1922) two Jews working in the service of revolution, 'a little flashily dressed, distinctly addicted to cheap jewellery', are told by the masked Drummond, 'My friends and I do not like your trade, you swine' before being beaten 'to within an inch of their lives' with the cat-o'-nine-tails. In 1939 the critic John Mair summed up the casualties in James Hadley Chase's first book, *No Orchids for Miss Blandish*:

Guys rubbed out	22 (with a rod, 9; with a tommy-gun, 6; with a knife, 3; with a blackjack, 2; by kicking, 1; by suicide, 1)
Guys slugged bad	16 (in the face or head, 15; in the guts, 1)
Guys given a workover	5 (with blunt instruments, 3; with a knife, 1; with burning cigarettes, 1)
Dames laid	5 (willing, 3; paid, 1; raped, 1)

The central feminine character in Latimer's *Solomon's Vineyard* can only get sexual pleasure after being hit, and one of the men obtains it only during the act of murder. In M. Scott Michel's *Sweet Murder* (1945) Wood Jaxon, the Marlovian private eye, is tied spreadeagled to a bed while an immensely strong and tall but girlishly pretty homosexual thug jams the lighted end of a cigarette into his mouth, lets it burn out on his chest, and beats him up again and again. These instances could be multiplied. Violence, much of it deliberately sadistic, had been an element in the thriller long before James Bond and Mike Hammer.

It would be unprofitable to welcome or regret this freedom of expression on ethical grounds. When C. H. B. Kitchin suggested in one of his detective stories that 'a historian of the future will probably turn, not to blue books or statistics, but to detective stories if he wishes to study the manners of our age', he was writing just before the Second World War and was far from having Mike Hammer in mind, but what he said remains true. The crime story reflects the prevailing ethic of its period in the attitude adopted by its writers towards police and criminals, crime and punishment. Because crime literature is based on giving the public what it wants, crime writers are more than usually sensitive to shifts of taste. This sensitivity is mostly unconscious; they simply find themselves in tune with a considerable section of the reading public on any given subject. To ask whether Agatha Christie would have written differently if she had been born half a century later is like asking whether a modern Shakespeare would have written in blank verse. The questions beg themselves by their absurdity. Nobody born in 1940 could possibly have thought like Agatha Christie, and so would not have written like her. To put the point in reverse, many recent crime writers would have written different kinds of books, or perhaps would not have written at all, a few years earlier. The present period has encouraged their talents, as it has discouraged those who feel a wistful yearning for the Golden Age.

Yet there is something more to be said. It may not be true that life imitates art as Wilde suggested, but all literature takes colour from its social surroundings and at the same time gives them a further element of meaning. Hammett and Chandler did not breed a class of young men who wanted to be Spades and Marlowes. What happened is that the sensibilities of these two writers produced such archetypal figures out of the American air, and fed them into the public consciousness through literature. Their acceptance by a large audience then helped to change the response of that audience, not just to private eyes but to the very nature of crime. This is one way in which popular art works, and the conditions of the past thirty years encouraged the production of crime and spy stories which were able to use crime literature as a form of popular entertainment to make moral or social comments about society. They encouraged also a good deal of gratuitous and sometimes disgusting violence, but along with such work went many crime stories that have returned to the spirit of the ancestor who preceded Poe: William Godwin.

· 13 ·

The Short Story's Mutations

(i) Decline

In *Queen's Quorum*, the 'History of the Detective-Crime Short Story as Revealed by the 106 Most Important Books Published in this Field since 1845', published in 1951, there is no hint of the short story's replacement by the novel as the dominant form, nor of its decline in quality. There is instead a triumphant progress from the 'Second Golden Era' to 'The First Moderns', 'The Second Moderns' and then 'The Renaissance'. Such conclusions did more credit to Ellery Queen's enthusiastic heart than to his analytical head. The Golden Age showed an immediate decline in the quality of short stories, and eventually in their number.

One reason for this has already been mentioned. The losses in circulation suffered by the kind of magazine that had nurtured the short detective story were slow but steady. The *Strand* clung for years to the formula that had brought success, which, as its historian has admitted, involved ignoring during the twenties 'the new poor, the decline of the larger country houses, the General Strike', and anything else that readers might find uncomfortable. The last Doyle story was published in April 1927, and although crime stories continued to appear they were with a few exceptions much inferior to those that had been published before the First World War. The *Strand* was not helped by the retention of an essentially Victorian editor, Greenhough Smith, until 1930. The circulation fell to 80,000 during the Second World War, and although its appearance was modernized, the paper that had grown up with Sherlock Holmes found no real reason for existence in the age of Philip Marlowe. By the time the last number appeared in March 1950, the flow of new short stories had almost stopped. It is typical of the magazine's backward look that, long before the end, they used a Sherlock Holmes story written in imitation of the master by Ronald Knox and illustrated in the manner of Sidney Paget.

In the United States the short story as a commercial article was replaced by serialized novels. The *Saturday Evening Post* had run the Thinking Machine and the Father Brown stories as series before the First World War, but in 1927 the serialization of Frances Noyes Hart's *The Bellamy Trial* provided a signpost to the future. The *Post* went on to publish a great many serializations of crime novels by Rinehart, Christie, Stout and others during the inter-war years. In 1927 also, *Scribner's* managed temporarily to check a steady decline in circulation with publication of Van Dine's *The Canary Murder Case*. In the same years these and other magazines carried comparatively few short stories of the classic Holmes length.

To say that the serialized novel had become more important for magazines than the short story is not to say that short stories were no longer written or that they failed to find print, only that there was a decreasing demand for them. In America the pulp magazines which relied on short stories flourished in these years, and there was a considerable development also of the 'short short story' of 2,000 words or less, which could easily be read in bus or train on the way home. Such a length gave no room for development of plot or character, or for anything more than the making of a single ingenious point, for instance that a man supposedly deaf has heard a casual remark made in another room, or that a man who claims to have been cut off from all communication during the past week knows the result of a football match that took place two days ago. Anecdotes of this kind can be entertaining both to write and to read, but a diet based on them soon becomes tiring.

Yet the short story's decline in these years was not only a matter of changes in editorial requirements. Crime fiction writers soon realized for themselves that the plot construction of a short story could be almost as demanding as that of a novel, and was far less rewarding. But again, one should not put too much stress on purely financial considerations. Allingham, Berkeley, Carr, Queen, Sayers, Van Dine (the names are taken almost at random) accustomed themselves to the leisurely pace of a novel, its accumulation of suspense and doubt, the final revelation and explanation that might take up some thirty pages. It is not surprising that some crime writers never attempted the short story, and that few between the Wars made it a major part of their work. The remarkable thing is that some of these stories were so good. Their merits are not those of Doyle in development of scene and character, or of Chesterton in revealing truths by paradox. The writers of short stories between the Wars attempted no more than the statement of a puzzle and its solution by clever detective work. Within these limits the short stories particularly of Queen, Sayers and Carr give a great deal of pleasure. Indeed, in some ways the short story is better suited than the novel to this kind of writing. That final snap of surprise can bring just as genuine a gasp of pleasure after a short period of suspense as after a long one.

This is notable especially in the case of Ellery Queen. The best of his short stories belong to the early intensely ratiocinative period, and both *The Adventures of Ellery Queen* (1934) and *The New Adventures* (1940) are as absolutely fair and totally puzzling as the most passionate devotee of orthodoxy could wish. At least one of the stories in the first book, 'The Adventure of the Bearded Lady', is a perfect example of this kind of problem story, baffling in its components but simple when they are put in their right places. Half a dozen others are almost equally good, and every story in these books is composed with wonderful skill. Some of the later Queen stories are interesting, but generally they do not come up to those in the first two collections, because the structure is looser, and there is not much compensation in the way of greater depth. Most of Carr's stories are compressed versions of his locked-room novels, and at times they benefit from the compression. Probably the best of them are in the Carter Dickson book, *The Department of Queer Complaints* (1940), although this does not include the brilliantly clever H.M. story 'The House in Goblin Wood', or a successful pastiche which introduces Edgar Allan Poe as detective.

Dorothy Sayers's short stories treat their subjects with an ease that most of the novels lack, and they are free from the worst excesses of Wimsey. Within the space of thirty pages there is mercifully no room for Wimsey—Bunter dialogue, although there is still some stuff that must seem strange to those who regard Sayers as a semi-realistic writer. 'Go back to your War Office and say I will not give you the formula,' cries a French royalist Count to Wimsey. 'If war should come between our countries – which may God avert! – I will be found on the side of France.' This is from a preposterous but rather enjoyable story called 'The Bibulous Business of a Matter of Taste', in which three Wimseys appear at a French château and have their credentials tested by a prolonged session of vintage and date naming. The collection that contains this story, *Lord Peter Views the Body* (1928), includes also the genuinely terrifying 'The Man with the Copper Fingers' and 'The Adventurous Exploit of the Cave of Ali Baba' which opens with a newspaper account of Wimsey's death, followed by his enlistment in some unspecified secret society. *Hangman's Holiday* (1933) contains the clever 'The Image in the Mirror' and a funny, quite uncharacteristic Sayers (no detective appears in it) called 'The Man Who Knew How'. *In the Teeth of the Evidence* (1939) offers two good stories in which Wimsey appears rather mutedly, and several odds and ends, including the delightful 'The Inspiration of Mr Budd'. Altogether, the short stories suggest that Dorothy Sayers might have been a better and livelier crime writer if she had not fallen in love with her detective.

These were mostly books by writers whose short stories were subsidiary to their novelistic talents. The same can be said of the short stories written by other crime novelists. The Poirot and Miss Marple short stories are far inferior to the novels, and so are Allingham's stories about Mr Campion. Several collections produced by Humdrums are no improvement on their longer work. Some other books mentioned in *Queen's Quorum* are either production-line work by writers who were at their best no more than efficient or, like the stories of Louis Golding and Damon Runyon, are remote from the ordinary concerns of the crime story. If the mere fact that a story dealt with a crime and its punishment was sufficient, then a miniature masterpiece like William Gerhardi's 'A Bad End' or a collection like Ambrose Bierce's *Can Such Things Be?* could not be ignored, but for the most part the real interest of these stories lies elsewhere.

After the First World War there were few writers for whom the short story was a natural medium of expression, as it had been for Doyle, Chesterton and Futrelle. Most often praised among them is H. C. Bailey (1878–1961), whose first collection of stories about Reggie Fortune appeared in 1920. It was followed by several other books of short stories and some Fortune novels, as well as novels about a sanctimonious and scoundrelly lawyer named Joshua Clunk. The Fortune stories were so successful that in the early thirties Bailey was regarded as one of a semi-mythical 'Big Five' among English detective story writers, the others being Christie, Crofts, Freeman and Sayers. He is now so disregarded that most of the books are out of print, although single stories may occasionally be found in anthologies. For those like me who find Fortune intolerably facetious and whimsical and the stories always affected, sometimes silly and at times obscure, this unanimity of disregard will seem perfectly justified. In case injustice may be done here it should be recorded that other critics have found that Bailey had 'a pretty sense of puzzle' (Sandoe) and that few writers produced 'puzzles more elaborately conceived or genuinely mystifying' (Haycraft).

The *Solange Stories* (1931) of F. Tennyson Jesse are sometimes mentioned as highly individual performances, but although they have a lucid and lively introduction dealing with her development of a woman detective with a special warning sense of evil, the stories themselves are disappointingly thin. Perfectly readable, but also disappointing after the praise lavished on them, are C. Daly King's collection of stories about *The Curious Mr Tarrant* (1935) and the stories about Henry Poggioli in *Clues of the Caribbees* (1929) by T. S. Stribling (1881–1965). Poggioli is an instructor in psychology at Ohio State University who becomes involved in cases set in Haiti, Martinique and parts of the West Indies. The stories themselves are slight, although they gain something from the originality of the settings. In the longest of them Poggioli is called in as 'the great American voodoo inspector' to demonstrate to Haitian Negroes that voodooism is nothing more than a superstition, and in 'A Passage to Benares' he is a murder suspect. It is suggested, indeed, that he has been hanged before the murderer's confession, although he survived to have more adventures recorded in *Ellery Queen's Mystery Magazine*.

These are the best work in a thin time. They represent a sharp descent from the great days of the short story, although there are felicities scattered along the way in the form of single tales. Among them are Aldous Huxley's 'The Gioconda Smile', a poisoning story based rather distantly upon an actual murder trial, Thomas Burke's chilling 'The Hands of Mr Ottermole', and 'The Perfect Murder' by Stacy Aumonier, a writer whose few genuine crime stories are well worth reading.

(ii) Revival

The short story's revival is linked directly with America, and partly with Hammett, Chandler, and their followers. Although the Continental Op stories were inferior to Hammett's novels, and many of Chandler's stories are the work of a man learning his craft, they gave a lead in theme and language to other writers. Take the first line of a Hammett story, a line like 'It was a wandering daughter job', or the evocation of the flavour of the desert town of Corkscrew in the story of that name, and you are in a world quite free from the gentility and snobbery of the Golden Age. But even more important than the existence of Hammett and Chandler as examples from which to learn, was the foundation in 1941 of *Ellery Queen's Mystery Magazine*. Here was a periodical which printed only short stories about crime and detection, and its influence upon the crime short story's development has been at least as great as that of the early *Strand*.

Ellery Queen, or half of him in the form of Frederic Dannay, exercised an active editorial interest from the beginning, and from the beginning he recognized that the form of the crime story was changing and that a successful magazine had to accommodate the old and encourage the new. *EQMM* was prepared to welcome equally a new story by Carr or

Allingham and the first short story of an unknown writer. They were ready to give the first prize in the yearly contest they inaugurated to stories which, it seemed to some of their readers, were not detective stories at all, like H. F. Heard's 'The President of the United States, Detective', or to a realistic story by an Italian-born writer. They gave special prizes for foreign stories, a gesture which produced in one year tales from Australia, Argentina (from Jorge Luis Borges), Portugal, the Philippines and South Africa. They have given at different times awards for the best first story, the best *tour de force*, the best piece of Sherlockiana, the best short short story, the best riddle story, and the best story by a college student. A full list of the prize stories in the yearly Queen's Awards, together with the new stories that have appeared in *EQMM*, is a roll of honour of the crime short story in recent years. It is also, as Queen claimed, a compendium of every possible kind of crime story. Some of the kinds are more important than others, not all of the stories are masterpieces, and some will madden anybody who has a fixed idea of what the crime story should be like. The permanently excited editorial style will not be to everybody's taste. Yet the value of the magazine far transcends any criticisms that may be made of it. No doubt short stories would have been written if *EQMM* had never existed, but they would have been much less various in style and interest, and almost certainly much poorer in quality. The editors have been directly responsible for encouraging the two most talented crime short story writers of the past thirty years.

In November 1946 the managing editor of the magazine told Fred Dannay on the telephone that a remarkable new story had come into the office. This was 'The Specialty of the House', the first story published by Stanley Ellin. The story is now so famous that there can be no harm in revealing that it is about the delicious lamb Amirstan which is the speciality (to revert to English spelling) of an inconspicuous New York restaurant named Sbirro's, that the meat in the dish is human flesh, and that it is unwise for any diner to accept Sbirro's invitation to enter his kitchen. Stanley Ellin (1916–   ) was a steelworker before he became a full-time writer, and although he has said that his idea of an ideal workroom is Proust's cork-lined chamber plus a typewriter, he is in most respects a strikingly unliterary character, interested in baseball, boxing and – surprisingly for an American – cricket. This earthy New Yorker from Brooklyn is, however, an exceptionally careful and easily dissatisfied writer who revises each page several times, and often tries out an opening sentence again and again until he 'hits one that feels right'. It was ten years before his first collection, *Mystery Stories* (1956), was published, and another eight before ten more stories were gathered between covers under the title *The Blessington Method*. His stories have been produced at an average rate of one a year.

Ellin has written several excellent novels, of which *The Eighth Circle* (1958) is the most notable, but his talent shows at its finest in his short stories. The great quality he has brought back to the crime short story is that of imagination. That concern with tricking the reader is all very well, but in the best crime stories it is subsidiary to the exercise of the imagination by which the writer becomes one with his subject. This is what makes us shiver a little when we read some of the Holmes stories. Ellin can be quite as ingenious as any Golden Age practitioner, but his ingenuity is turned to ends which produce the authentic shiver. The little final twist is a turn of the knife in the reader's sensibility. It is because he can imagine what might persuade a little man defeated by life to commit murder ('The Cat's-Paw'), or the existence of a society to ease a way out of life for old people who are a nuisance to the young or middle-aged ('The Blessington Method'), or what it is like to be a public executioner, that his work is a landmark in the history of the crime short story. His finest pieces go beyond the usual limits of the genre and turn into fables, occasionally tender but more often sharp, about the grotesque shapes of urban society and the dreams of the human beings who live in it.

The talent of Roy Vickers (1889–1965) was less remarkable than that of Stanley Ellin and was manifested late in his writing career, but it was wholly distinctive and operated particularly in the medium of the short story. Vickers wrote many crime novels from the twenties onwards, but these books bear no mark of being produced by the same man who wrote the short stories which began with the invention of the Department of Dead Ends, an imaginary branch of Scotland Yard in which the details of all unsolved murder mysteries are kept. Vickers began to write the Dead Ends stories in the thirties, but found it hard to sell them, because their realistic tone was utterly incompatible with the requirements of magazines at the time. It was not until Ellery Queen discovered 'The Rubber Trumpet' and one or two other stories in the dusty pages of *Pearson's* and asked if there was a series of these tales, that Vickers was moved to revive his original idea. 'The Department does not grope for points missed in the investigation [but] keeps an eye open for any unusual occurrence to any of the persons who were once in the orbit of an unsolved murder,' as Vickers himself put it. When at last a collection of stories appeared in hard covers, as *The Department of Dead Ends* (1949), the brilliance of the conception was at once appreciated. A rubber trumpet thrown out of a railway train provides a link with seventy-seven other rubber trumpets apparently sold over the counter of a chemist's shop, to bring George Muncey to justice, a begging letter which turns up in the Department two years after the apparently motiveless murder of Gerald Raffen leads directly to the murderer, and so on.

Vickers's method is generally to provide the setting for the crime, show it being carried out, and then go on to the accidental discovery that lays a trail to the criminal. He follows in this the pattern of the inverted story, but uses it with more flexibility and sophistication than its inventor. He also improves on the originals by giving almost every story a deadly probability. Many of the cases have a suburban setting, and the murderers are often respectable people, people like us. To quote Vickers again: 'Together we must reach a moment in which we agree that a particular pressure of circumstance might well prove too much, not indeed for ourselves but perhaps for our neighbours.' This might be a little dull but in fact it is not, because Vickers has his own, far from mechanical, ingenuity, exemplified in a story like 'The Man who Murdered in Public', where George Macartney is acquitted of forcibly drowning his wife because the two earlier 'accidents' in which women have been drowned cannot be put in as evidence in relation to the third. George is eventually caught by one of those felicitous oddities that are the hallmark of the Dead End cases. The story obviously had its origin in the career of George Joseph Smith, the 'Brides in the Bath' murderer, and a number of the other tales looked glancingly at real English murder cases.

Between the near-fables of Ellin and the near-documentation of Vickers, the modern crime story offers a great deal of entertainment and some serious writing. The six stories in *Knight's Gambit* (1949) weigh lightly in the whole balance of William Faulkner's achievement, but they are undoubtedly more deeply conceived than most crime stories. One of them, 'An Error in Chemistry', was submitted for the first Ellery Queen Detective Short Story contest, and won second prize. The stories deal with the detective exploits of Gavin Stevens, county attorney, who is in these tales rather like Uncle Abner, although in the whole Faulkner saga (he appears in several novels) he is developed as a very different figure. Some of the stories were published long before they were gathered up in book form, and they show Faulkner's interest in the mystery story as a form. The detective stories about Johnson and Boswell of Lillian Bueno McCue (1902   ), who used the name of Lillian de la Torre, collected in *Dr Sam: Johnson, Detector* (1946), are perhaps the most successful pastiches in detective fiction. *EQMM*, again, was responsible for their first publication. Miss de la Torre caught happily the tone and weight of Johnson's conversation, and rightly made the puzzles almost incidental to the relationship between biographer and subject. One may like or dislike pastiche of any kind, but here it is certainly done on a high level.

Much else of interest has appeared in recent years. Patrick Quentin's *The Ordeal of Mrs Snow* (1961), contains several excellent stories, and some gems lie uncollected under the Quentin and Q. Patrick labels. Ruth Rendell has published three collections of short stories, *The Fallen Curtain* (1976), *Means of Evil* (1979) and *The Fever Tree* (1983), which are most successful when they offer strongly ironic endings. H. R. F. Keating has written some delicately amusing stories which have not yet been bound between covers. Roald Dahl's *Someone Like You* (1953) and *Kiss Kiss* (1960) contain gruelling tales within the criminal canon, including in particular 'The Way up to Heaven' and 'Lamb to the Slaughter', with its literally perfect disposition of a murder weapon. Patricia Highsmith's vividly imagined tales in *Eleven* (1970),[1] *The Animal Lover's Book of Beastly Murder* (1975) and *Little Tales of Misogyny* (1977) mostly concern crimes, although few are what we generally recognize as crime stories. It is in the short story that the boundaries of criminal literature have been most markedly extended.

It is, again, important not to give a wrong impression. Many crime short stories continue to be written with nothing but entertainment in mind. Among the best are Crispin's *Beware of the Trains* (1953), his posthumously published *Fen Country* (1979), three collections of Appleby stories by Michael Innes, and Michael Gilbert's Petrella tales. There are some hundreds of short stories written by the prolific Edward D. Hoch (1930–), although the most ingenious remain uncollected in volume form. Some of these stories, and many others written by British and American authors, suffer from the fact that they were commissioned by newspapers and magazines who confined their writers within a very brief space. Yet it is a mark of the short story's revival that an English publisher has issued successfuly every year since 1969 a collection of new stories under the title *Winter's Crimes*, and that other anthologies appear every year, reprinting material from magazines. The annual publication of *Winter's Crimes* is a real achievement, but although the stories are new, almost all, naturally enough, are by established writers. A continuous flow of good crime stories presupposes the existence of a market for new

1. In America *The Snail-Watcher and Other Stories*.

writers, and in Britain there is still no such market. It is true today, as it was a decade and more ago when this book was first published, that the crime short story still flourishes chiefly through *EQMM*.

· 14 ·

Crime Novel and Police Novel

(i) The crime novel

The detective story has changed into the crime novel. Such a statement needs not so much justification as definition. A comparison of the main features in the two kinds of book may help in showing that they are really not the same article with a different label.

DETECTIVE STORY	CRIME NOVEL
Plot	*Plot*
Based on a deception which may be mechanical (locked room), verbal (misleading remarks), concerned with forensic medicine (poisons, blood groups, fake prints) or ballistics. Book is constructed backwards from this deception, revelation of which is the climactic point to which everything else leads.	Based on psychology of characters – what stresses would make A want to kill B? – or an intolerable situation that must end in violence. No deceptions of locked-room or faked-print kind, no obscure poisons. Most often the problem is something like: 'Has A really killed B, and if he has what will happen to him?' Book is constructed forwards from such a problem.
Detective	*Detective*
May be professional or amateur, and if amateur may run detective or inquiry agency, or get involved by chance in criminal cases. Always at the centre of story's action, most often the hero, and generally a keen observer who notices things missed by others.	Often no detective. Occasionally a detective runs through a series of stories, but rarely shown as a brilliant reasoning machine. Most often the central character is just somebody to whom things happen.

Method

If the crime is murder (it almost always is), method may be bizarre or misleading, e.g., the victim appears to have been shot but was in fact poisoned. Sometimes the method may be highly ingenious, as in a locked-room mystery, or itself puzzling, as in a poisoning case where everybody ate and drank exactly the same things.

Clues

As essential element. There will be perhaps a dozen of them in the story. The detective may explain their meaning at the time, or deductions may be left to the reader.

Characters

Only the detective is characterized in detail. Otherwise characterization is perfunctory, particularly after the crime when people become wholly subsidiary to plot.

Setting

Mostly confined to what happens before the crime. Later plot and clue requirements take over and setting (school, newspaper office, theatre, etc.) fades.

Social attitude

Conservative.

Method

Usually straightforward, rarely vital, although ballistic or forensic details may play an important part.

Clues

Quite often no clues in the detective story sense.

Characters

The basis of the story. The lives of characters are shown continuing after the crime, and often their subsequent behaviour is important to the story's effect.

Setting

Often important to the tone and style of the story, and frequently an integral part of the crime itself, i.e., the pressures involved in a particular way of life lead to this especial crime.

Social attitude

Varying, but often radical in the sense of questioning some aspect of law, justice or the way society is run.

Puzzle value	*Puzzle value*
Generally high. The detective and the puzzle are the only things that stay in the memory.	Sometimes high, sometimes almost non-existent. But characters and situation are often remembered for a long time.

The distinctions are real, the articles different. The distinctions are exaggerated a little here because the lines of differentiation are frequently crossed. There are crime novels which contain surprises as stunning as those of the best detective stories, although they are obtained by different means, as in Ira Levin's *A Kiss Before Dying*. There are detective stories, like some of those written by Michael Gilbert, which offer characterization that is far from perfunctory. The categories are useful, though, because the aims of the detective story writer and the crime novelist are basically different. The detective story is concerned first with setting a puzzle for the reader, and as Chandler put it in a letter, 'to get the complication you fake the clues, the timing, the play of coincidence ... to get the surprise murderer you fake the character, which hits me hardest of all, because I have a sense of character'. The crime novelist is most often a fictionally split personality. Half of him wants to write a novel about people affected by crime, but the other half yearns to produce a baffling mystery. This split almost down the middle is very evident in Chandler's own work, and recently in the work of Ruth Rendell. Chandler might say that 'those who say the problem overrides everything are merely trying to cover up their own inability to create character and atmosphere', but often in his early books the atmospheric brilliance that came to him as naturally as breathing is used to cover up his inability to devise a plot. The crime novelist tends to make the story secondary to the characters, the detective story writer concentrates on the puzzle to the exclusion of reasonable behaviour. Chandler thought that this was inevitable, that 'something must always be sacrificed', but this is not true. When the fusion of puzzle and characterization is perfect, as in *The Glass Key*, you have books produced in the form of crime novels that have a claim to be considered as works of art.

The range of talent working within the crime novel is very wide. This form of sensational literature is so flexible, and in its revival so comparatively fresh, that writers are trying to use it in very different ways. There are crime novelists who aim more or less consciously at blending the elements already mentioned into a story that has many of the values of a novel, and a few who work with a fairly distinct moral or social purpose.

There are many who have given up most of the detective story's apparatus and offer a lively setting and credible characterization, but still write with a lightness of attitude that marks their books 'For Entertainment Only'. There are writers who attempt a realistic view of police work and procedure, writers whose books are basically psychological studies, and a few who have brought into the crime story the unusual element of wit. And although spy stories are dealt with separately, it would be wrong not to mention here the remarkable transformation of the spy story in the hands of John Le Carré, Len Deighton and other writers into a kind of literature that gives room for the sharpest kind of comment on the realities of power and violence.

The divisions that follow are again to a certain extent artificial, and may be thought objectionable, but they do seem to me real. They are meant to define intention, rather than achievement. Serious writers can be boring and pretentious, and along with most people I would prefer to them entertainers, who by definition entertain. Yet there are differences. The best books of Emma Lathen seem to me as wholly enjoyable as anything in modern crime writing, but the kind of pleasure they give is different, not in degree but in kind, from that given by the work of Patricia Highsmith. Emma Lathen may be regarded as a descendant of the Golden Age writers, although she writes much better than most of her forebears. Patricia Highsmith owes almost nothing to them. Other examples could be given, but I hope the point is made that some distinctions are unavoidable in this account of the growth of the crime novel in its various forms.

(ii) Serious crime novelists

The writer who fuses characters and plot most successfully is Patricia Highsmith (1921–   ), the most important crime novelist at present in practice. This statement will not receive general assent in her native America, and it is curious that American critics, who are so generous to British writers, have been slow to recognize outstanding home-grown talents. For more than a decade Hammett was regarded as just another writer of pulp stories, and Chandler, when he came to England, discovered with delight that 'over here I am not regarded as a mystery writer but as an American novelist of some importance ... there is none of that snobbism which makes a fourth-rate serious novelist, without style or any real talent, superior by definition to a mystery writer'. Highsmith has observed that in France and England (she could have added Scandinavia) 'I fare much better as to prestige, quality of reviewing and – proportionately speaking – sales, than in America'. Crime stories have always been the Cinderellas of literature so far as reviewing is concerned, but in Europe the best of them receive serious treatment. Perhaps it should be added that Highsmith is an acquired taste, which means a taste that some never acquire. When I was reviewing crime fiction regularly, Victor Gollancz used to write to me before going on holiday asking me to recommend the best books of the year published by other firms than his own. (Many of them, thanks to his critical susceptibility and intelligence, appeared in his own yellow covers.) He then bought these books and took them away with him. At my insistence he bought one year *The Two Faces of January*, which he disliked intensely. To his letter in the following year he added a postscript: 'Please – no Patricia Highsmith.'

Most of Highsmith's books have their origin in some sensational idea. In her first novel, *Strangers on a Train* (1949), a young man who meets another in a train proposes that each of them shall murder a person whom the other wishes to see dead. Since neither killer will have any connection with his victim there is no reason why these should not be 'perfect murders'. In *The Blunderer*[1] (1954) a clumsy amateur killer sets out to copy a crime committed by a more professional one and finds himself being pursued by the murderer. Such tricky plot devices are often used by very inferior writers – Baroness Orczy used the *Strangers on a Train* plot for one of her 'Old Man in the Corner' stories – but in Highsmith's hands they are starting points for finely subtle character studies. She recurs often to the attraction exerted on the weak by the idea of violence. In *The Two Faces of January* (1964), when the emotionally footloose Rydal Keener sees the petty crook Chester MacFarland kill a man, his immediate reaction is to attach himself to Chester and his wife rather than to report the affair to the police. In the opening scene of *Those Who Walk Away* (1967) Ray Garrett is shot at and wounded by Coleman, but again his reaction is to link himself more closely to the would-be murderer rather than to attempt to escape from him. It may be said that this is not true to 'life', but this means only that it is not the way most people would behave. It is true and convincing in the life of Highsmith characters, who find themselves linked to each other by the idea of crime. There are no more genuine agonies in modern literature than those endured by the couples in her books, who are locked together in a dislike and even hatred that often strangely contains love.

Behind such relationships there are ideas about the relations of people

1. In America *Lament for a Lover*.

within society that strike a distant echo of those views held by Godwin. Without being directly concerned with politics, Highsmith implicitly suggests that in a society where most people are imprisoned within the mechanisms of organizations, social groups or families, criminals are potentially free. Her heroes are therefore often criminals, heroic in the sense that they are the most likeable people in the story. Her personal expressions of her ideas are often naive, but in this case unequivocal:

> Criminals are dramatically interesting, because for a time at least they are active, free in spirit, and they do not knuckle down to anyone ... I find the public passion for justice quite boring and artificial, for neither life nor nature cares if justice is ever done or not.

Such a comment helps to explain why the books of hers that many people like best are those about Tom Ripley, an apparently likeable young American who lacks any moral sense, so that when necessary he will forge, cheat and murder to achieve a given end. *The Talented Mr Ripley* (1957) was published a long while before its sequel, *Ripley Under Ground* (1970), which has been succeeded by *Ripley's Game* (1974) and *The Boy Who Followed Ripley* (1980). Highsmith enjoys Ripley as a character, and perhaps because of this has been self-indulgent in relation to him, so that his exploits verge on the preposterous in the later books. She is also determined to avoid the label 'crime writer', and her two most recent novels (Ripley aside) are not crime stories. It is as a crime novelist, nevertheless, that she has written best, and one hopes that she will return to recognition of this.

All her work shows a professional ability to order a plot and create a significant environment, something evident in the mid-Western background of *People Who Knock on the Door* (1983), but it is when she is treating criminal themes that she brings a particular characteristic intensity of feeling to the central figures. Violence is necessary to her, because the threat or actuality of it fires her best writing, and the problem she faces in relation to its use is a way of co-ordinating sensationalism of theme with subtlety of treatment. The deadly games of pursuit played in her best books are as interesting as anything being done in the novel today.

Highsmith has been discussed first because her approach makes her an exemplar of talented novelists whose spur to writing comes from an interest in crime and its outcome, but nothing in the way of a ranking order is being suggested, and the writers presented below are given in an order roughly chronological. The first two books of Margot Bennett (1912–80) were published just after the end of the Second World War, and few works in the genre have a stronger period flavour. Within the detective story's limits she worked, as Graham Greene observed, with wit and a sense of character, in writing with the desperate high spirits of the time about shortages and the black market and the problems of people at home in wartime but lost in the large acres of peace. *Time to Change Hats* (1945) contained, Greene said, 'the finest evacuee family I have encountered since Evelyn Waugh's *Put Out More Flags*'. In the four novels she wrote after the War the high spirits changed to a kind of sorrowful wit, most evident in *The Widow of Bath* (1952) and the cunningly devised *The Man Who Didn't Fly* (1955). Here are two people, once in love, meeting again after a long time: 'They sat and looked at each other, thinking of the shared past, but they were like painters of different schools working on the same scene, and their separate pictures were almost unrelated.' Sometimes the dialogue sounds like that of an English Chandler, at moments like that when her doom-laden hero in *The Widow of Bath* meets a beautiful woman whose activities once landed him in prison: ' "Are you as luxurious, greedy, mercenary, unscrupulous, selfish, faithless, ambitious, and lax as ever?" ' he asks, and she replies: ' "I'm a civilized woman." ' Often she is both observant and funny, as in her comment about the seaside home of a retired judge who has spent some time in the Colonies, that 'it was a Folly, a merino millionaire's folly; perhaps there were some carved sheep on the lawns', or in her view of the judge himself, 'an obsolete battleship, who believed that his guns could still roar'. Turn to almost any page in her books and you will find an unexpected and right turn of phrase.

These talents are put at the service of a skill in plot construction that is never mechanical, although it is sometimes too intricate. She uses as mere incidents tricks that would serve another writer as material for a plot. In *The Widow of Bath* a girl is presumed to have left her clothes in a shed and then drowned while swimming. In fact she has been murdered, but what makes the Inspector say: ' "Why don't you think about the clothes in the swimming shed? What was missing from the picture?" ' There is a dress, underclothes, handbag with lipstick and other things, purse ... what is missing? ' "Wouldn't she take a towel if she went swimming?" ' There are a dozen clever deceptions in the book, twice as many as most writers would have given us, and certainly more than are needed. *The Man Who Didn't Fly* has a plot just as ingenious, but simpler. Four men arrange to fly to Dublin but only three board the plane, which crashes over the Irish Sea. Which of the four men didn't fly? The puzzle and the solution are as good as could be wished, and they run perfectly with Bennett's sense of character and the constant flame of her wit. A real talent was lost when, after 1958, she gave up the crime story.

That the sympathies of both Highsmith and Bennett are radical is evident from their books. John Bingham (the writing name and the family name of Lord Clanmorris, 1911–   ) is by temperament a conservative, a man likely to deprecate Highsmith's sympathetic feeling for criminals and the idea that they are 'free in spirit'. His first book, *My Name is Michael Sibley* (1952), however, is about an innocent man who tells lies to the police and is then pounced on, played with, endlessly interrogated, with each fresh questioning tightening the ropes around him. The book is a classic example of the crime story's new direction. The murder in it remains officially unsolved, and we know from the beginning that Michael Sibley is innocent. The question that holds our attention from the first chapter until the result of the trial at the end is, what will happen to this innocent man? Unlike the earlier followers of Francis Iles, Bingham is able to dispense with the element of surprise and still tell a wholly fascinating story.

A large part of this fascination rests in his accurate account of police interrogation, something which had rarely been attempted in the British crime story. We learn nothing about his Chief Detective-Inspector and Sergeant outside the limits of the case. They are the embodiment of potentially hostile officialdom, polite English versions of Chandler's policemen, but equally conscious of their power.

The Chief Detective-Inspector was a broad-shouldered man well above average height. I should say he was in his late forties. He had a round head, with closely cropped fair hair, receding slightly at the temples, and a brick-red face so keenly shaven that it seemed to radiate hygiene and good health. His features were regular, the nose and jaw clean-cut, but the lips were thin and the general impression you had was of a hard character in which sympathy, or indeed any of the more human emotions, had long since died ... He did not impress me as the sort of man who would have a single one of those endearing little habits or whimsical sayings which are so often attributed to police officers.

The Sergeant is, on the surface, a little different, more relaxed and even slightly sporty, but basically equally anonymous and cold. The two policemen, at first polite and casual, play the wretched Sibley, giving him line and then slowly reeling him in with each fresh interrogation, as he makes a statement, and then a revised statement, and at last a third admission of all his previous deceptions and untruths, after which they triumphantly land him gasping in a prison cell. In its time the book was wholly original, and although Bingham has been flattered by imitators, it remains supreme in its kind.

Bingham is a very variable writer. At his best he communicates as well as anybody writing today that uneasy feeling of violence moving under the surface of everyday life. *Five Roundabouts to Heaven* (1953)[2] and *The Paton Street Case* (1955)[3] are admired by some readers more than his first novel. He goes in very little for the usual deceptive tricks of the trade, but the sequence of small surprises in *A Fragment of Fear* (1965) show that he can manage them as well as anybody when he chooses. His recent work has shown a sharp decline.

So has that of Nicolas Freeling (1927–   ). Freeling began with a central character, Inspector Van der Valk, a Dutch version of Maigret, a figure distinctive enough to be remembered, yet inconspicuous enough to lead the author into criminal cases fulfilling his credo that

> Murder, and any other crime, is not a part of entertainment, but an integral part of life. We are all murderers, we are all spies, we are all criminals, and to choose a crime as the mainspring of a book's action is only to find one of the simplest ways of focusing eyes on our life and our world.

Basing himself on these ideas, which would probably receive assent from all the writers mentioned in this section, Freeling moved towards the creation of character studies which are also crime stories, from his first book, *Love in Amsterdam* (1962). He looks with a sympathetic eye – or Van der Valk does, which is much the same thing – at the springs of criminal activity, which he sees almost always as some kind of obsession. The combination of a tragic love story with a smuggling investigation in *Gun Before Butter* (1963)[4] shows his talent almost at full stretch, but probably the best of his books, and the one most clearly expressing what he is trying to do, is *Criminal Conversation* (1965). The anonymous letter sent to the police, with which it begins, turns out to be the work of a banker, 'one of the half-dozen most important men in Holland', who is accusing a fashionable neurologist of murder. The incident leads to a series of discussions and arguments between Van der Valk and the suspect which present a fascinating contrast, not of cat and mouse, nor even of accuser and accused, but of different styles and temperaments, the policeman's coarse but subtle, the neurologist's refined, charming, calm. The breaking down of this calmness to the point when, as Van der Valk says, the doctor realizes that ' "I'm the only friend he's got" ' is the real subject.

2. In America *The Tender Poisoner.*
3. In America *Inspector Morgan's Dilemma.*
4. In America *Question of Loyalty.*

In *A Long Silence* (1972)[5] Freeling killed off Van der Valk, although he has been revived since then in a few short stories. Probably Freeling felt, as others have done, that the detective who appears in a series of books imposes limitations on what can be suggested and said, offering too many easy options both to writer and reader. He has been replaced sometimes by the almost anonymous Castang, once by Van der Valk's widow Arlette. On other occasions there has been no detective. Unfortunately, with the departure of his detective Freeling seems to have lost his way as a writer.

Some of his attitudes have been taken over by Janwillem van de Wetering (1931–), who has so far stayed with the three Dutch policemen introduced in his *Outsider in Amsterdam* (1975), romantic Sergeant de Gier, bullet-headed Adjutant Grijpstra, and the little grey-haired Commissaris who is their boss. The police conversation is convincingly jokey, although de Gier occasionally sounds too much like Marlowe or Ross Macdonald's Lew Archer. The crimes are unusual in their settings – a communal religious society, Tokyo with the Japanese Mafia taking a hand, Maine in a hard winter. Van de Wetering spent some time at a Japanese Zen Buddhist temple. He was also a member of the Amsterdam Municipal Police, and enjoyed the work despite, or because of, the fact that he never made an arrest. In a recent interview he strongly resisted the idea that he was trying to 'do anything' more than 'tell a story', but still his books have a quirky religious feeling about them, blended with an air of relaxed flower-strewing anarchism. *Outsider in Amsterdam* and *The Blond Baboon* (1978) are probably the best of them. All are engaging, although if one puts Van de Wetering's detectives up against Maigret or Van der Valk, they are seen to be something less than original creations.

Kenneth Millar (1915–83), who wrote his best books under the name of Ross Macdonald, was the lineal successor to Chandler, as Chandler succeeded Hammett. These three are the truly considerable writers in the tradition that began in the pulps. Macdonald's early books, written under his own name, are uneven, but they show the vividness in the use of metaphor and simile which from the beginning pulled his work out of the anonymous ruck. *Blue City* (1947), the best of these early books, is about the son of a murdered man coming back to a mid-Western town to find his father's killer. The development owes something to Hammett, but the turns of phrase are striking ('His face had thinned and died, so that his smile was like carefully-folded paper') and so is the quality of observation

5. In America *Auprès de Ma Blonde*.

that sees

Mr Dundee's wig-brown hair, carefully parted in the exact centre of his egg-shaped skull ... his fat, laundered little face and his dark little eyes, his very hard white collar and his pale-blue tie which was held in place by a gold-plated initialled clasp.

In the first half-dozen Lew Archer stories the setting is always California, sometimes its rich face and often its dirty backside. The plots are densely complicated, there is a lot of gun-play. The books are written with the exuberance of a man intoxicated by his own skill with epithets. Chandler criticized one of them much too harshly for saying that a car was 'acned with rust' and for calling the words and drawings on lavatory walls 'graffiti'. There doesn't seem anything wrong with these words (Chandler's own suggested 'spotted' and 'scrawlings' are simply weaker), although in the books as a whole there are rather too many of them. If you turn to almost any page you are likely to be jerked to attention rather than lulled into repose, and that must be a good thing. A random opening of pages in three different books, all of them early Archer, gave 'He had a bulldog face whose only expression was a frozen ferocity intended to scare off trespassers ... I caught glimpses of glass-and-aluminium living-machines gleaming like surgical equipment in the clinical moonlight ... Geoff had lived too long among actors. He was a citizen of the unreal city, a false front leaning on scantlings.' There is sometimes a sense of strain about such writing, but often it is finely appropriate to the frenetic world that is being described.

Later Macdonald's work changed greatly, a change that he dated from *The Galton Case* (1959), a story which was 'roughly shaped on my own early life, transformed and simplified into a kind of legend'. Archer is now used quite deliberately as 'not so much a knight of romance as an observer', or sometimes almost a father confessor, to whom emotionally susceptible or injured people pour out the stories of their past. This later work can again be divided into two kinds, the books that show an interest in psychology but still use the mechanics of the crime story, and others in which the primary concern is psychological with the puzzle a secondary thing. In all of them the quality of the observation gives pleasure. The view of California as a place of immense beauty made ugly by man's insistent drive towards the use of more sophisticated technology is expressed with passion, and there is much sympathetic characterization, especially of the young. All of these later books are good, and it is only naming personal preferences to mention *The Zebra-Striped Hearse* (1962) and *The Far Side of the Dollar* (1964) among those that are predominantly puzzles, and *The Underground Man* (1971) and *The Blue Hammer* (1976) among the psychological stories. A good deal of subtlety is used in some of the last books in blending the criminal theme with something that echoes it symbolically, like the mystery of the truth or falsity of the Chantry portrait in *The Blue Hammer* and the forest fire in *The Underground Man*. Macdonald largely fulfilled his ambition to use the crime story as a vehicle for conveying psychological truths. He achieved what Rex Stout was trying to do in some of the books that preceded the arrival of Nero and Archie.

How should one rank Macdonald in relation to Hammett and Chandler? In the later books his intentions were so different from theirs that no meaningful comparison is possible. Perhaps his talent might have flowered more finely if he had upon occasion discarded Archer, a possibility he was contemplating seriously near the end of his career. It might also have flowered in different directions, for the later stories are all variations on the theme of the discovered past, and that theme is controlled by Archer's presence. But this should not be taken as denigration. Macdonald's achievement is wholly individual, unique in the modern crime story.

Hammett, Chandler, Ross Macdonald: with them the line of the hard-boiled crime story really ends. There are plenty of books containing scenes of thuggish violence and sado-masochistic sex, but the writing in them is no better than that of the forgotten *Black Mask* storytellers, and indeed they might be called *Black Mask* up to date. Of those who have continued in the genuine private-eye tradition the most talented is Roger L. Simon (1943–), whose first book in the genre, *The Big Fix* (1974), was done with a sharp eye for the modern. The opening places the story instantly in the years of student protest, the late sixties. They could have been written in no other lustrum:

The last time I was with Lila Shea we were making love in the back of a 1952 Chrysler hearse parked across the street from the Oakland Induction Center. Tear gas was seeping through the floorboards and the crack of police truncheons was in our ears. I could barely hear her little cries over the wail of sirens.

The detective is Jewish Moses Wine, the story is about a Democratic Presidential candidate who is being damaged by unwanted extreme Left support, the lush, dotty Californian background is beautifully done. Chandler and Macdonald up to date? Not quite, but Simon looked like the most promising new writer in the tradition for a long time. *The Big Fix* is still worth looking for, but two later books showed the promise unfulfilled. Simon's tendency to an excess of jokiness was shared by Andrew Bergman, whose *The Big Kiss-Off of 1944* (1974) and *Hollywood and LeVine* (1975) are lively enough, but lightweight compared with the real masters.

The writer most often mentioned as the lineal descendant, of Chandler in particular is Robert B. Parker (1932–   ), who has taken his Boston-based detective Spenser through a series of books beginning with *The Godwulf Manuscript* (1973). These are all perfectly readable – the best is the second, *God Save the Child* (1976) – but the debt to Chandler is so great as to make the writing ludicrous at times. The stories are not helped by making Spenser a jogger and an expert amateur cook. *Looking for Rachel Wallace* (1980), in which Spenser is hired to look after a lesbian writer on a publicity tour, begins well but fades away. It does, however, suggest that Spenser may have a future independent of Marlowe.

'Among the crime writers who have come into prominence since the war she has few peers, and no superior, in the art of bamboozlement. She presents us with a plausible criminal situation, builds it up to a climax of excitement, and then in the last few pages shakes the kaleidoscope and shows us an entriely different pattern from the one we have been so busily interpreting.' I wrote these words about Ross Macdonald's wife, Margaret Millar (1915–   ) a long while ago. They still seem true, although one would have to add the qualification 'at her best'. She is one of those novelists whose imagination is sparked off by the element of mystery, and the four 'straight' novels she published in the forties and early fifties are much inferior to her best mystery stories. Even as a mystery writer her early books were comparatively commonplace. It is the half-dozen books beginning with *Beast in View* (1955) that show the full scope of her skill as a novelist whose chosen theme is almost always a mystery with roots deeply hidden in the past.

The skill is shown at its finest in *How Like an Angel* (1962), which begins when Joe Quinn, a former casino cop at Reno who has lost his money gambling, lands up at the home of the True Believers in California, out in bleak mountainous country forty-five miles from the nearest large town. The True Believers is a religious cult whose members believe that they are preparing for the ascension of a Tower which has five levels, of the earth, trees, mountains, sky, and at the top 'the Tower of Heaven where the Master lives'. Nothing could better show the difference between the Golden Age story and the crime novel than the treatment given to similar groups by Allingham and Marsh, compared to that of Millar. For them the cult is merely a background, ridiculous and distasteful. Millar treats it seriously, describing its beliefs, physical situation and adherents. The practical good sense of Sister Blessing, the silence of Brother Tongue of Prophets, the excitement when a new convert arrives to join the slowly disintegrating group, are conveyed with a powerful sense of pathos and absurdity, joined to respect for a way of life. The tension of the novel is partly created by the contrast between the simplicities of the group and the complexity of the investigation which Quinn undertakes on behalf of Sister Blessing into the background of Patrick O'Gorman, who apparently died five years earlier in a car accident. The puzzle is there all right, and its solution on the last page lives up to those phrases used about Millar's work, but by that time many readers will have become so much concerned with the fate of the characters that the problem itself is a secondary thing.

The best of the other Millar books show her ability to create an atmosphere of uneasiness and terror which in other hands might have become merely Gothic, but in her case is used to show developments based on the conflict of character. *Beast in View*, with its perfectly fair bit of conjuring on which the whole story depends, *The Soft Talkers* (1957),[6] *The Listening Walls* (1959), with its apparent double bluff and brilliant trick ending, and *A Stranger in My Grave* (1960) are all very good. Millar's recent books have been less firmly plotted, and only occasionally successful.

Among the most interesting and extraordinary recent work in the crime story is that of George V. Higgins (1939–). Higgins was a Boston lawyer and Assistant Attorney-General in Massachusetts, and his crime stories are based on a knowledge of criminals, the kind of people they are and the language they use. The characters in Higgins's books, from *The Friends of Eddie Coyle* (1972) onwards talk with a heightened naturalism that embodies the hesitations, repetitions, emphases, of ordinary speech. Almost all are crooks or policemen, and the early novels are nine tenths conversation or monologue, with thoughts and motives obliquely conveyed through speech full of criminal slang and colloquialisms, and punctuated with swear words used automatically. The effect is not dreary but at times almost poetic, like that of a Compton-Burnett brought up in Boston's combat zone.

The best Higgins books are wholly original in approach as well as language. *The Digger's Game* (1973), *Cogan's Trade* (1974) and *The Judgment of Deke Hunter* (1976) are all brilliant novels that tell their criminal stories with sometimes baffling indirectness. The end of *Cogan's Trade* gives an idea of the quality of dialogue which builds up in layers, so that you appreciate a page more than a paragraph, a chapter more than a page. Cogan is a gunman, his trade is murder, and he has done a job at short notice in which he has killed several people. He complains that he is not being paid enough, and then reflects on the real villain of the story, whose name is Dillon. Dillon, who double-crossed everybody and has set up all

---

6. In America *An Air That Kills*.

these shootings, has just died – not been murdered (as one might think and even hope), but died of a heart attack. Cogan is talking to the car driver who has brought him the money for his work. The driver is in awe of Cogan, but frightened even more by the memory of Dillon.

'Well, how about that?' the driver says. 'Dillon's dead. Son of a bitch.'
'He wasn't a bad guy actually', Cogan said.
'No', the driver said, 'no, I guess he wasn't. He wasn't a bad guy.'
'He always', Cogan said, 'he never, well, I knew Dillon a long time, right? It was Dillon, really, got me started, said I oughta be doing something that'd be around and like that, you know? He was the guy that really plugged me in. I knew Dillon a long time.'
'Sure', the driver said. 'I had a lot of respect for him.'
'Sure', Cogan said, 'so'd I. You know why?'
'You were afraid of him? ' the driver said.
'Nah', Cogan said. He finished his beer. 'Nah, it wasn't that. It was, he knew the way things oughta be done, right?'
'So I'm told', the driver said.
'And when they weren't', Cogan said, 'he knew what to do.'
'And so do you', the driver said.
'And so do I', Cogan said.

Those are the last words of the book.

I return to Britain, and to criminal gentility. Shelley Smith (the name used by Nancy Hermione Bodington, 1912–   ) began by writing conventional stories about slightly simple women in danger, more sophisticated versions of the Rinehart novel. In the thirties such books were one of the chief variants of the orthodox puzzle, and in Britain Ethel Lina White wrote several, of which *The Wheel Spins* (1936) was probably the best. Smith's *Come and be Killed* (1946) showed a development of this plucky-little-lady-in-trouble theme. Florence, dim, dullish and neurotic, makes a half-hearted attempt to commit suicide, and then runs away from the nursing home to which her busy sister has sent her. When she meets the weatherbeaten and apparently kindly Mrs Jolly we know that Florence is in trouble, and prepare ourselves for her hairbreadth escape from death. Not so. Florence is murdered by jolly Mrs Jolly, and the book is the portrait of a murderess rather than of a woman in trouble. Mary Roberts Rinehart, one might say, has turned into Francis Iles.

Good though *Come and be Killed* was, it hardly prepared one for *The Lord Have Mercy* (1956).[7] Here Shelley Smith used the conventional background of middle-class English village life, the Conservative dance,

7. In America *The Shrew is Dead*.

Dr Barnardo's fête, little dinner parties, to show the worms of hatred and frustration working away under the surface. The butch lesbian ready to leave her clinging partner and the local doctor's frigid, bitchy wife are particularly good. After the wife's death from an overdose of barbiturates everybody goes on behaving as they might do in real life. The final crime which resolves the situation has a fine inevitableness about it. Even better in its specialized kind is *An Afternoon to Kill* (1953), a *tour de force* which may enthral, amuse or infuriate, but certainly won't bore any reader. The ending, the cause of such emotions, is a genuine surprise.

Roy Fuller (1912–) has written three crime stories at a middle stage in his principal literary career as poet. All are marked by the exactness and elegance of his poems and other novels, but perhaps the most successful is *With My Little Eye* (1948). The sub-title calls the book 'A Mystery Story for Teen agers', but this is deceptive, for it means only that murder and other crimes are seen through the eyes of an intelligent adolescent narrator. The light sophistication of the tone is conveyed in the first paragraph, with its apology for kicking off with 'a boring explanation': 'It would be pleasant to start with the astonishing thud of the pistol shot, but then the explanation would have to come in the middle of the excitement, which would be even more boring.' A little-known book, *With My Little Eye* is in its small way a perfect example of a modern crime story, finely constructed and balanced, with the solution to the various problems that baffle Frederick French (what could make a man move from one bookmaker to another on a racecourse, putting five pounds on every one of the nine horses in a race?) dropping perfectly into place. *The Second Curtain* (1953) finds George Garner, a timid publisher's reader, nursing the hope that through the box files in which he keeps the whole of his correspondence he will one day be acknowledged as 'a sort of Horace Walpole'. Garner becomes involved in the problem posed by the disappearance of his constant correspondent and old friend Widgery, and his quest for the truth about Widgery leads up to an abyss of violence, into which he looks for a moment before flinching away. Again beautifully composed, the book emphasizes like some others mentioned here how little rather than how much violence may be used in a successful crime story. *Fantasy and Fugue* (1954) looks back to Godwin in its central character who is both hunter and hunted. It is less successful than the other books chiefly because the theme is treated with a too insistent Freudianism.

The most interesting crime writers to emerge in Britain during the past decade are without doubt P. D. James (1920–) and Ruth Rendell

(1930–   ), and this is true even though James's first book appeared in 1962 and Rendell's two years later. James's work, at first glance, seems to contradict a good deal of what has been said about the progress of the crime story. She has been called a natural successor to Sayers (the initial P stands for Phyllis), and it is true that she shows the same care in plotting, has the same desire to ensure the accuracy of minor points, plus an almost obsessional zest in describing furniture and fittings, and like Sayers gives us dialogue that is convincing rather than entertaining. But the differences are more important than the surface similarities, and they rest in the fact that she has pushed, as a modernist must, against the boundaries of the classical detective story. At first she regarded detective fiction only as a useful apprenticeship for writing novels, but 'after I had done three or four [detective] novels, I realized that in fact the restriction . . . could almost help by imposing a discipline, and that you could be a serious novelist within it'. Her innovation has been chiefly in terms of subject, so that *The Black Tower* (1975) is set in a home for incurables, and *Death of an Expert Witness* (1977) creates a forensic research laboratory in East Anglia with splendid solidity. And she can be formidably realistic in a way that would never have been attempted by Sayers or any other Golden Age writer, as in the following passage from *Shroud for a Nightingale* (1971). A trainee nurse is demonstrating the intragastric feeding of milk by tube, with another nurse in the role of patient. The girl administering the feed

lifted the funnel high over Nurse Pearce's head and began slowly to pour the milky mixture down the tube. The class seemed to be holding its breath. And then it happened. There was a squeal, high-pitched, horribly inhuman, and Nurse Pearce precipitated herself from the bed as if propelled by an irresistible force. One second she was lying, immobile, propped against her mound of pillows, the next she was out of bed, teetering forward on arched feet in a parody of a ballet dancer. And all the time she screamed, perpetually screamed, like a stuck whistle.

The milky mixture has been replaced by carbolic acid.

The way of the innovator is not easy, nor always successful. James's most celebrated book, *Innocent Blood* (1980), is not a detective story but the account of an adopted girl's search for her real parents, and the dramatic and tragic results of her discoveries about them. The book is in the end cosy rather than, as it should have been, uncomfortable to read, and in *The Skull beneath the Skin* (1982) she returned to orthodox detection and brought back Cordelia Gray, the woman detective who had appeared in *An Unsuitable Job for a Woman* (1972). It should be added that James probably does not think of herself as an innovator, but simply as, in her own words, 'a very English writer' who happens to have strayed into criminal fields. It is true that thirty years earlier she would have been a distinguished representative of the Golden Age, to set beside Marsh and Allingham. It is the pressure of the times that has made her a modern.

Ruth Rendell's first book, the ingenious *From Doon with Death* (1964), introduced Detective Chief Inspector Reginald Wexford who, she has said, was 'born at the age of 52' and was 'a man because like most women I am very much still caught up in the web that one writes about men because men are the people and we are the others'. The Wexford books are orthodox crime stories, set in a mid-Sussex town, and the Inspector is equipped with a wife, daughters who provide occasional problems, friends, and a puritanical sidekick named Inspector Burden, who is inclined to distrust modern youth. Some of the stories have stunning surprise endings, but it is the subjects that divide them from the work of the Golden Age. One book involves transvestism, another is based on the hatred members of a family feel for each other – and the hatred is based on personality, not on the problems of an inheritance. Her subjects justify the remark of a wit who said that in a Rendell novel a couple is not a happy thing to be. Some of the books are about sexual frustration, which is powerfully conveyed without use of a single sexual word, and little in the way of sexual description.

The Wexford books have inevitable similarities of approach, and it is little more than personal preference to pick out *Murder Being Once Done* (1972), *Some Lie and Some Die* (1973) and *Shake Hands For Ever* (1975) as particularly good, although the choice does emphasize that the most accomplished Wexfords are found in the seventies. In her chosen area, which seems always something like suburbia, and among her chosen characters, middle-class or a little lower, Rendell's ear and eye are unerring. The conversations between these people are real, and they convince also when Wexford talks to them. If one wanted to introduce a foreigner to the flavour of British urban life, Ruth Rendell's novels would serve as well as any of those by writers more highly regarded, in part because they don't write crime stories.

Rendell herself prefers the other books she writes, which offer studies in abnormal psychology leading on to violence. In an interview she said that she read Freud, Jung and Adler, but little criminology, and remarked also that she often felt personal disaster to be imminent. 'Some kind of disgrace, humiliation, suffering, pain, disaster, poverty, famine ... It is a neurotic state. I wish I didn't have it. I have it.' She added that many of her characters have it too, and it appears in her books as a flaw in the personality that leads to violence when put under some kind of emotional stress. Again the basis of the flaw is often sexual, like that of Arthur Johnson in *A Demon in My View* (1976), who keeps a dummy woman in his cellar, and finds ecstatic pleasure in strangling her every few days. This book, and *A Judgement in Stone* (1977) are the best of the stories concerned with the psychology of a murderer. Anybody who experiments as freely as Rendell is taking considerable risks, and there are books which fail (*The Face of Trespass* and *Master of the Moor* are two) because the central figure simply does not carry conviction. Taking them all together, Wexford and gruelling chillers, humdrum police work made interesting and criminal psychology mostly made plausible, Rendell's work blossomed magnificently in the seventies.

Superintendent Andy Dalziel, overweight and impolite, and the almost intellectual Inspector Pascoe, the creations of Reginald Hill (1936–), bear some relationship to Wexford and Burden, but are less successfully dovetailed into the novels where they appear. Hill has yet to fulfil the promise of his awkward but intelligent early novels, and this seems to be because Dalziel and Pascoe often put a brake on the progress of an interesting story. *Deadheads* (1983) is a case in point. Is Patrick Aldermann a multiple murderer or an innocent man? The problem is neatly posed and cleverly developed, the writing alert and amusing (horsy Daphne's rangily athletic movements 'divert the eye from the basic equininity of the total bone structure'), but the standard police investigation gets in the way, and what might have been a tale to put beside *Before the Fact* peters out rather tamely, although with a pleasing ambiguity. Hill's best book to date is *The Spy's Wife* (1980), a believable and moving novel, which shows what he can do when he gives his policemen leave of absence.

There are not many recent European writers who can be considered seriously in the context of the crime novel, but their contribution is particularly interesting because it is so unlike that from Britain or America. Friedrich Dürrenmatt (1921–), the Swiss playwright and novelist, is unquestionably the most notable of them. Dürrenmatt writes in German, and has obviously been much influenced by Expressionism. His work is relentlessly moralistic, and every social point is driven home with the insistent irony of an Emil Jannings film. The most important of his short novels is *Der Richter und sein Henker*, translated as *The Judge and His Hangman* (1954), a book masterly in its control of the crime story medium for the author's symbolic and moral purposes. Inspector Barlach, an old detective who knows that he is dying, uses criminal means to trap the master-criminal he has been hunting over a period of forty years. Barlach's behaviour often seems unintelligible or stupid but in fact has its own logic. In this book Dürrenmatt uses much of the apparatus of the detective story. Why did young Lieutenant Schmied wear evening dress on days which he marked with a 'G' in his diary, what happened to the body of the dog killed by Barlach's assistant, Chanz, when the dog attacked the Inspector? The apparatus is used as part of a fantastic game which Barlach is playing with the other characters, and which Dürrenmatt is playing with the reader. The revelation of the murderer comes as a surprise, but it is subservient to the points the author is making about the nature of justice and the need to extirpate evil by violence.

Dürrenmatt's other crime stories do not fuse the investigatory and symbolic elements quite so successfully, but they are all remarkable for their originality. *Der Verdacht*, translated as *The Quarry* (1962), finds Barlach in hospital, slowly recovering from what had been thought a fatal illness. The doctor treating him thinks he identifies, in an old picture from *Life*, a German concentration camp doctor who took pleasure in operating on inmates without anaesthetics. Has this man committed suicide, or is he in fact still alive and the head of a clinic which takes in only wealthy patients? There follows a struggle of wits and wills between Barlach and this man, which is also a struggle between freedom and nihilism. 'Freedom is the courage to commit crime, for freedom itself is a crime,' the doctor says, adding: 'I devote myself to that which made me free – murder and torture.' Again, his destruction is achieved only by the use of a force greater than his own.

Das Versprechen, translated as *The Pledge* (1958), is about the transformation of Inspector Matthäi from an emotionless machine into a man with a passion for justice, intent to discover the murderer of three young girls. In pursuit of this man Matthäi becomes for years a petrol station attendant, and with the utmost ruthlessness uses another young girl as bait for the killer. The bait is not accepted, the girl becomes a sluttish prostitute, the defeated Matthäi sinks into a sodden wreck. At the end of the story it is revealed that he was 'a genius, more so than any of your fictional detectives', and that all of his deductions were correct. Again, what might have been a mere clatter of ironies is kept finely under control.

Dürrenmatt's use of coincidence and fantasy is justified by his moral force. This cannot be said of the two French writers, Pierre Boileau (1906–) and Thomas Narcejac (1908–), who collaborate as Boileau-Narcejac, or of Jean Baptiste Rossi (1931–) who uses the pseudonym of Sebastien Japrisot. Boileau-Narcejac and Japrisot are rather like a blend of Gaboriau and Leroux, combining the realistic detail of the one with the implausible or outrageous surprise endings of the other. Boileau-Narcejac usually presents us with a sexual tangle which looks straightforward, and then reveals a previously laid plan which is always ingenious but often strains credulity. A good example is *The Living and the Dead* (1956). Here a detective down on his luck is hired by his old friend, Gévigne, who is now a rich man. Gévigne wants his wife, Madeleine, watched, not because he suspects adultery but because her behaviour is strange and apparently suicidal. The detective follows Madeleine, falls in love with her, saves her from an attempt at drowning, is present when she kills herself by jumping off a tower. In fact he is being used as a dupe. Madeleine is indeed dead, killed and disfigured by her husband who threw her off the tower, and the 'Madeleine' known to the detective is Gévigne's mistress, whose behaviour was designed to provide a witness who would say that the dead woman was suicidal. The idea is ingenious, but the plan has as many holes as a watering-can. *Heart to Heart* (1959) similarly sacrifices probability for immediate trick effects, and so does *Spells of Evil* (1961), a sexual triangle which is not what it seems. In Japrisot's *Trap for Cinderella* (1962) we are confronted with the problem of whether a girl badly burned in a fire and then equipped with a plastic face is really who and what she seems to be. Yet although there is something strained and artificial about these writers, it has to be said that their often outrageous deceptions really do deceive, much more dramatically than those of most contemporary British and American crime novelists.

The work of the Swedish writer Peter Wahlöo (1926–75) was of two different kinds. He wrote two novels which combine the moral symbolism of Dürrenmatt with a flavour of Orwellian fantasy. *Murder on the Thirty-first Floor* (1966) and *The Steel Spring* (1970) make their points about dictatorship and paternalism through the medium of crime, and Chief Inspector Jensen, who appears in both books, is trying to discover the nature of society while dealing with what is generally called criminal activity. The books that Wahlöo, as Per and not Peter, wrote in collaboration with Maj Sjöwall (1935–   ) were less ambitious and more successful. These police investigations carried out by Inspector Beck, a gloomy version of Freeling's Van der Valk, might be called 'Police Novels' except that the authors are more interested in the philosophic implications of crime than in police routine. Sjöwall and Wahlöo were using the form of the police novel to make left-wing and even directly political points. They planned and wrote a series of ten novels (the last, *The Terrorists*, appeared in 1977) which were to become increasingly outspoken in revealing the nature of Sweden, 'an ideologically pauperized and morally debatable so-called welfare state of the bourgeois type', and by extension of other bourgeois states. For their purpose Beck was an ideal figure, a version of the modern anti-hero, a man inclined to doubt the validity of his own actions. Whether or not the view of modern Sweden and its police force is accurate, the results are both powerful and fascinating. In one book, *The Locked Room* (1973), the collaborators daringly used the convention of the John Dickson Carr books and added to it a police procedural which was also an exposure, at times wildly farcical, of modern police techniques. Confessions are recorded on faulty tapes, the criminals are misapprehended in an empty apartment. It is taking great risks to treat your policemen seriously in some books, farcically in others. Sometimes we find ourselves resenting such a change in approach, sometimes the narrative drive of the stories is damaged because social points are made too obviously. But the best of the series (*Roseanna*, *The Abominable Man*, *The Terrorists*) are among the most original modern crime stories, and Sjöwall/Wahlöo sometimes succeeded in doing things that no other crime writers even attempted.

Things that are never really attempted, for example, in the work of Ross Thomas (1926–   ) or James McClure (1939–   ), even though most of Thomas's books concern social corruption of one kind or another, and McClure's books about the Afrikaner Lieutenant Tromp Kramer and his Zulu sidekick Sergeant Zondi look at South African racial problems in a way that has led one critic to compare them with Alan Paton and Nadine Gordimer. Distinctions are inevitably arbitrary, but for this arbiter both Thomas and McClure do little more than use corruption in America, race feeling in South Africa, as top dressing for lively thrillers and mysteries.

With that said, there is no doubt of the liveliness. Thomas's *The Fools in Town are on Our Side* (1971) is about a Southern city in the hands of crooks; his best book *The Porkchoppers* (1972) deals with terrorism by trade unions; *The Money Harvest* (1975) tells how a Mafia mobster plans to rig the wheat market. Thomas's dialogue is vivid and amusing, his gangsters convincingly heartless and deadly (the respectable killer of *The Porkchoppers* is particularly chilling), he is good at devising an intricate plot and gradually revealing its details. These talents are accompanied by unusual limitations. Several books contain long flashbacks, often interesting in themselves but irrelevant to the course of the story. Sub-plots proliferate, minor characters loom large and disappear for a hundred pages, and – most damagingly – almost all of the books have marshmallow at the core. The heroes are various, both in appearance and colour (black in *The Seersucker Whipsaw*, yellow in *Chinaman's Chance*), but they are so farseeing and intelligent as to be practically indestructible. One feels admiration when reading almost every Thomas book (his subsidiary work as Oliver Bleeck is not recommended), but irritation is never far away.

McClure's Tromp and Zondi stories show the law of diminishing returns already frequently observed. The first of them, *The Steam Pig* (1971), and *The Caterpillar Cop* (1972), which succeeded it, were cleverly devised murder mysteries whose solution involved some point of racial behaviour. The relationship between beer-swilling Tromp Kramer and his sergeant is on Tromp's side that of one whose confidence in his superior colour is such that he is able to treat the black subordinate tolerantly, while always making clear who is master. But such a relationship must be very limited for the purposes of fiction, and in later books like *The Sunday Hangman* (1977) and *The Blood of an Englishman* (1980) Tromp is much less rude and crude, Zondi is treated almost as an equal, a book has for subtitle 'A Kramer and Zondi Novel'. The results are still entertaining, but most of the early realism has been washed away.

Looking at the work of these writers it is possible to make a rough division between those who have abandoned the puzzle element in most of their work (Highsmith, Bingham, Freeling, Smith) and those who retain it in a changed form like James and Rendell; or between those who use the crime story primarily to investigate human personality and those chiefly concerned with expressing an attitude towards society, like Bennett, Macdonald, Dürrenmatt and Sjöwall/Wahlöo. But although such divisions cast some illuminations, the important thing is that these variously talented writers have chosen deliberately to use the form of the crime story as a way of expressing their insights. Almost all might have successful careers as what is ambiguously called straight novelists.

And so to Borges, Jorge Luis Borges (1899–   ), whose omission from the previous edition of this book brought both sharp and sorrowful rebukes to its author. There can be no doubt that Borges is interested in, even fascinated by, British crime and adventure literature. 'I saw London through Dickens and through Chesterton and through Stevenson,' he once told an interviewer, and Chesterton's verve, colourfulness and disregard of realism hold particular attractions for him. The problem in code or cypher, the double personality, the labyrinthine puzzle, all these aspects of detective fiction play a part in Borges stories. His concern, however, is with surrealistic and not logical explanations, so that a story may contain other stories within it, the whole making a Chinese box of tricks, or a Russian doll. Almost all Borges stories challenge at some point the convention of realism, so that any apparently straightforward situation presented to us is likely to have its reality questioned or destroyed within a few pages. Every time a book is read or re-read, Borges has said, in a remark that makes his own work an ideal hunting ground for structuralists, it is modified.

It follows that Borges's interest in the detective form is limited to Golden Age puzzles. It is their mechanical ingenuity he values, the tricks played with time, fact or identity. Most of the writers discussed in the last few pages would hold little interest for him. Essentially Borges's connection with the crime story is parodic, and it is not surprising that the detective who sits solving crime puzzles brought to him in a prison cell is named Isidro Parodi (*Six Problems for Don Isidro Parodi*, published in 1942 but translated into English in 1981). The solutions are unconvincing, the stories merely fanciful or jokey, but the book is, as admirers will say, minor work. Father Brown appears in one story, naturally enough a fake Father Brown. Major Borges tales, however, are similar to minor ones in convincing or amusing only on the level of jokes. 'Ibn-Hakkan-al-Bokhari' lampoons Chesterton in its outrageousness; half a dozen stories in *Ficciones* (1944, translated 1962) contain jokes about the classical detective story, or peep under its skirts looking for a dreadful secret which turns out to be about a man peeping under the skirts of the detective story looking for a dreadful secret which turns out ... 'An Examination of the Work of Herbert Quain' tells us that Quain's first novel failed because *The Siamese Twin Mystery* (by Ellery Queen, although this is not mentioned) was published almost at the same time, and 'The Garden of Forking Paths' and 'Death and the Compass', often claimed as masterly short crime stories, are no more than games played by a writer amusing himself with the *idea* of the puzzle rather than making an effort to construct one. 'The Form of the Sword' and 'Theme of the Traitor and Hero' are similarly comments made on the spy story, amusing (a word which gets a great deal of work when one is writing about Borges) and clever, but nothing more. Most of Borges's stories are, in his own phrase, 'guessing games, or parables' that have no decisive answer. They could be considered as attacks on the superficiality of the short detective story, but they are in no other way examples of it.

Alain Robbe-Grillet (1922–) is the avant-garde writer most often mentioned after Borges in connection with the crime story. *The Erasers* (1953, translated into English 1964) certainly contains a detective, Wallas, who is at the centre of the action in the sense that everything is seen through his eyes, but Robbe-Grillet is interested in the technique and minutiae of detection, not its ultimate end. A woman crosses the street, several kinds of fish are displayed in a window, a man in a black overcoat and hat comes out of a house, it is five minutes to eight when Wallas enters the Place de la Préfecture. All is described as if under Holmes's magnifying glass, but are these things important to the story? To this Robbe-Grillet's implicit answer is: what story? Dozens of stories are contained in what Wallas sees. The contrasts between the particularity of Wallas's vision, the surrealist atmosphere in which he moves, and the frequent repetition and echoing of conversational phrases to give an air of meaningfulness to everything that happens or is noted, work very well to create a crime story which remains in a formal sense an unsolved mystery. *The Erasers* was put forward for the yearly award given by the British Crime Writers Association for the best crime novel of the year, and one critic felt its rejection so strongly that he resigned from the awards panel.

A similar technique is used in *The Voyeur* (1958) and *Jealousy* (1959). Again we are almost wholly confined to what the central character feels and sees, but we have moved much further from the orthodox crime story in the sense that the crime in *Jealousy*, if it takes place at all, is provided by the reader's imagination rather than being 'actual'. In *The House of Assignation* (1966, translated 1970) three different possibilities are offered about the way in which Edouard Manneret has been murdered, and the point for Robbe-Grillet is *not* to discover the 'real' one. For him as for Borges, one of the limitations of Kafka would be that his fictions always offer a decisive, even though an ambiguous, answer to the problems of his protagonists. Again like Borges, Robbe-Grillet prefers multiple possibilities, and *The Erasers* is the only book of his that comes within the canon of the crime story.

Italy has produced a single very curious example of the avant-garde crime story, Umberto Eco's *The Name of the Rose* (1980, translated 1983). The time is the fourteenth century, the scene a rich Franciscan abbey, the murders multiple, the detective William of Baskerville. William owes something to Conan Doyle, in appearance and conversation as well as in name, but the book's elaborate periphrastical jokiness is more reminiscent of Borges, of Nabokov, even of Baron Corvo. The novel has won prizes, and one notes a French view that 'in the entertaining guise of an erudite detective story, it is also a vibrant plea for freedom, moderation and wisdom', while feeling that the entertainment is buried deep under an erudition not lightly worn, and that the plea for moderation is reached only through William's disproving of several kinds of chop-logic. A reader lacking interest in religious ritual and theological argument, like this one, may pull through to the end with relief rather than admiration.

(iii) Entertainers

The essential distinction between serious novelists and entertainers is one of attitude. The writers mentioned previously in this chapter have in common the fact that they are all to some degree emotionally involved in their work. Their books offer personal and individual feelings about the world and society. The entertainer thinks instead of what will amuse his audience, and if an idea or a subject seems likely to disturb it is put aside. Often the entertainer shares the preconceptions of the audience so completely that no adjustment is necessary. This is obviously true of Christie and the early Queen, less true of Sayers and the later Allingham – to take examples almost at random – but even the less orthodox entertainer tries not to injure the susceptibilities of the reader. In our time there are many skilful writers who put into their books little or nothing of their own personalities. Now that the old rules no longer apply, they are able to treat lightly and amusingly many subjects that would not have been touched thirty years ago.

Emma Lathen in America, Michael Gilbert in Britain, are two outstandingly skilful writers of this kind. Emma Lathen is the pseudonym of Mary J. Latsis and Martha Henissart. Her or their detective stories, produced at the rate of roughly one a year since *Banking on Death* (1961), offer mysteries that are solved by John Putnam Thatcher, the silver-haired Senior Vice-President of the Sloan Guaranty Trust in New York's Wall Street. One reads Lathen primarily for the always shrewd and often funny descriptions of Thatcher's relationships with other people connected with the Sloan who are drawn into cases – the tetchy President, Bradford Withers, the pessimistic Everett Gabler, who is the most trusted of Thatcher's section chiefs, the emotionally erratic Tom Robichaux – and for the settings, which often play an important part in the story, and are always done with a convincing show of knowledge. They range from a power struggle in a car company (*Murder Makes the Wheels Go Round*, 1966) and a rather similar struggle in an Oriental rug business (*By Hook or By Crook*, 1975), to racial problems on Wall Street (*Death Shall Overcome*, 1966).

It is apparent that Lathen has a thorough grasp of banking procedures, and the best of the stories are firmly centred on Wall Street dealings. *Murder against the Grain* (1967) and *Accounting for Murder* (1964) are among the best. In the first of these, Sloan finds itself threatened with the loss of a million dollars when a shipment of grain for the Soviet Union proves to have been loaded on the basis of forged documents, and in the second an implacable little man named Clarence Fortinbras (author of 'Fortinbras on Accounts Receivable') presses an investigation into the affairs of a firm called National Calculating, and is murdered for his pains. Lathen always knows exactly what she is doing, and does it with supreme confidence and a humour that is never over-emphasized, although in recent books the formula seems to be wearing a little thin. Attempts by Lathen, using the name of R. B. Dominic, to develop a second string to Thatcher, in the person of a liberal Congressman named Ben Safford, have not been particularly successful.

The first novel by Michael Gilbert (1912–) was *Close Quarters* (1947), an orthodox detective story of what might have been pre-1939 vintage. It even included a map of the Cathedral Close as ornamentation for an ecclesiastical murder case. Gilbert quickly moved away from this classical pattern, and in *Smallbone Deceased* (1950) made splendid use of his professional legal knowledge to construct a puzzle that also offered a nicely comic view of life in the office of Horniman, Birley and Craine, solicitors. Since that time Gilbert has wavered between a wish to be fairly realistic and a feeling that one shouldn't be too serious in a crime story.

He is not afraid to experiment with settings – one of his best books, *Death in Captivity* (1952),[8] is set in a prisoner-of-war camp – and in *The Crack in the Teacup* (1966) he concentrates very successfully on some apparently petty crookedness in the affairs of a local council. *The Body of a Girl* (1972) explores the social background of a society, but as always with Gilbert shrinks from digging very deep. 'What is a writer to do if he is not allowed to entertain?' Gilbert has asked, but the point being made in this book is that he may entertain and still do something more. In fact Gilbert has gone some way in this direction with *The Night of the Twelfth* (1976), and perhaps his best as it is certainly his most individual book, *Death of a Favourite Girl* (1980),[9] in which a powerful portrait of a less than scrupulous policeman is combined with a teasing puzzle.

Successful comic crime stories, short or long, are rare. One turns away with a shudder from the many Holmes parodies, and with not much more cheerfulness from the conscientiously crazy detective stories of the English Pamela Branch and the Americans Craig Rice and Elliot Paul, but the postwar period has produced two successful writers of crime comedy. The first book by Joyce Porter (1924–), *Dover One* (1964), introduced one of the most successful inefficient detectives in crime fiction. Chief-Inspector Dover is a fat, lazy, beer-swilling boor who leaves all the actual work to

8. In America *The Danger Within*.
9. In America *The Killing of Katie Steelstock*.

his assistant, Sergeant MacGregor, and either stumbles across the solution to a crime by accident or takes credit for MacGregor's leg-work. The climax of *Dover One* is both gruesome and funny. Unfortunately that law of diminishing returns operates most powerfully in relation to comic detectives, and having established Dover's characteristics in her first book, Porter has not found it possible to do much more than repeat them less effectively in later ones. Her books introducing another comic detective, the Hon.-Con, are best left unbroached.

The work of Colin Watson (1920–82), however, has triumphantly survived similar problems. In his hands fireworks of comedy go up as they are meant to do in a dazzling show of stars, instead of spluttering miserably into darkness. All of his books are genuine mysteries, and all gain from being placed in the firmly realized country town of Flaxborough, with its once-popular Moorish Electric Theatre which is later the Alhambra Billiards Club, and its slyly lecherous respectable citizens. Watson also deals tactfully with his comic characters. Harcourt Chubb, Flaxborough's Chief Constable, is pompous and sometimes obtuse, but not merely silly. *Hopjoy Was Here* (1962), his most notable performance, contains some brilliant comedy about a Bond-like secret agent who is investigating the disappearance of Hopjoy, one of his men. Here again the portrait of 'the man known as Ross' never slips over from engaging comedy into unbelievable farce. The later Watson stories, in which the chief figure is a demurely crooked spinster named Miss Teatime, are less convincing than the earlier ones, but he remains the rarest of comic crime writers, one with the gift of originality.

It may have been noticed that the entertainers tend to use a series detective (the inconspicuous Inspector Purbright runs like a vein of common sense through Watson's books), but that his detectival skills are often deprecated rather than emphasized. This is certainly true of H. R. F. Keating's Inspector Ghote of the Bombay Police, who often teeters on the edge of a disastrous mistake without ever actually tipping over. The development of Keating (1926–   ) has been interesting. He began with four elliptically written books, at times semi-surrealist in style. *A Rush on the Ultimate* (1961) was perhaps the best of them, but all are interestingly odd. *The Perfect Murder* (1964) introduced the often naive, occasionally shrewd Ghote, who has been the central figure in several later books. These have a good deal of charm, although they tend to be devised too much as demonstrations of Ghote's reactions to a particular place. *Inspector Ghote Hunts the Peacock* (1968), for instance, shows him on a first visit to London. Ghote is prepared to be delighted by everything English, from policemen to the Tower, is distressed when he discovers colour prejudice, and makes a disastrous mess of delivering a speech. His reputation is saved, however, when he unwittingly finds a clue that leads to the discovery of an opium cache, and almost as unwittingly solves a crime relating to an Indian girl. The picture of Ghote in London is delightful, but as a crime story the book is less than satisfactory. *Inspector Ghote Goes by Train* (1971) is similarly amusing and informative about Indian train travel, but disappointingly slight as a puzzle, and *Filmi, Filmi, Inspector Ghote* (1976) has a splendid setting in the Indian filming of *Macbeth* which tends to swamp the plot.

As often happens, the creation of a series detective has hampered Keating's desire and intention to write seriously. (He has written four 'straight' novels, among which *A Long Walk to Wimbledon*, 1978, set in a ruined London, is a finely imaginative work.) *The Murder of the Maharajah* (1980), along with *The Perfect Murder* his most successful crime story, is set in the thirties and shows what Keating can do when free of Ghote. The picture of the puckish, malicious Maharajah of Bhopore, cheating at chess and delighting in playing practical jokes on his guests, is brilliantly done, the English Resident Adviser and local District Superintendent of Police are well sketched, the puzzle is genuinely baffling.

Wobble to Death, the first crime story by Peter Lovesey (1936–   ), won a crime novel competition. The book used as very effective background an actual endurance race held in London in 1879, and introduced the stolidly intelligent Sergeant Cribb, who has appeared in several other crime stories set in the last twenty years of the nineteenth century. The first novel showed occasional wobbliness in plotting, but the later books are written with assurance, with some excellent interplay between Cribb, his pompous superior Inspector Jowett and his subordinate Thackeray. The details are well researched, whether they deal with bare-fist fighting in *The Detective Wore Silk Drawers* (1971), spiritualism in *A Case of Spirits* (1975), or Irish dynamiters in *Invitation to a Dynamite Party* (1974).[10] Occasionally one has the feeling that there is too much setting, too little plot, but in general the balance is maintained. Lovesey regards the books as Victorian police procedural novels, but they are nearer to period social comedies with thriller and puzzle elements. *A Case of Spirits* offers a particularly ingenious murder method. Ingenuity is also the hallmark of his best crime story, *The False Inspector Dew* (1982), which contains a twist

10. In America *The Tick of Death*.

or turn of the plot every fifty pages, with a coup near the end which will surprise most readers. The setting is the Cunard liner *Mauretania*, the year 1921, and the false Inspector Dew himself contributes to one of the cleverest criminal comedies of the last few years.

One of the likely, or at least possible, spin-off benefits of a series detective is that he may be used for TV. This has happened to Inspector Purbright and Miss Teatime, to Inspector Ghote and Sergeant Cribb. It happened also to James Hazell, ex-copper, ex-lush, temporary barman, bouncer and bum, and private detective. Hazell is the creation of P. B. Yuill, a name masking the identities of novelist Gordon Williams (1939–   ) and football player and then manager Terry Venables. The authors were, as is not unusual, disappointed by the TV version of Hazell, who is made more conventionally heroic and more comic than in the three books about him. In these the detective, first met in *Hazell Plays Solomon* (1974) while recovering from a broken ankle sustained when 'some reluctant clients in Fulham had slammed a car door on it three or four times', is a blend of a Cockney Marlowe and one of those battered optimists who come up from any disaster merry and bright. Well-observed details of scabby contemporary London, convincing dialogue including some real or invented rhyming slang for which Americans might need a glossary, an adroitly designed puzzle to solve – the trilogy completed by *Hazell and the Three Card Trick* (1975) and *Hazell and the Menacing Jester* (1976) were among the lightest and brightest books of their respective years. But perhaps the authors expected too much, perhaps they got bored with their hero. Whatever the reason, there has been no fourth Hazell novel. The three are well worth looking for in paperback.

(iv) The standard article

The level of writing in the crime story has improved greatly in the past thirty years. Where Golden Age characters were all cardboard cut-outs except the detective, modern ones often come to life without their creators' intentions, perhaps sometimes against their will. Many crime stories are still barely literate in their writing and crass in their depiction of people and events, but the standard article is of far higher quality than in the past. Arbitrary distinctions must again be made, both in mentioning briefly a dozen writers who will be felt by many to deserve more detailed consideration and more ungrudging praise, and in ignoring fifty others who are bound to regard as incomplete and unsatisfactory a book of this kind that does not include their names. Here are some skilful writers whose books may stir readers with blood less sluggish than mine. I have put them into categories that can only be called rough and ready.

The Women's Novel: (By which is meant work always written, and I guess most eagerly and often read, by women.) Joan Aiken's (1942–) early books, notably *Trouble with Product X* (1966)[11] show her Gothic romanticism at its best. Similarly Gothic is Celia Fremlin (1914–), with *Uncle Paul* (1955) distinctly memorable. Chillers rather than thrillers are produced by these writers. Equally chilling is Ursula Curtiss (1923–), with something nasty always to be found in the domestic woodshed. *The Noonday Devil* (1951) is among the best of her books. Elizabeth Ferrars (1907–), stylish and witty, with agreeable touches of malice, has never completely fulfilled her talent. *Enough to Kill a Horse* (1955) and *Hanged Man's House* (1974) are recommended. Christianna Brand (1907–) has often written too hectically for her own good. *Green for Danger* (1944) is her most popular book, *Cat and Mouse* (1950) her best.

Orthodox Practitioners, whether of detective stories or of thrillers which contain a puzzle element: Andrew Garve (1908–), who has now given up writing, was happiest with thrillers. *The Megstone Plot* (1956), *The House of Soldiers* (1961) and *Murderer's Fen* (1966)[12] are all unusually good in their kind. John D. MacDonald (1916–) is – at least in his native America – one of the most overrated modern practitioners. The highly praised Travis McGee books, each with a different colour in the title, but much-of-a-muchness in merit, show his undoubted competence. Michael Underwood (1916–) has produced during the past thirty years, at the rate of roughly one a year, soundly written books that benefit greatly from his vast knowledge of legal procedure. *The Juror* (1975) is one that shows him at the top of his form. Donald Westlake (1933–) began with near-Hammett, then found a successful niche as writer of funny crime stories. Are they funny? I can restrain my mirth, but others have found *The Busy Body* (1966), *The Spy in the Ointment* (1966) and others positively side-splitting. Westlake doubles as Richard Stark, trebles as Tucker Coe.

Makers of Waves, who have given us something new in detectives: Joseph Hansen (1923–) has created the first series homosexual detective, Dave Brandstetter. A good idea, but Brandstetter as he moves mostly around California Gaydom seems a dull, sentimental fellow. One awaits the first Lesbian P.I. Not the first but the most distinctly Jewish detective is Rabbi David Small, the invention of Harry Kemelman (1908–). Rather too much about old Jewish customs and modern Jewish

11. In America *Beware of the Banquet.*
12. In America *Hide and Go Seek.*

attitudes for me, but *Friday the Rabbi Slept Late* (1964–) and the others are undoubtedly clever books. *Tuesday the Rabbi Saw Red* (1973), which introduces the hero to academic life, is a personal favourite. The invention of a Navajo detective named Joe Leaphorn by Tony Hillerman (1925–) showed courage. Unfortunately there is something essentially unexciting about such a figure (for British readers, anyway, who don't know their Navajo from their Sioux), but *The Blessing Way* (1969) and *Dance Hall of the Dead* (1971) are soundly conceived and written books.

And my apologies to the fifty others.

(v) The police novel

The police novel, or the police-procedural as it is now called, concentrates upon the detailed investigation of a crime from the point of view of the police, and in the best examples of the kind does so with considerable realism.

This is a recent development, not to be confused with the work of the Humdrums, which sometimes traced the course of a police investigation, but did so rather superficially, and often from the lofty viewpoint of a Superintendent.

The classical detective story is generally unsuitable for adaptation to cinema or TV because the half-burnt match, the particular shade of lipstick on the cigarette end, the lifted fingerprint, are visually uninteresting. In recent years, however, the cinema has coped successfully with Christie through lavish star-studded productions, and TV with Sayers by turning the stories partly into costume drama, partly into period comedy. The routine of police work, however, makes excellent TV, and went along with the police-procedural novel from the beginning. The American TV series *Dragnet* and the British *Z Cars* and *Softly Softly* have been succeeded by many others. The best, like *Kojak* and *Hill Street Blues* in the US, *The Sweeney* and *The Gentle Touch* in Britain, are agreeably zestful, and please by their vivid language and their sentimentalized but not wholly untrue vision of the sectarian comradeship inside the police.

Considerable variety is offered within the police novel, although it rarely has the salty quality of the best TV. One possibility, soon seen and used, was that of showing half a dozen cases going on at the same time, all handled by a single officer. This became a speciality of J. J. Marric in Britain and Elizabeth Linington, under three different names, in the US. The early Ed McBain stories developed in considerable detail the links between detection and forensic work, with reproductions of important clues in the text. Later McBain turned to characterization of the various detectives, giving each a distinct personality and the lion's share in a particular book. Hillary Waugh has exploited successfully the operations of a small police force, and its relationship to other forces in dealing with matters outside its own boundaries.

The early police novels had great zest and freshness (McBain's first books appeared in 1956, Marric's first Gideon book a year earlier), but their limitations soon became apparent. A fair degree of realism is possible, but it canot be pushed too far for fear that the book might be as dull as the actual days of a policeman. The division of interest between several unlinked cases means that some are more interesting than others, so that one hurries through the pages dealing with the attempt to identify a crook practising a long-firm fraud to get back to the absorbing hunt for a child-killer. Laboratory details can be fascinating, but they have to be informed by some human interest that often strains credulity. Details of the lives and loves of the detectives are often brought in so that they may be, again improbably, personally involved in the cases they set out to solve. There are similar improbabilities in other kinds of crime story, but they are particularly damaging to the police novel because surface realism is of its essence.

The most consistently skilful writer of police novels is undoubtedly Ed McBain (1926–) in his 87th Precinct stories. Under the name of Evan Hunter he has written some very successful novels, and he has used other pseudonyms, but the formula of the police novel suits his talent particularly well. The TV series adapted from his stories and characters lacked the force and liveliness of the books. McBain began with Steve Carella, a detective working for an unnamed big city police force, and equipped him with a wife named Teddy, who is beautiful but both deaf and dumb. As the series developed Carella's fellow detectives, like Cotton Hawes who was named after Cotton Mather, and the Jewish Meyer Meyer whose father thought it would be an excellent joke to duplicate surname and first name, were introduced. Sometimes several detectives appear in a book, sometimes only one or two. The cases vary from the macabre to the comic, and the stories are told largely in crisp, believable dialogue between detectives and suspects, or between the detectives themselves. Often the dialogue has a nice note of deadpan comedy. Here is Cotton Hawes in *'Til Death* (1959), thinking he may find a suspect in the bathroom:

> The door to the bathroom opened. A slender man wearing eye-glasses stepped out, zipping his fly.
>
> 'Anybody else in there?' Hawes asked him.

'What?'

'In the bathroom.'

'No', the bespectacled man said. 'Of course not. Who else would be in there with me?' He paused. Indignantly he said, 'Who are you?'

'Water Commission', Hawes said. 'Just checking.'

This is the characteristic McBain tone. '*Til Death* is actually not one of the better books, involving as it does the wedding of Carella's sister and bringing in the family complications that lend themselves to the characteristic McBain weakness of sentimentality, but the dialogue carries it along. The sum of the books has given us an informative and never boring account of police procedure, some good puzzles, excellent chases, occasional psychological insights, much variety of plot and incident. A good view of McBain's varied skills can be got from *Cop Hater* (1956), *The Mugger* (1956), *Like Love* (1962), *Sadie When She Died* (1972) and *Guns* (1976). The best McBains are short, Simenon-length books. His longer novels, like *Ice* (1983), are much less successful.

J. J. Marric was one of the many pseudonyms used by John Creasey (1908–73). The name was derived from his own and his wife's initials and the Christian names of his sons Martin and Richard. The early books about Commander George Gideon of Scotland Yard's CID are the best things in Creasey's large output. A CID Inspector who once lived next door to Creasey asked, 'Why don't you show us as we are? You don't have to put in the dull part.' The portrait of Gideon is an attempt to do this, and it is excellent up to a point, although in the end it is marred by hero-worship and lack of humour. Apart from Gideon the strengths of the books are those of other Creasey work, an apparently inexhaustible flow of ideas and the ability to generate excitement in describing action. The weaknesses are lack of the imagination necessary to vary the police novel formula, and a level of writing at its best no more than pedestrian.

Once the idea of telling three or four stories between one set of covers had been devised it quickly became rather too easy a way of writing tales that were fairly effective when counterpointed, although none of the individual incidents would have stood up on its own. This applies to the work of Elizabeth Linington (1921–), who under her own name writes books about a Los Angeles detective named Ivor Maddox, and under the names of Dell Shannon and Lesley Egan about other Los Angeles detectives named Lieutenant Luis Mendoza and Sergeant Andrew Clock, as well as about Vic Varallo of the Glendale police. The Linington stories are efficient and readable, but she clearly has much less direct knowledge of the LA police than McBain has of New York or Creasey of Scotland Yard.

If a single book had to be chosen to show the possibilities in the police novel which are outside most crime fiction, no better example could be found than *Last Seen Wearing* – (1952) by Hillary Waugh (1920–   ). This remarkably realistic novel opens with the disappearance of Marilyn Lowell Mitchell, a pretty eighteen-year-old freshman at Parker College, Bristol, Mass. We see the wheels move slowly as her friends become alarmed, the housemother rings Lowell's father in Philadelphia, her address book is examined, a telephone call is reluctantly made to the police. Thereafter we follow the investigation as Chief Frank W. Ford and Detective Sergeant Burton K. Cameron conduct it, with all its false trails, fending off of newsmen, consultation with parents, teachers, friends. Perhaps Creasey should have ignored that advice not to put in the dull part of police work, for it is the 'dull part', the painstaking checking of every lead until it peters out, that Waugh makes most interesting. By treating seriously the anguish of the parents and their certainty that their daughter would not have done anything they did not approve, he produces some fine character studies. And the ending has the neatest possible twist, with one of the chief characters never appearing on stage at all.

Like other writers of the police novel – and he preceded both McBain and Marric – Waugh was confronted with the problem of writing similar books sufficiently varied to keep the reader's interest. He replaced Ford and Cameron with Fred C. Fellows, Chief of a small-town police force, and his right-hand-man, Detective Sergeant Sidney Wilks. Fellows and Wilks have more humanity than the earlier detectives – indeed Fellows is a little too folksy for some tastes – and the small-town atmosphere gives their work a personal flavour. *Last Seen Wearing* – remains Waugh's best book, but several of the later ones manage to be realistic without dullness. *That Night It Rained* (1961) and *Pure Poison* (1966) are particularly good. In 1968 Waugh abandoned Fellows, and his replacement by a Manhattan detective named Frank Sessions and then by other investigators has not had happy results.

Should the books of Chester Himes (1909–   ) be classed as police novels? It is hard to know what else to call them, and his black detectives, Coffin Ed Johnson and Grave Digger Jones, make an exhilarating black comic comment on the activities of all other policemen. *Cotton Comes to Harlem* (1964) was the first Himes crime story to receive much attention. From that time onwards he recorded the activities of these fierce thugs in a world more thuggish still, in rattlingly vigorous prose, and with equal feelings for violence and comedy. Coffin Ed has been quick on the trigger ever since a hoodlum threw a glass of acid in his face, and when we first meet Grave Digger he has been off duty for six months after being shot up, although 'other than for the bullet scars hidden beneath his clothes and the finger-size scar obliterating the hairline at the base of his skull where the first bullet had burned off the hair, he looked much the same'. The humans among whom the detectives move in the eight novels about them are credulous, lecherous, treacherous, greedy and savage. Coffin Ed and Grave Digger are savage too, although they are not monsters masquerading as heroes, like Mickey Spillane's Mike Hammer.

There are other practitioners of the police novel, but none who equals McBain in variety of treatment, or Marric in handling several stories at once, or Waugh in originality. It does not seem likely that there will be much further extension in the range of this kind of crime story.

A brief account of my own work was given in the original edition by the late Edmund Crispin. At my request H. R. F. Keating, until recently crime critic of *The Times*, has provided another view. Keating writes:

Julian Symons has been called, with justice, the high priest of crime writing in Britain, both on account of his pioneering and high-achieving fiction and of his work as a critic, most notably and influentially perhaps in the first edition of this volume itself. He has been made a Grand Master of the Mystery Writers of America.

His fiction may be divided broadly into two modes, the ingenious and the perceptively probing. In the first he is hard to excel for sheer cunning. Many of his short stories, of which difficult form he is a memorable exponent, are of this kind, together with the novels The Man Who Killed Himself (1967) *and* The Plot against Roger Rider (1973), *a virtuoso dance for puppet people.*

But his chief success has been in using the crime novel to comment with a certain icy power on contemporary society, or occasionally in books set in late Victorian days on the everlasting hypocrisies. He has said himself that he sees no better vehicle for showing the violence behind bland faces. In The Colour of Murder (1957), The End of Solomon Grundy (1964), The Players and the Game (1972) *and others, he laid bare in prose of fastidious clarity the degeneration in society, abuse of power , and the fads of what might be called Colour Magazine Man.*

Yet he is not all sombreness. Seldom far from satire, in The Man Who Lost His Wife (1971) *he reached a hilarious scathingness arousing comparison with Evelyn Waugh. Only occasionally does he allow himself some plotting too hastily plucked up. Only sometimes does the obliqueness of his customary approach produce a negative ambiguity.*

15

Big Producers and Big Sellers, Curiosities and Singletons

(i) Big Producers, Big Sellers

There are several crime and thriller writers who, although they have not influenced the development of the form, and few of their books are of individual interest, must be noticed in a study of this kind. They are authors who have written a great many books, or who were and in some cases still are immensely popular, the Big Producers and the Big Sellers.

In general their work has a machine-like nature that removes it from the sphere of literary into that of sociological consideration. A popular character is devised, the formula for treating him established, and it is then just a matter of producing stories to feed the demand. If there are too many stories about one character, a new series may be started with another. Much crime fiction is of this kind, a ready-made product like cornflakes or puffed wheat. The Big Producers are among those who have filled that need most efficiently. They are alphabetically listed here.

LESLIE CHARTERIS is the pen-name of Leslie Charles Bowyer Yin (1907–   ), who has been writing stories about The Saint, 'the Robin Hood of Modern Crime', for nearly half a century. The Saint is a compound of the most obvious features of a romantic hero, put down in terms of cliché. He is 'always immaculately dressed', has 'luxurious tastes', and is a 'connoisseur of food and wine', although he does not go much further along these lines than knowledge of where you can get a succulent steak or 'the best omelette in North America'. The stories about him occasionally have a pleasant double twist, as in *The Saint in New York* (1935), in which he disposes of a number of the city's nastier gangsters only to find that he has been doing so with the help of the biggest gangster of all. They are too often written with the sort of rhodomontade that makes Charteris say that somebody has 'a weakness for the stuff that maketh glad the heart of man', meaning that he likes drink. For those who can endure the Saint's total invincibility and self-satisfaction, his adventures are lively and marked by some touches of humour.

*

The output of René Raymond (1906–   ), who became famous as JAMES HADLEY CHASE, is eighty-odd books, including those written as Raymond Marshall. Raymond was a traveller for the book wholesalers Simpkin, Marshall when he wrote *No Orchids for Miss Blandish* (1939), which has already been mentioned. Five years after its publication it was said that the book had sold 500,000 copies, and probably no other book by Chase has had anything like the same sale.

In France Chase has been compared with Dostoevsky and Céline, but such critical absurdities can spring only from the glamour given by translation, or by cinema adaptations which in some cases show subtleties that the books do not possess. At worst the writing in his books is shoddy, at best like secondhand James M. Cain. In his attack on *No Orchids* George Orwell acutely remarked that the prime motive of a book apparently concerned with violent sex was really power. This remains true of almost all Chase books, whether they are about gangs who hate everybody or individuals who hate each other. Love, where it occurs, is often used as a means of obtaining dominance over another individual.

REGINALD SOUTHOUSE CHEYNEY (1896–1951), who added Peter Evelyn to these given names, had a varied career as bookmaker, hack journalist and unsuccessful song-writer before in 1936 he published his first full-length work of fiction, *This Man is Dangerous*. The man was Lemmy Caution (i.e., 'let me caution') and thanks to Caution and another detective named Slim Callaghan, Cheyney was able in 1944 to publish audited sales figures showing that he had sold more than $1\frac{1}{2}$ million copies in the year. At his peak he sold 300,000 copies a year in the US (astonishingly, since much of his dialogue was in ludicrous pidgin-American) and 900,000 in France.

Cheyney was a precursor of Spillane in his zest for violence, and in exploiting a public taste for cruelty. (He had been an early, and active, supporter of Mosley's Fascists.) Lemmy Caution is the first 'good' man in crime fiction to torture for pleasure, while giving an assurance to the reader that he can enjoy it too because Caution is on the 'right' side. These unlovely books contain much more violence than sex, in spite of the promise in such pseudo-American titles as *Dames Don't Care* and *I'll Say She Does*.

One can safely say that JOHN CREASEY produced more books than any other twentieth-century writer. At his death the number was over 600, but he kept a reserve stock of unpublished work, which continued – perhaps even continues still – to appear after his death. From 1932 onwards he published seven to fourteen books a year, written under more than twenty different names, each representing a particular kind of story. The reader of a book by Michael Halliday knew that it would have a psychological flavour, an Inspector West story was a mixture of police work and thrillerish detection, and a book about the Baron (said by Jean Cocteau to be his favourite character in crime fiction) was essentially an adventure story.

Creasey's Gideon books, written as J. J. Marric, have already been mentioned. His stories are notable for the ingenuity of the ideas with which he overflowed, for his slight attention to sex and his total avoidance of cruelty. Unfortunately the writing of the books is never equal to their often clever conception, and his people think and behave with a schoolboyish naïveté.

ERLE STANLEY GARDNER (1889–1969) had 135 million copies of his books in print in America alone, in the year of his death. His complete output included eighty-odd of the Perry Mason stories that brought him real success in his forties. The first was *The Case of the Velvet Claws*, which appeared in 1934. Later he added the D A series dealing with a country district attorney, the Bertha Cool and Donald Lam books written as A. A. Fair, and others.

Gardner took great trouble to make sure that every detail of his intricate plots was right. When he wrote about ballistic or medical matters he always had authority for what he said, but his speciality was the law. He had spent more than twenty years practising law in California, and the knowledge he gained was put to good use in the Perry Mason stories, which hinge on points of law, forensic medicine or science. The T V series reflects the cunning legal tricks, and also the total lack of characterization. Upon the whole the early Mason stories are the best, although Gardner achieved a pleasant flexibility in the lively, often funny A. A. Fair stories.

The world created by E. PHILLIPS OPPENHEIM (1866–1946) in his 115 novels and 39 books of short stories had the virtue of resembling in some degree his own life after the age of forty, when he disposed of the family leather business. His chief success came after the First World War, with books like *The Amazing Quest of Mr Ernest Bliss* (1919)[1] and *The Great Impersonation* (1920). During the years between 1923 and the Depression neary thirty of his novels, stories and articles were sold in America to popular magazines and the *Chicago Tribune*. These sales alone brought in

1. In America *The Curious Quest of Mr Ernest Bliss*.

more than $350,000 during the period, and America was his principal source of income.

The Riviera was Oppenheim's favourite stamping ground, and the best of his books are set there. In an article about him, Reg Gadney quotes from a newspaper interview in 1919 when he said: 'I am a maker of stories while you wait. Sex is dropping a little. Crime is coming in. A good sound story is what they want.' This seems fair enough, if one adds the large lacing of snobbery given to all the stories. Oppenheim women are frighteningly elegant rather than sexy, his heroes remember Eton and the Guards, his plotting is crude. He provided the edge of snobbery as he dictated the stories in the intervals of yachting, visiting casinos, fishing and making love, and left the editing of them to his series of young girl secretaries. He was called the Prince of Storytellers, but a better name would have been the Great Escapist.

MICKEY (Frank Morrison) SPILLANE (1918–) makes his appeal to the human desire for power, like Chase and Cheyney. He is a more efficient writer than either of them, and more explicit in linking sex and violence. Power is the law to Spillane's Mike Hammer, who says, 'The cops can't break a guy's arm to make him talk, and they can't shove his teeth in with the muzzle of a .45 to remind him that you aren't fooling.' Hammer can and often does do these things, and they are described with relish. When he breaks a man's fingers and then smashes an elbow into his mouth, the 'shattered teeth tore my arm and his mouth became a great hole welling blood' while 'his fingers were broken stubs sticking back at odd angles'.

The treatment of sex has a clinical interest. Women are seen as sexually desirable objects, and there are a good many descriptions of their bodies, but intercourse is often replaced by death and torture. In *I, The Jury* (1947) Charlotte, the beautiful psychiatrist, makes several unsuccessful attempts to get Hammer to bed. At the end, when she proves to be a multiple murderess, he shoots her in the stomach. ' "How could you?" ' she asks incredulously, and he replies, ' "It was easy." ' At the end of *Kiss Me Deadly* (1952) the apparently lovely Lily is revealed as 'a horrible caricature of a human' whose body has been burned so that it is 'a disgusting mass of twisted, puckered flesh from her knees to her neck'. Hammer goes on to burn her to death so that she becomes 'a mass of flame tumbling on the floor with the blue flames of alcohol turning the white of her hair into black char and her body convulsing under the agony of it'.

These are early Spillane books. Later ones I have read are less crude, but little less distasteful. The most nauseating and disquieting thing about these books is that Mike Hammer is the hero.

Of all the Big Producers EDGAR WALLACE (1875–1932) was the only one who possessed genuine imaginative talent, shown most clearly in his crime plays *The Ringer* and *On the Spot*, but present also in some of his 173 books, of which roughly half were crime stories. He made no notes beyond a list of the characters' names, and when writing serials rarely knew what was going to happen in the next instalment. His characters, apart from the detective, hardly exist, although Wallace had a wide knowledge of crooks and their language, which he used to good effect.

Wallace came to real success late in life, after a career in which he had been war correspondent, racing journalist and crime reporter. His first crime story, *The Four Just Men* (1905), published at his own expense, gave no solution to the problem of how the Just Men had killed the Foreign Secretary. Wallace offered a prize of £500 for the correct solution, with disastrous results. Many correct solutions were sent in, and the costs of production, advertising and prize money were not covered by the sales. Failure had been his companion too long for him to use his talents with any care when, in the last decade of his life, he wrote successful plays and books that sold in millions. The best of his crime stories are *The Crimson Circle* (1922), in which the 'amazing psychometrical detective' Derrick Yale is pitted against Scotland Yard, the ingenious *The Clue of the New Pin* (1923) and the preposterous but enjoyable *The Fellowship of the Frog* (1925). The most clearly realized of his detectives is the absent-minded spinsterish Mr J. G. Reeder, and *The Mind of Mr J. G. Reeder* (1925)[2] is probably his best collection of crime stories. The German Chancellor Konrad Adenauer was a great admirer of Wallace's work, and he retains considerable popularity today.

The enormous sales of the crime and adventure stories written by DENNIS WHEATLEY (1897–1977) indicate how low is one literary level of popular success. A characteristic Wheatley book contains chunks of pre-digested history served up in a form which may appeal to readers with a mental age of twelve. *Come into My Parlour* (1946), which Wheatley thought 'one of my better stories' begins with the invasion of Russia in 1941. When the satanic-looking Gregory Sallust meets his chief Sir Pellinore Gwaine-Cust he is told that 'whether we like the Bolshies or not, Winston was one hundred per cent right to declare that any enemy of Hitler's is a friend of ours', although 'They haven't shown up any too well

2. In America *The Murder Book of Mr J. G. Reeder*.

– so far'. Sallust's reply is that 'If the main German armies had not gone into Russia this summer they wouldn't be sitting on their bottoms' – and we are off on another bit of potted history for the ignorant. Much of the dialogue is on the level of Sir Pellinore's jovial ' "Drat the boy!" ', and a typical piece of third-person narration begins 'Having partaken of Sir Pellinore's Lucullan hospitality ...'

Two recent writers must be mentioned, because although not Big Producers they are emphatically Big Sellers. Frederick Forsyth (1938–) was a journalist and roving reporter when he wrote *The Day of the Jackal*, a book rejected by three publishers but selling in millions when it reached print in 1971. Forsyth has no pretension to anything more than journalistic expertise, and his books tell you about things – making bombs, running guns, obtaining false passports – rather than about people. His first novel is, by general agreement, better than the others, but all are candidates for examination in that unwritten history of modern literary taste. So also are the immensely successful books of Robert Ludlum (1927–), who has written under other names. A personal inability to finish any Ludlum book, because of the crudeness of the writing and the frequent absurdity of the subject matter, absolves me from detailed comment.

(ii) Curiosities and singletons

Within this portmanteau I have put all sorts of odds and ends, books of merit by neglected or otherwise commonplace writers, observations that didn't fit in easily elsewhere, oddities and minor discoveries. Other readers will have worthy singletons of their own, and the fields of crime fiction abound in curiosities waiting to be unearthed. I hope that some of my singletons may be new, even to those with a wide knowledge of the form.

GEORGE ANTHEIL (1901–59), who was, in the twenties, the 'bad boy' of avant-garde music (his 'Ballet Mécanique' for sixteen pianos, some buzzers, an airplane propeller and an electric drill, among other instruments, was much admired by Ezra Pound), wrote two crime stories under the name of Stacey Bishop. I have read only the first of these ventures into 'glandular criminology', and certainly *Death in the Dark* (1930), with its several apparently impossible murders solved by an investigator who talks often about Pound and behaves rather like Philo Vance, is an extraordinary performance.

There are a good many ASSOCIATIONS of crime writers. The two most important are the MWA (Mystery Writers of America) and the CWA (the British Crime Writers Association). MWA was founded in 1945, has

four 'regional chapters', and is undoubtedly the most influential organization of crime writers. It sponsors yearly Edgar Allan Poe awards ('Edgars')
for first novels, short stories and several other categories of work
associated with crime stories. The one most highly regarded is the award
for the 'Best Mystery Novel' of the year. MWA also gives occasional
Grand Master and other special awards, all celebrated at a yearly dinner.
A publication, *The Third Degree*, is sent to all members.

CWA was founded in 1953 at the initiative of John Creasey, who was
largely responsible for nursing the association through its first shaky years.
Like MWA it publishes anthologies, and it produces a monthly news-
sheet, *Red Herrings*. It gives a Golden Dagger award for the best crime
novel of the year, a Silver Dagger for the runner-up, and a special first
novel award. In recent years these have been financially supported by the
Arts Council, more lately by Securicor. The awards are made at a yearly
dinner.

There are no organized bodies of crime writers in Germany, Holland
or Italy, or if there are I have not discovered them. France has an
association called 813, the title of an Arsène Lupin novel. It is not confined
to writers, but includes crime buffs of all kinds, including those devoted
to crime movies and comic strips. The event of the year is the Festival du
Roman et du Film Policiers de Reims, where films are shown, talks are
given, champagne is drunk. Crime Writers of Canada, or CWC, is no more
than two years old, but already has a membership that includes 42 native
criminal practitioners. The Poe-Klubben, which has its headquarters in
Copenhagen, draws its members from all over Scandinavia, although
Sweden has its own separate organization. (Indeed, it is said to have four.)
Discussion of crime stories at Scandinavian meetings is much better
informed, and on a higher critical level, than among any other group.
There was, at least a few years ago, a flourishing association of crime
writers in Japan.

The Detection Club has already been mentioned. Membership of it is
by invitation (unlike MWA and CWA, for which anybody with professional qualifications is eligible), and its activities are mainly those of a
dining club. There are Sherlock Holmes societies in many countries, with
names which vary from the staid 'Sherlock Holmes Society of London' to
the 'Speckled Band of Boston'.

In the Heat of the Night (1965), the first crime story of JOHN BALL
(1911–   ), was an excellent detective story almost in the Golden Age
style, which introduced the colour problem by way of a black detective

named Virgil Tibbs, who is set to swim against the tide of feeling in a bigoted little Southern town. Ball's later work has been much less successful.

GORE VIDAL (1925–   ), novelist and critic, wrote three detective stories in the early fifties under the name of EDGAR BOX. *Death in the Fifth Position* (1952), *Death Before Bedtime* (1953) and *Death Likes It Hot* (1954) are all lively stories. Their sexual outspokenness, which caused some comment at the time, seems mild enough to generations brought up on Lady Chatterley and Myra Breckinridge.

In 1945 the poet and novelist Ruthven (Campbell) Todd (1914–78) wrote twelve detective stories in six months under the name of R. T. CAMPBELL. One of them was written in three days. They were published in England by the small and soon defunct firm of John Westhouse, and are now rare. A pleasant uncertainty prevails about the publication of four among the twelve books. Did *The Hungry Worms are Waiting* ever see print, or did Westhouse go broke first? No copy of it is known to have appeared in any specialized bookseller's list.

VERA CASPARY (1904–   ) has written a number of crime stories, among which *Laura* (1943) is done with unusual wit and style, particularly in the sections written by the aesthetic criminologist Waldo Lydecker, a figure based on Alexander Woollcott. The book was made into a successful film, with Clifton Webb playing Lydecker.

My own long-held belief that ARNOLD BENNETT (1867–1930) wrote crime stories has been rather shaken by serious reading of them. Among what Bennett called his Fantasies, the potboilers he wrote to pay for more serious but at the time less successful work, *The Loot of Cities* (1905) is a collection of stories in the Raffles vein but less stylish, about rich Cecil Thorold, who fiddles crooks and other dubious characters out of their money, and generally dispenses justice. *Buried Alive* (1908) is a ridiculous novel about an artist so reclusive that he allows his dead valet to be buried in Westminster Abbey instead of himself, and later has to prove his own identity in court. *The Grand Babylon Hotel* (1902) is an almost equally absurd story of intrigues involving an American millionaire named Theodore Racksole and his daughter. All are written in a tone of uneasy facetiousness.

CRITICISM of crime stories has always been bedevilled by the question of whether they should be corralled separately or reviewed with other novels. In theory the latter is preferable, but in practice crime stories which go out with other novels are rarely reviewed at all. So they are hived off, and in the process treated necessarily as inferior literature.

In general reviewing is too kind, making little distinction between books well and badly written. It is disturbing to find, in English crime reviews of the thirties, quite notable books and evident rubbish being treated on the same level by reviewers as intelligent as Sayers and Milward Kennedy. The British situation has improved in some national papers, and so has the American, so that reviewers are allowed to give individual treatment to what they regard as an exceptional book.

Among the splash and dash of his Hornblower novels, C. S. FORESTER (1899–1966) wrote two low-toned but compelling crime stories. In *Payment Deferred* (1926) a hard-up bank clerk murders a distant relative, buries him in the backyard and suffers ever after. *Plain Murder* (1930), which shows another suburban murderer caught in tangles largely of his own devising, is equally gripping but marred by some improbabilities.

Reputation for a Song (1952), the first novel by a north-country English barrister, EDWARD GRIERSON (1914–75), sprang from the Iles tradition. The exposure of a family skeleton in the household of a country solicitor leads to murder, and then comes the account of a trial, done with great skill and assurance. This is an outstandingly interesting account of crime as it is committed and endured.

Of the detective stories written by FRANCES NOYES HART (1890–1943), only *The Bellamy Trial* (1928) has distinction. Based on a famous American case of the period, it is remarkable for the care with which it gets the feeling of a courtroom. Like an actual trial it is slow, repetitive, at times obscure. These are hardly recommendations, yet the method is justified by the powerful climax and the semi-hypnotic effect of the courtroom buzz upon the reader.

A Taste of Honey (1941) by GERALD HEARD (1889–1971) is about death caused by a strain of Italian bees which sting like hornets. They are used by an apiarist to kill a man who has already used the bees to commit his own undetectable murder. Long-windedly philosophical, it has curiosity value only.

Rose Louise Hovick (1914–70) wrote two detective stories under her stage and striptease artist name of GYPSY ROSE LEE. Much the better is *The*

G-String Murders (1941),[3] a ribald book about the murder of stripper La Verne in the lavatory with its newly acquired throne. Her second book, *Mother Finds a Body* (1942), contains the splendid malapropism, spoken by a woman on leaving a party, 'I'm going. I find the company very uncongenital', but is upon the whole much inferior. After these two books the author returned to stripping the Gypsy Rose.

A Kiss Before Dying (1953), the first crime story by IRA LEVIN (1929–), showed clearly that if there are no brand-new tricks to be played on the reader, the old ones can be made to look new in sufficiently cunning hands. Rex Stout called the book 'a masterpiece of the *genre*', and if that overstates the case it is only because the story changes style and becomes thrillerish after the surprise has been sprung half-way through. In comparison with the earlier novel his second book, *Rosemary's Baby* (1967), seemed forced and unconvincing. On the screen, strangely, it seemed more plausible.

MEYER LEVIN (1905–81) wrote only one crime story. *Compulsion* (1956) is closely based on the Leopold and Loeb case. Its originality lies in the psychoanalytical interpretation of the murderers' actions, which is relentless and persuasive. There have been many documentary case histories that read like fiction, among them Truman Capote's *In Cold Blood*. Levin was the only writer to reverse the process. Worth looking for.

The Defection of A. J. Lewinter (1973) was a first spy story by ROBERT LITTELL (1939–), who worked on *Newsweek*. Lewinter defects, but from West to East, for reasons that seem incredible to both sides. Pawkily funny, knowledgeable, and pleasantly lighthearted in the depiction of the obsessed Lewinter, this is a really original book. Its successors have been contimental, eccentric, or both.

NAP LOMBARD was the curious name used by Pamela Hansford Johnson (1912–83), who collaborated with her husband Gordon Stewart on two detective stories, *Tidy Death* (1940) and *Murder's a Swine* (1942). Lord Winterstone, known as Lord Pig, is the hero of these two period pieces. Pamela Hansford Johnson's second husband was C. P. Snow.

The detective story to end detective stories was published in 1937 by Ernest Wilhelm Julius Borneman (1915?–), under the name of CAMERON MCCABE. *The Face on the Cutting-Room Floor* seems to be a tautly-told detective story about the murder of a film actress whose part in a film has

---

3. In Britain *The Striptease Murders* (1943). The only connotation of G-String in Britain at that time was in connection with violins.

been completely eliminated in the cutting-room. McCabe, the narrator, is tried and acquitted. It is then revealed that he was in fact the murderer.

So far the apparent novel. But all this is only a demonstration of what the 'detective story' is like. The heart of the book is in the epilogue, told by a minor character named A. B. C. Muller. In this epilogue Muller considers McCabe as a man who became a murderer 'merely through a concurrence of certain typical present-day tendencies, each of which can be found in almost every contemporary big-city middle-class man'. But was McCabe the murderer? Muller examines the case against other figures in the story, including the detective Smith, to show that they would also fit the murderer's role. He then offers a critique of the detective story as a form by assuming that *The Face on the Cutting-Room Floor* has already been published, and fitting remarks made by critics about other detective stories to his own book. The critics include Cyril Connolly, W. H. Auden and Cecil Day-Lewis. Muller observes that 'the possibilities for alternative endings to *any* detective story are *infinite*', and shows this by ending the epilogue with Muller himself killing one of the characters in the novel. The whole thing is a dazzling, and perhaps fortunately unrepeatable, box of tricks.

The book was republished in 1974, and another edition appeared in the US in 1981, with an 'Afterword' written by the author. This revealed that Borneman was an exile from Nazi Germany who later worked with Orson Welles on a projected film of the *Odyssey* and the *Iliad*. In 1960 he headed the German TV Federal Network, and he is now teaching sexology at Salzburg University. His sexological investigations have revealed, he says, little evidence of penis- but much of bosom-envy.

The single crime story written by JOHN MAIR (1913–42), whose review of *No Orchids* has been quoted, was *Never Come Back* (1941). Mair rightly called the book 'an intellectual thriller', and it is in the first class of its kind. There is a very modern cowardly hero who broods on poisoning his Fascist girlfriend but knows that he will never do it, and the excitement of a man on the run. It is a little like John Buchan up to date, and in everything essential remains up to date today. Those who search for old Penguins may find the book, but why is it not reprinted?

DEREK MARLOWE (1938–   ) has written two crime stories marked by original ideas, which yet fall short of being wholly original. In *A Dandy in Aspic* (1966) a double agent is assigned to kill himself. Very good: but the plot faintly echoes *The Big Clock*, the dying fall of the prose is reminiscent of Le Carré. *Somebody's Sister* (1974) is pastiche Chandler of high quality, with a flavour of seriousness. Marlowe always writes extremely well, he is full of good ideas, and one keeps hoping that he will find a criminal theme that completely fits his talent. So far this hasn't happened.

WADE MILLER is one of the several pseudonyms under which Bill Miller (1920–61) and Bob Wade (1920–   ) produced books of no more than average competence, although their Max Thursday stories are of interest. Their first book, *Deadly Weapon* (1946), stands out from their other work by the cleverness with which wool is pulled over the reader's eyes, blinding him to what is really a logical and obvious conclusion. This is also an out-of-print Penguin.

PERIODICALS for readers, fans and students of the crime story flourish, particularly in the US. The most important is *The Armchair Detective*, which comes quarterly from 129 West 56th Street, New York 100019. The subscription is at the time of writing $20. Every issue contains well-researched articles about crime writers – Michael Innes, Robert B. Parker, Anthony Price in recent issues – along with 'departments' which keep up to date with American paperbacks, reissues, TV and cinema. The emphasis is strongly American, the articles are valuable as source material rather than criticism, there are quarterly 'newsletters' about Stout and Sayers of interest only to ageing groupies. In spite of such limitations, this is an indispensable magazine. Others are for fans only, like the *Rohmer Review* and *Huntress* (for devotees of the TV *Avengers* series). France has several magazines, the most important being the monthly *Polar* and the more scholarly *Enigmatika*, edited by Jacques Baudou, director of the Reims Festival. Sweden has *Dast*, edited by Iwan Hedman, which is strongly slanted towards thrillers on all levels from Wheatley upwards, and *Jury*, which contains articles about American, British and Scandinavian writers. Some of the *Dast* material is in English. A Japanese newsletter called *The Maltese Falcon Flyer* is said to exist, but I have not seen it. Norway has a lively-looking magazine called *Alibi*. Britain has nothing at all. It should be emphasized that the interest of all these magazines is in the information they contain, rather than the criticism they offer.

The Ingenious Mr Stone (1945) is a surprising piece of work. In describing 'the methods used by Lysander Stone in solving the Langdon-Miles problem', the author, ROBERT PLAYER (1905–78), has used the several narrators and the leisurely manner of *The Moonstone*. The book is notable for the evident enjoyment with which it is written, its humour, and the outrageous (as late as 1945) use of more than one successful disguise. Player wrote other crime stories, some wonderfully eccentric in their titles (*Let's Talk of Graves, of Worms, & Epitaphs*), but none up to the Lysander Stone story. His pseudonym concealed the identity of Robert Furneaux Jordan, who also wrote about architecture.

The use of PSEUDONYMS by writers of crime fiction deserves a separate essay. Why do so many resort to them? On the surface it may be a matter of convenience, or of a publisher's insistence that too many titles under a single name will flood the market, or of a snobbish feeling that writing crime stories is a low pursuit. Yet there is surely something beyond or beneath all this. The essence of crime stories is that they conceal something, and it is psychologically appropriate that the author's identity should also be hidden. Is it going too far to suggest that through use of a pseudonym writers are able to indulge secret thoughts, and write about subjects which they would otherwise have found it difficult to approach? Certainly there is room for a thesis on 'The Hidden Self: Personal Concealment and Revelation in the Crime Novel' by some industrious student.

Arthur Sarsfield Ward (1883–1959), better known as SAX ROHMER, was discovered in the early fifties living in the New York suburb of White Plains, a small, grey, nervous man who was able to report that Dr Fu Manchu was not only still alive, but had greatly changed in character. He remained a villain, but was now 'flat out against the Communists and trying to help democracy' instead of trying to establish a personal domination over the world, a domination against which the dogged Nayland Smith, even though he was the Burmese Commissioner and 'empowered to control the movements' of the British CID, struggled at times almost alone.

The Fu Manchu stories are absolute rubbish, penny dreadfuls in hard covers, interesting chiefly in the way they reflect popular fears of the 'Yellow Peril', which in these books, as a character remarks, is 'incarnate in one man'. The doctor's hands are like claws, he generally wears a little cap on his 'amazing skull', his green eyes are like 'an emanation of Hell'. The stories proceed with little regard for possibility, and several of the books include scenes in which Smith and his friend Petrie face torture. One or two other Rohmer books are a little better, and the short stories in *The Dream Detective* (1920) about Moris Klaw, who has dreams which help him to solve crimes with the assistance of his somnambulistic daughter Isis, have a sort of ludicrous logic about them which is amusing in small doses.

PETER SHAFFER (1926–   ), later a highly successful dramatist, wrote with his twin brother ANTHONY SHAFFER, whose affectionate send-up of Golden Age stories in his play *Sleuth* was much acclaimed, three detective stories, two under the name of Peter Anthony and the best, *Withered Murder* (1955), in their own nominal colours.

Sudden Death: Or My Lady the Wolf (1886) by Britiffe, fourth Baron SKOTTOWE (1857–1925) is a curiosity among curiosities, the first transvestite detective story. In the opening chapter the narrator, Buchanan, sees an unidentifiable woman push a man off a cliff. The crime remains unsolved, and a little later Buchanan meets a dashing, slender young man named Gordon Leigh with whom he becomes very friendly. Leigh has, as all his male friends agree, 'something peculiarly nice and attractive about him'. Two more murders are committed, one victim being a woman to whom Buchanan had become engaged. Suspicion falls on a woman named Astarte who has the reputation of being 'the most reckless heartless cruel daredevil that ever walked the earth for man's undoing', and in the final chapter Astarte and Gordon Leigh are revealed as identical. Astarte/Leigh has lived 'sometimes as a man, sometimes as a woman, but more often as the former because I liked it better'. Undone by her love for Buchanan, she confesses her crimes and takes poison. Skottowe wrote one or two historical studies and textbooks, but no other novels.

The first book written by C. P. SNOW (1905–80), later Lord Snow, was a detective story, *Death Under Sail* (1932), a work orthodox in the tradition of the period, but written with what was already a distinctive skill in characterization. *A Coat of Varnish* (1979), produced when his talent was failing, is a ponderous, unsuccessful book. One or two of the 'Strangers and Brothers' series, notably *The Masters* (1951) and *The Affair* (1960) have a puzzle element, and Snow had a wide knowledge of crime fiction.

CHRISTOPHER ST JOHN SPRIGG (1907–37) reversed the usual pseudonymous course by producing under the name of Christopher Caudwell the poems, essays on politics and culture, and the philosophical work *Illusion and Reality* by which he is remembered as the most interesting Marxist theorist of his generation. His detective stories were written without a protective mask. He produced eight of these lively, but orthodox (and unpolitical) books between 1933 and 1937, when he was killed fighting on the Republican side in the Spanish Civil War. *The Perfect Alibi* (1934) is among the best of them. All are out of print.

The historian and biographer FRANCIS STEEGMULLER (1906–   ) wrote three smoothly sophisticated crime stories during the forties under the name of David Keith, and then abandoned the form.

Among the readable books written by DARWIN L. TEILHET (1904–64), some in collaboration with his wife, Hildegarde, is a work of considerable distinction. *The Talking Sparrow Murders* (1934), which was Teilhet's own work, is a mystery story set in Germany just after the Nazi accession to power. It is worth reading, both for its picture of the time and place, and as an unusual blend of spy story and mystery.

Gorky Park (1981) is an over-praised but still interesting novel by MARTIN CRUZ SMITH (1942–   ). The style is crude, the characters wooden, but the picture of a Russian 87th Precinct cop hedged by bureaucratic fences and betrayed by colleagues is unusual and convincing.

LAURENCE VAIL, one time husband of Kay Boyle and Peggy Guggenheim, wrote a spoof detective story, *Murder! Murder!* (1931), in which the hero kills, or thinks he has killed, dozens of people in Paris. ('Sated after three successful crimes, two parricides, one death-rape, I sit at a café, order a glass of cognac. I feel discouraged.') Is Martin Asp a multiple murderer, or is the whole thing a book-long drinking bout? Often funny, equally often boring, a stylishly written curiosity.

Some will feel indignant at finding the Chinese detective stories of R. H. VAN GULIK (1910–67) placed among curiosities. Yet what else can they be called? The traditional Chinese or Japanese 'detective story' is a tale of crime and punishment, in which it is part of the convention that the criminal shall be known from the start. The reader's pleasure (or the listener's, for most of the tales had an oral tradition) came from the magistrate's trapping of the villain. The Chinese tales were so far removed from Western feeling that in them animals, and even objects, might take voice and give damning evidence.

Van Gulik, who was for some time the Dutch Ambassador in Malaya and Japan, began by translating Chinese stories published in the eighteenth century, and then branched out into fiction of his own, still purporting to be based on the cases of Judge Dee, who appeared in the original work. The later books in particular are no more than well-informed pastiche.

Among the saccharine family chronicles of SIR HUGH WALPOLE (1884–1941) are a few books tart as damsons. Like many sentimentalists Walpole had a feeling for fear and cruelty, and both get into his neglected thriller, *Above the Dark Circus* (1931). As he conceived the book it was to be 'all Piccadilly, crowds and corpses, with a jolly villain and no sadism', but sadism comes in against his intention in the picture of the mean-faced Pengelly, with his love for the blackmail game, which, he says, can't be touched for fun and excitement. *Portrait of a Man with Red Hair* (1928) is also marked by genuine psychological creepiness.

The Labour MP ELLEN WILKINSON (1891–1947) was called Red Ellen because of the colour of her hair, although her political views were also fiery. Her one detective story *The Division Bell Mystery* (1932) is a lively performance, so unconcerned with party politics that the hero says: 'A bread-march was not like England.' Murder is done in a committee room of the House of Commons, by the pleasing method of a revolver fixed in the division bell grating, which fires through the grating at the sound of the bell.

16

A Short History of the Spy Story

(i) Before the Second World War

It has been said already that crime fiction is a hybrid, and that too much categorization is confusing rather than helpful, but within the hybrid form detective stories and crime novels are of a different strain from spy stories and thrillers. The lines of demarcation are uncertain, but everybody recognizes their existence. It would be absurd to consider John Buchan and Eric Ambler together with R. Austin Freeman and Agatha Christie, but equally silly to ignore them in a book of this kind. It seemed best to give a separate chapter to spy stories and thrillers.

The spy story owed its existence to awareness of the threat to national security implied in professionally organized spying, and also to the slow realization that the spy's activities may be both intricate and dangerous. In Elizabethan times Walsingham established a considerable spy network, and under Napoleon's reign Fouché, the Chief of Police, became known as the spy-master, but no books were written about an occupation regarded as unpleasant and unglamorous. In 1771 the first edition of the *Encyclopaedia Britannica* defined a spy as 'a person hired to watch the actions, motions, &c. of another: particularly of what passes in a camp', adding that 'when a spy is discovered, he is hanged immediately'. The phrase finds an echo in the first spy novel known to me, J. Fenimore Cooper's *The Spy* (1821). Harvey Birch the pedlar, known to be a spy for the British during the American War of Independence, is called a traitor by the American Major Dunwoodie, who says: 'I should be justified in ordering your execution this night.' Birch survives, and is in fact the hero, a double agent whose real allegiance is given to his own country. The book's sub-title is 'A Tale of the Neutral Ground', and although *The Spy* is not a very good novel, it anticipates in some respects the ambiguities of the modern spy story. Cooper thinks of the spy in exclusively military terms — there is a subsidiary plot about a young English officer who has gone behind the American lines to see his family, and who, although not a spy, is sentenced to death as one because he was not in uniform and was wearing a ridiculous disguise. Cooper's spy is conceived as an important but humble figure, and he was not used as a central character by any other novelist until late in the nineteenth century. The entertaining *The Battle of Dorking* (1870), by the military historian Sir George Chesney, dealt with an imaginary invasion of England but, rather surprisingly, did not mention spies, perhaps because the author felt their activities to be regrettably unsporting.

The development of the spy story was directly linked to the inventions that came in the wake of the Industrial Revolution. As the breech-loading rifle replaced the muzzle-loader, and the quick-firing *mitrailleuse*, Gatling and Maxim guns threatened the effectiveness of some other weapons, and naval power increased with the development of dreadnoughts and submarines, and aeroplanes turned from dream into possibility and then reality, a real threat was implied in the theft or copying of secret plans and documents. The highly developed industrial countries were those with the most inventions to be uncovered, and this was the primary reason why the spy story had its origins in Europe.

It was first exploited by William Le Queux (1864–1927). If Le Queux's biographer is to be believed (something by no means certain), Le Queux himself was a British Secret Service agent both before and during the First World War. Such agents were not well paid and, again according to the biographer, Le Queux's books were written chiefly to defray the heavy expenses of Secret Service activities. Le Queux was a journalist and his first novel, *Guilty Bonds*, appeared in 1890, after he had visited Russia and written for *The Times* a series of articles on the revolutionary movement and the condition of exiles in Siberia. *Guilty Bonds*, which dealt with a political conspiracy, was banned in Russia, and so was *A Secret Service* (1896), which had a Jewish Nihilist hero, and treated in some detail the anti-Jewish pogroms after the assassination of Alexander II.

During the next thirty-odd years Le Queux wrote more than a hundred books, of which perhaps a quarter were spy stories. His low opinion of his own work was not shared by the Prime Minister Arthur Balfour, who, when discovered reading Le Queux, asked: 'Are you criticizing my taste in literature?' The stories are poorly written and full of padding, especially in the treatment of love affairs, but they are laced with a good deal of material obviously based on considerable knowledge of military and political affairs. Le Queux followed faithfully the current line of military thinking, according to which France was regarded as the prime danger to British security until the end of the nineteenth century, when it was replaced by Germany. *England's Peril* (1899) begins with the murder of Lord Casterton, who has been protesting in Parliament about our inadequate military preparations, a constant theme in the press at the time. His face is shattered beyond recognition, and at the end of the book it turns out that he has been the victim of an explosive cigar given him by his wife. She is in love with Gaston la Touche, who under cover of being an explorer is the chief of the French Secret Service, and is after the plans of Portsmouth Harbour. In *The Great War in England in 1897* the French have joined hands with the Russians in an invasion of Britain, and in *His Majesty's Minister* (1901) a French spy operating from a cottage between Staines and Kingston has tapped the private wire between Windsor Castle and the Foreign Office.

In *The Invasion of 1910* (1905), however, the enemy had become the Germans, and in the preface to *Spies of the Kaiser* (1909) Le Queux warned his readers that England was 'in grave danger of invasion by Germany at a date not far distant', and suggested that 5,000 agents of Germany were active in Britain, being paid between £10 and £30 a month. This collection of stories, although full of absurd dialogue, contains interesting details like drawings of 'the new British submarine' and 'the new British Army aeroplane'. When the First World War began Le Queux went about armed, with a hand on the revolver in his pocket ready for an attack which never came. His fictional occupation had been heavily damaged by the impact of reality, and the post-war books lack the zest which slightly redeems the early ones.

By the early years of the century it had been established that the Germans were the enemy, although in the Sexton Blake penny dreadfuls the Kaiser was treated with respect until the outbreak of the First World War. The first spy story with any literary pretensions, *The Riddle of the Sands* (1903) by Erskine Childers (1870–1922), is about two young Englishmen who stumble across some German exercises for the invasion of Britain, exercises taking place in the Friesian Islands. This is one of the best spy and adventure stories ever written, from the well-judged leisureliness of the opening which describes the disillusionment suffered by young Carruthers of the Foreign Office when he joins his friend Davies on what he expects to be a lazy holiday on a luxury yacht and finds that is the only member of the crew on a little seven-tonner. There is a lot of well-described detail about the business of managing a small boat in difficult waters, all of which is a necessary prelude to the very exciting fog-bound journey in a dinghy through the narrow waters of the Memmert Balje that is really the climax of the story. The conversion of Carruthers from a peevish dandy to a resourceful amateur agent is excellently done, through the contrast of his character with that of the verbally clumsy but practically skilful Davies, and the whole story has immense charm, vivacity, and an underlying idealism that takes for granted the way in which an honourable man must behave.

It is accepted that such a man cannot be a spy. The Englishman acting for the Germans, who calls himself Dollman is, Carruthers says, 'the vilest creature on God's earth'. But what about the young men? '"Mightn't we come to be spies ourselves?"' Carruthers asks, and Davies responds indignantly that they have a right to expose Dollman because '"If he's in with Germany he's a traitor to us ... If we can't do it without spying we've a right to spy."' This is the first adumbration of the double standard by which They are viewed as spies pursuing evil ends, while We are agents countering their wicked designs with good ones. For Buchan, Oppenheim, 'Sapper' – in fact for all spy writers before Maugham and Ambler – the moral problem involved in spying was thus easily solved.

The tragedy of Childers's own life had a relationship to the morality of spying. During the First World War he worked as an Intelligence Officer, was several times mentioned in despatches and received the D.S.C. Afterwards he devoted his life to working for an independent Irish Republic. He was principal secretary to the delegation which negotiated an Irish Treaty with the British Government, but opposed it in the interest of full independence. He joined the Republican Army fighting against the newly established Irish Free State, was captured by Free State soldiers, court-martialled and shot. This undoubtedly gallant and honourable Anglo-Irishman was regarded by both British and Irish governments as a traitor and renegade at the time of his death.

The slipperiness of identifying books as 'spy' stories is shown by consideration of the two novels by Joseph Conrad (1857–1924) about revolutionary agents, The Secret Agent (1907) and Under Western Eyes (1911). The material of these books is that of spy stories – in the first an attempted Anarchist outrage in London's Greenwich Park which follows fairly closely the details of an actual incident, in the second the activities of the counter-agent Razumov. Yet although one critic has said that Conrad 'pioneered the political detective novel in English', these books seem distinct in spirit from both detective and spy stories. Verloc and Razumov are both double agents, the first to be treated seriously in fiction, but it is not the nature of the double agent that interests Conrad so much as the desire to capture 'the very soul of things Russian' in these self-destructive figures. Both stories have a dimension of seriousness that is not present in Childers or John Buchan, but the real thing is that for Conrad spying is not an end but a means. The end is the (in Conrad's view) wholly evil nature of revolution, in which spies play naturally their loathsome part. An earlier version of *Under Western Eyes*, called *Razumov*, was much more concerned with the personal problems of the central character. In the published book the conspiracy seems at times to have been grafted on to the original manuscript for the sake of excitement.

After the First World War began, spy stories became unequivocally nationalist in tone and right-wing in political sympathy. Sometimes these feelings were expressed with the moderation of John Buchan, sometimes with the crudeness of 'Sapper', but the underlying assumptions were always there. The enemy in books written up to 1920 was almost always Germany, later joined and superseded by Soviet Russia. Sometimes there is treachery at home, inspired from abroad. So Buchan's Richard Hannay, in *The Thirty-Nine Steps* (1915), finds somebody impersonating the First Sea Lord at a meeting of the Defence Council and walking out with all their plans. In *Mr Standfast* (1919) the treatment of the conscientious objector Launcelot Wake is tolerant but condescending. He is allowed to retain pacifist feelings, and dies heroically in carrying a vital message across a river ('"That's too damnably dangerous"', Hannay says, '"I won't send any man to certain death"'), but of course Buchan could not allow Wake to adhere firmly to his principles by a refusal to be involved. At the end of *Bulldog Drummond* (1920), the first of his four rounds with Carl Peterson, Drummond discovers that a gigantic conspiracy to over-throw the Government by means of a General Strike is being backed by Moscow gold, and that people whose names are household words secretly support it. How can such things be? The American Jerome K. Green explains it in simple terms: '"They're out for Number One, and when they've talked the boys into bloody murder, and your existing social system is down-and-out, they'll be the leaders in the new one."' Drummond is horrified. '"Why can't they be made to understand, Mr Green?"' he asks. '"The working-man – the decent fellow –"'

Buchan and 'Sapper' are compared only because they used similar material. Buchan was a talented writer, 'Sapper' a producer of blood and thunder. John Buchan (1875–1940) regarded himself as a serious politician and an amateur novelist. During the First World War he was Director of Information and then Director of Intelligence. Later he was for eight years an MP, was created Baron Tweedsmuir, and became Governor-General of Canada. He had a busy official life, but along with his determination to be one of the men who counted (the phrase was Arnold Bennett's) went a high romanticism expressed particularly in the stories about Hannay, a character founded upon one of his military heroes, 'Tiny' Ironside, who later became a Field-Marshal. Buchan blended invention with material drawn from his own knowledge in these tales. Perhaps the best of the Hannay books is *Greenmantle* (1916), in which the hero, helped by his friends and by the American agent Blenkiron, acts as a spy – although the word is never used – trying to stop the Germans from raising the Islamic prophet Greenmantle for military ends. The books, like those Buchan wrote about Edward Leithen, are tales of adventure as well as spy stories. The author's own word for them was 'shockers', and in their unsophisticated kind they are very good.

The real name of 'Sapper' was Herman Cyril McNeile (1888–1937). The Bulldog Drummond stories that made him famous are markedly xenophobic, and full of clichés of phrase and situation. A girl has 'a skin like the bloom of a sun-kissed peach', Drummond is 'a sportsman and a gentleman. And the combination of the two is an unbeatable production'. Europeans are rarely referred to except as wops and dagos. The plots are absurd, but undeniably have their ration of excitement.

The essay by W. Somerset Maugham (1874–1965) on 'The Decline and Fall of the Detective Story' (1952) is upon the whole not very original, with its observations that there is little room for humour and none for love interest, and its insistence that 'fine writing is out of place'. All this had been said before. The stories in *Ashenden* (1928), however, which sprang from Maugham's own experience in the Secret Service, were something new in spy fiction. After the easy, absurd assumptions made by Buchan, 'Sapper' and Oppenheim, the Ashenden stories have the reality of a cold bath. The detached nature of 'R', Ashenden's chief, the rejection by Ashenden as absolutely useless for fiction of stories like one told him by R about the beautiful blonde who drugged a Minister's drink and took the secret papers (it would have seemed original to Le Queux, usable to 'Sapper'), set the scene for an attempt to treat the business of spying with much more realism than had been considered possible. The characterization has no particular subtlety, but is marked by a downbeat levelling tone which insists that spies and their masters are in many ways ordinary people – the ruthless, powerful R cannot face tipping a waiter without fearing that he will make a fool of himself. Spies may have to use the services of a killer like the Hairless Mexican, and they can make mistakes, as in the assignment when the Mexican kills the wrong man. An Englishman in the pay of Germany is no longer the vilest creature on God's earth, but simply a man who may be bribed to act as a double agent. This double agent turns out to be an amiable character, but when it has been decided that he is untrustworthy, a trap is laid for his destruction. The Ashenden tales are among Maugham's best work as a short story writer, and they had as great an influence on the development of the spy novel as Iles's books had on the crime story. Their morally neutral attitude provided the ground on which Ambler and later writers worked, and R's coolness about killing was to be adopted and adapted by Ian Fleming.

A neutrality that is not only moral but also political and personal weakens Ashenden himself, so that he comes through less as a character than as a piece of litmus paper on which events produce a reaction. In the six novels he wrote before the outbreak of the Second World War, Eric Ambler (1909–   ) infused warmth and political colour into the spy story by using it to express a left-wing point of view. In a sense these books turn 'Sapper' and Buchan upside down. The central character is an innocent man mixed up in violent events, who slowly comes to realize that the agents and spies working on both sides are for the most part unpleasant but not important men. They murder casually and without passion, on behalf of some immense corporation or firm of armament manufacturers whose interests are threatened. These, rather than any national group, are the enemy. *The Dark Frontier* (1936) is the first and least important of these books, but it contains a prophetic note in the possible detonation of the first atomic bomb, and also reflects Ambler's own feelings at the time, put into the mouth of the atomic physicist Professor Bairstow:

> It looked too as if there would always be wars ... What else could you expect from a balance of power adjusted in terms of land, of arms, of man-power and of materials: in terms, in other words, of Money? ... Wars were made by those who had the power to upset the balance, to tamper with international money and money's worth; those who, in satisfying their private ends, created the social and economic conditions that bred war.

The conclusion is emphasized in the conversion of Schimler from social democracy to Communism in *Epitaph for a Spy* (1938), in the friendly portrait of the Greek Communist Marukakis in *The Mask of Dimitrios* (1939),[1] and particularly in the activities of the Soviet agent Zaleshoff, a broad-shouldered, pleasantly ugly man who is always helping innocent Englishmen out of trouble, incidentally for his own ends. A nice Soviet spy? It seemed a contradiction in terms, but such unorthodoxy helped Ambler to keep what was sometimes shop-worn material looking bright and fresh.

1. In America *A Coffin for Dimitrios.*

The political side of the books lay under the surface. Almost all the best thrillers are concerned, in one form or another, with the theme of the hunted man, and these books are no exception. Ambler was fascinated by European cities, and his hunts take place against convincing backgrounds in Istanbul, Sofia, Belgrade, Milan. He was interested also in the problems of frontiers and passports, so that the difficulty of moving from one country to another plays a large part in the stories. And he showed from the beginning a high skill, which became mastery, in the construction of plot. His finest book of this period, a masterpiece in its kind, is *The Mask of Dimitrios*, in which flashback follows flashback in the attempt of the crime novelist Latimer to trace the career of the dead Dimitrios, and there is little direct action until three quarters of the way through the book. To develop interest through a book composed in such a way is a mark of the highest technical skill. The story sparkles with incidents like the interview with the retired spy, or the account of the white slave traffic, that could be extracted as separate stories, yet continue to advance the plot.

Once the convention of the agent as hero had been questioned by Maugham it collapsed, and from the mid-thirties onwards the spy story and thriller became for British writers a vehicle through which to ask the questions about society which still could not be easily expressed in the detective story. The novels that Graham Greene (1904–   ) wrote in the thirties and called 'entertainments' are mostly thrillers, with an attitude towards the corruption of international politics which is not very different from Ambler's. The theme of hunter and hunted is strong in these stories. Often the two are interchangeable, and sometimes the villain is seen as a kind of pathetic hero. Typical figures of this sort are Anthony in *England Made Me* (1935),[2] who is in love with his sister but unable to do anything about it, the paid assassin Raven in *A Gun For Sale* (1936),[3] the boy gangster Pinkie in *Brighton Rock* (1938), and 'D', the agent of a government resembling the Spanish Republican Government in *The Confidential Agent* (1939). And the figure of the hunted man is often, although not so plainly, seen in Greene's later work, in books like *The Power and the Glory* (1940),[4] *The Comedians* (1966) and even *A Burnt-Out Case* (1961), in which Quarry is pursued by the emissaries of the public world from which he has tried to escape.

The thirties thrillers and *The Ministry of Fear* (1943) are very typical books of the decade, using the symbols of the time, the railway station

2. In America *The Shipwrecked*.
3. In America *This Gun for Hire*.
4. In America *The Labyrinthine Ways*.

and the journey to the border, symbols now replaced by the airport and the plane itself. All are equally alien to easy human communication. (One abandoned Greene book had the almost super-typical thirties title, *The Other Side of the Border*.) These are fine novels and thrillers, yet one senses that there was for their author something limiting as well as liberating about the form. It gave scope for comment on society, but much less for the interaction of personalities that for Greene was the real stuff of the novel. The masterly opening of *Brighton Rock*, for instance, is not really necessary to the problems of Pinkie which are the heart of the book.

Greene has defended the thriller as a form, suggesting that it should not be regarded patronizingly, yet there is something defensive about his own labelling of some books as 'entertainments'. Does he mean that they are not serious, or that his other works may not entertain? In any case the distinction helps to perpetuate the snobbishness which he deprecated, although the effects of the entertainments are often as serious as those of his other novels. They are not upon the whole achieved through deeply perceptive characterization, but by the vision of places and objects seen both in themselves and as symbols, in a way that has made several of them the basis of successful films. The entertainments resemble his other novels more than they differ from them. It cannot truly be said that he is like Conrad, a novelist who has occasionally used the thriller's apparatus. He is rather one who begins with the material of a thriller, and then sometimes loads it with a weight of meaning that is too great for the form to bear. Greene was obviously aware of this problem, although he would not have stated it in quite the same way, and it is triumphantly surmounted in such late novels as *The Comedians* and *The Honorary Consul* (1973), where the thriller element is perfectly integrated with the form of the story. *The Human Factor* (1978), an outright spy story, is much less successful.

(ii) The modern spy novel: pipe-dream and reality

During the Second World War Anthony Boucher remarked on the wave of British patriotism which 'led almost every top-flight mystery writer to save the Empire from Fascism by the intervention of his star detective', adding that their work 'brought to international espionage a literacy and dexterity hitherto lavished on purely private murder'. One can see that it may have looked like that at the time, but what is most noticeable now is the weakening of the tendency towards realism engendered by Maugham and developed by Ambler.

For the most part writers simply grafted the theme on to their usual detective story pattern, sometimes with engaging results, as in Allingham's *Traitor's Purse* (1941),[5] but still producing work closer to the detective than to the spy story. A book like *Rogue Male* (1939)[6] by Geoffrey Household (1900–), which begins when the narrator is caught by the police watching the terrace of an unnamed dictator's house through the telescopic sights of his rifle, and develops into an exciting pursuit story, is closer in spirit to the spy story than is the work of the detective story writers who fitted the spy story into their usual setting and characters. Michael Innes's books offer the only exception to this generalization. His spy stories, which began with the very literary *The Secret Vanguard* (1940), in which directions are conveyed through an invented stanza added to Swinburne's 'Forsaken Garden', are secondary to his detective stories, but entirely different from them. A great deal of romantic excitement is generated in *The Journeying Boy* (1949),[7] *Operation Pax* (1951)[8] and *The Man from the Sea* (1955).[9] These books, closer to Buchan than to Ambler, have a fine romantic freedom that is rarely present in the later detective stories. But in spite of Innes and Household (who has never equalled his early performance) the renaissance of the spy story clearly dates from 1953 and the publication of *Casino Royale*,[10] the first novel by Ian Fleming (1908–64). For roughly fifteen years the spy story as developed by Fleming, le Carré and Len Deighton became the most exciting form of sensational fiction.

Fleming is the heir of Buchan and 'Sapper', and James Bond was a more sophisticated version of Bulldog Drummond. The ethos which orders his actions is very much the same. As Kingsley Amis has pointed out, 'throughout all Bond's adventures nobody English does anything evil', and Amis found this acceptable, as he thought that to use foreigners as villains was merely 'a convention older than our literature'. In essence the Bond pipe-dream was the 'Sapper' pipe-dream converted to the mood of the fifties. So although Bond is a patriot prepared to suffer torture for his country, he is also a killer who works for pay, and his brand-name code of behaviour does not prevent him from laying all the girls. In the fifties readers responded to Bond because he provided an excitement lacking in their lives. Into the British post-war atmosphere of virtuous puritanism he

5. In America *The Sabotage Murder Mystery*.
6. In America *Man Hunt*.
7. In America *The Case of the Journeying Boy*.
8. In America *The Paper Thunderbolt*.
9. In America *Death by Moonlight*.
10. In America *You Asked For It*.

brought a celebration of physical pleasures, including those of sadism and masochism. He was a perfect pipe-dream figure for organization man, because he was an organization man too, but unlike the standard model was individually powerful. He could act, he could destroy, he appeared to be free. In America the books at first had little success, at least partly because there was no Welfare State to which Bond could provide the antithesis. As Fleming's biographer has pointed out, the growth of Bond as a mythical figure, with its accompaniments of brand-name shirts, shoes, drinks, cigarettes, games, came after the immense success of the first Bond film made in 1962, two years before Fleming's death. Later films have turned Bond from a cult into a joke, as they have moved further from reality to dependence on deplorable gimmicks.

It would be wrong to see the Bond books wholly in sociological terms. The insistence that Bond was satisfied only by the very best, and the desire to put a brand name to everything, seem in retrospect harmless vulgarity. The books are blood and thunder thrillers, done at first in a strongly personal style and with a convincing appearance of expert knowledge. If it is true, as his biographer says, that Fleming relied for technical details on other people, and that 'it is hard to think of a single subject on which he was a genuine expert', then he was a very skilful assimilator. The first half-dozen Bond books are excellent sensational entertainment. They are very much on a level, and to pick out *Casino Royale* and *From Russia with Love* (1957) is to state a personal preference. Later Fleming became bored with Bond, and the books lost the freshness that was one of their charms.

The difference between pre- and post-war attitudes can be seen very clearly in Eric Ambler's work. The feeling that lay behind the early novels could not survive in a world where shadowy cartels and puckish Soviet agents were evidently a long way from reality. Ambler's later books show a constant effort to come to terms with the new world, to find subjects and narrative forms that would enable him to write with the ease and understanding shown in the pre-war novels. It cannot be said that he has altogether succeeded. Some of the later books, like *The Night Comers* (1956)[11] and *The Levanter* (1972), reflect Ambler's interest in machines and the way they work, others move uneasily between comedy and suspense like the two Abdul Simpson stories. *The Care of Time* (1981) begins brilliantly with a journalist being tempted into working on what purports to be the memoirs of the Russian Nihilist Nechaev, but shows some clashing of gears when we come to the real heart of the plot.

11. In America *A State of Siege*.

The difficult years have brought their rewards, however, in Ambler's finest novel, *Doctor Frigo* (1974), where the deliberate Maughamish detachment of the later work finds its full justification in a political crime story told with great subtlety and skill. The narrator is a doctor working on an island of the French Antilles, whose father was murdered twelve years earlier, either by a left-wing group or by the ruling military junta. Through complex but credible plot devices the emotionally icy Doctor Frigo is drawn into a plan for replacing the junta by an exiled liberal. As always when working at his best, Ambler manages with very little violence, and the fireworks of action are held back until the last part of the book. *Doctor Frigo* is a masterly piece of work, one that justifies the detachment that has sometimes seemed like a world-weary loss of interest. Ambler is never less than a very accomplished writer, but here, as in *The Mask of Dimitrios*, what impresses one most on putting down the book is the skill shown in the Victorian accomplishment of conceiving and carrying through a plot.

Fleming represented *a* mood rather than *the* mood of the period in Britain. David Cornwell (1931–   ), who used the name of John le Carré for his first book, *Call for the Dead* (1961),[12] was a member of the Foreign Service at the time of its publication. This spy novel was followed by a good straightforward detective story, *A Murder of Quality* (1962). Neither book had more than moderate success, but *The Spy Who Came in from the Cold* (1963) found a response almost equal to that roused by the Bond books, although of a different kind. The Bond stories were enjoyed as pipe-dreams, le Carré's for their approach to reality. They offered, again, something new in the form.

It is right, I think, to see two traditions in the spy story as in the crime novel. The first is conservative, supporting authority, making the implicit assertion that agents are fighting to protect something valuable in society. The second is radical, critical of authority, claiming that agents perpetuate, and even create, false barriers between 'Us' and 'Them'. Fleming belongs to the first tradition, le Carré's early work to the second. The texture of his writing owes something to Maugham and Greene, but his material is most firmly rooted in the revelations about Soviet agents that shook Britain in the fifties. The messages of the unjustly neglected first novel, and of the *Spy* and its successor *The Looking-Glass War* (1965), are that authority is not benevolent but often destroys those who serve it, that espionage and counter-espionage work is often fumblingly uncertain in

12. In America *The Deadly Affair*.

its aims and effects, that 'Our' men may be personally vicious and 'Their' men decent human beings – and, most of all, that an agent is often a weak and not a strong character, powerless once he has been caught in the spy net.

The special qualities of these books are their sense of place, their sense of doom, their irony. The irony is most powerful in the *Spy* because there it is most closely associated with the fates of individuals. As layer after layer of deceit is lifted in the story, and the cynicism with which 'London' has used its own agent is revealed, the effect is to show the two apparently opposed organizations on one side, and helpless human beings like Leamas and Elizabeth on the other. Le Carré shows a strong sense, both here and in *The Looking-Glass War*, that spying is a sort of game in which, without wearing comic noses or any sort of disguise, people pretend to be what they are not. The whole apparatus of the trial in the *Spy* is a game, and so of course are the ridiculous, out-of-date operations in the later novel. And the purpose of such party games is betrayal: this is what is required of human beings by the players 'sitting round a fire in one of their smart bloody clubs'.

Le Carré's later progress has been for the most part dismaying. He moved gradually away from the spy story with well-written novels that were less warmly welcomed, until the disastrously bad *The Naive and Sentimental Lover* (1971) was greeted with almost unanimous disapproval. He then returned to the spy story and his central character George Smiley, but this was Smiley with a difference, no longer a faceless organization man but now almost unequivocally a hero. *Tinker, Tailor, Soldier, Spy* (1974), *The Honourable Schoolboy* (1977) and *Smiley's People* (1980) are all long, complicated, funereally slow. Le Carré retains his skill in orchestrating a book, but the prose is ponderous, the obliquities often unnecessary. And the difference is one of approach as well as manner. The work of the Centre is now distinctly idealized, and although spying may still be a rather dirty business, the men of the Centre are now seen as modern patriots defending the bad against the worse. In early books the security services, both bureaucrats and men in the field, are shown as conscienceless people playing destructive games. The revelation of *Smiley's People* is that even the Russian spymaster Karla is human.

It should be added that this is a minority view, and that the three books mentioned have been immensely successful. The criticism made does not apply to *The Little Drummer Girl* (1983), a novel about the Arab–Israeli struggle, in which the complexities of the plot are fully justified, and the narrative has the pace and energy that the Smiley trilogy lacks.

Through Fleming and le Carré, pipe-dreams and reality, the spy story in Britain flowered remarkably. Of the several writers half-way between the two, William Haggard and Anthony Price are the most interesting. William Haggard is the pseudonym used by Richard Henry Michael Clayton (1907–   ). The operations of Colonel Russell of the Security Executive, from his first appearance in *Slow Burner* (1958), are marked by a feeling for aristocratic attitudes, linked less with birth than with behaviour, that is unusual in the modern spy story. Haggard is a right-wing romantic of the Buchan kind (Colonel Russell would surely find Drummond much too violent, and Bond distressingly vulgar) who has an agreeable streak of realism. Russell is capable of getting on perfectly well, on a basis of *Realpolitik*, with his Soviet opposite number, but cannot bear the liberal equivocation of his own country's politicians. *The Arena* (1961) and *The Unquiet Sleep* (1962) are among the best of his books. Later Haggards (he writes roughly a book a year) are subject to the usual law of diminishing returns, and show also an unpleasant liking for ruthlessness, an eagerness for drastic solutions to political problems. Colonel Russell's old-world clubland realism is seen increasingly to hide a distinctly thuggish mentality.

Conservative feelings rather than right-wing sentiments are expressed in the work of Anthony Price (1920–   ). He has put it well himself, when saying that he takes the view that Our Side is good and Their Side bad, whatever may be the individual vices of Us, the individual virtues of Them. He asks gently whether such a view is old-fashioned. Romantic is the word I should use, and perhaps he would not resist it. The romanticism is gentlemanly, not violent, but there is a slight sense of reading ancient history in Price's ingenious linking of past and present. In *Other Paths to Glory* (1974) a historical investigation of the First World War battle of the Somme is found to have a dangerous relevance to the present day, and a similar approach is made in most of his books, successfully in his first novel, *The Labyrinth Makers* (1971) and with a difference in *The '44 Vintage* (1978), which shows us his central characters David Audley and Jack Butler at the beginning of their careers. In *Our Man in Camelot* (1976) and *Tomorrow's Ghost* (1979) the division of interest between past and present works less well. But the division seems in itself a device almost calculated to dispel excitement, and for me it does, so that I admire the ingenious dovetailing but am rarely greatly stirred by the result.

(iii) You know I know you know I know you know

The above line from Thom Gunn's poem expresses very well the over-elaboration and over-subtlety that has turned too many spy stories into ingenious absurdities. The concept of the double agent, when first conceived, was a surprising one, as it turned out that Their man was really one of Ours: but such surprises lose freshness in the spy story as quickly as on TV, so that further complexity was needed to provide the necessary shock. Very well: Their man occupies an important position in one of Our intelligence services. He feeds back information to Them because We have turned him, and is really one of Ours. So readers think: but his allegiance is finally to Them, so that he is one of Theirs put in place by a double deception. Why not, however, a triple or quadruple deception, why not complicate things further by setting one of Our intelligence services at work against another, and then do the same thing for Them, so that in the end real information is taken to be false by one department and genuine by another, is replaced by information that is (as one might say) genuinely false . . .

Such Silver Age conceits are the end of something that at first was marked by real feeling. The spy story is an excellent medium for expressing the deceptions and self-deceptions of twentieth-century man, as the careers of many spies from Sorge to Philby have shown, and the complications offered in the early books of Len Deighton (1929–   ) from *The Ipcress File* (1962) onwards gave a real new turn to the form. His anonymous central character is a working-class boy from Burnley, opposed to authority, who dislikes or distrusts anybody outside his own class. This archetypal sharp boy is set down in an immensely complex world, in which people and their motives are hardly ever what they seem. The early Deighton stories – *Horse Under Water* (1963), *Funeral in Berlin* (1964), *Billion Dollar Brain* (1966) – are elliptically, sometimes too elliptically, told, but their sudden shifts are extremely effective and the technological expertise is not there just for show. Deighton's fascination with what in another writer would be gimmicks comes through, like Kipling's feeling for machinery, and there is something almost lyrical about his recreation of the lives of agents, as well as something knowing. From *Billion Dollar Brain*, his finest performance in this period, one carries away admiration for the intricate plot and the characterization of the clownish Harvey Newbigin, but even more for the evocation of General Midwinter's dotty neo-Fascist organization in Texas and the wonderfully vivid picture of the shooting in the snow outside the Russian train. Writing of this kind, combined with the constant crackle of his dialogue, makes Deighton a kind of poet of the spy novel.

For such writing freshness is essential: but the freshness doesn't last, or as Ross Macdonald put it, the blaze of youth is not to be recaptured. Deighton was a youthful writer when he began, and those first four books are written with enviable verve. Like le Carré and Ambler he felt the need of a different strategy, and he has experimented in trying to find one. The result has been some commonplace or poor books that, in his own phrase, offer plastic trees instead of real wood: but the result also has been his two best novels, *SS-GB* (1978) and *Berlin Game* (1983). The first provides a series of puzzles in a picture of Britain under Nazi rule after Hitler's invasion in 1941. It sounds an unpromising theme, but Deighton handles it with such tact and effective understatement that the occupation becomes entirely plausible. The book is as good in its highly original kind as it could be, unlike its unhappy successor, *XPD* (1981), which shows the tricky nature of this history-as-it-might-have-been variant. *Berlin Game* gives us a central character very like the original Burnley boy, with much the same chips on both shoulders, but a little tamed or at least more discreet. This book, notable like *Doctor Frigo* for its avoidance of violent action, has replaced the verve of youth with subtleties of design and sophistication.

Deighton has survived, sometimes triumphantly, sometimes shakily. The field around, however, is littered with corpses of writers, once promising, who have been driven frantic by the Double-Triple-Quadruple Syndrome. In 1972 I suggested that 'it would be in everybody's long-term interest if a moratorium could be declared on the writing of spy stories for the next ten years'. Far from that happening, spy stories of all kinds from fiction to faction have appeared, in quantities that seem to increase yearly. Some are ridiculous, many merely dull, or silly without the exuberance that sometimes redeems equally absurd TV series and films. TV series like *The Man from Uncle*, films like those made from the Bond books, succeed by a refusal to take themselves or the spy story seriously. The viewer's reaction to these romps among machinery is not bafflement but laughter. Over these books and their writers it is kind to drop a veil of silence.

Among them, however, is a newcomer of talent. *The Miernik Dossier* (1973), the first novel by Chales McCarry (1929–   ) was called by Ambler 'the most intelligent and enthralling piece of work I have read for a very long time'. The book is constructed wholly from documents – letters, memorandums, debriefing notes, secret tapes – but this usually deadening approach succeeds here because of the quick shifts of style and feeling as several agents, each with a particular axe to grind, try to discover whether the emotional, hard-drinking and high-smelling Pole Tadeusz Miernik truly wants to defect, or is under instruction to do so for some propaganda purpose. The characters are credible and sharply defined, the action sometimes puzzling but always concerned with the central problem of Miernik's sincerity, the ending richly ambiguous. The book had the stamp of authenticity that might be expected of a writer who had been ten years in the CIA, but also showed a certainty of touch and tone surprising in a first novel.

Unhappily, McCarry has never equalled *The Miernik Dossier*. His Company man Paul Christopher, placed centre stage in all the later books, is a pipe-dream hero of the most implausible kind, a one-time poet, successful with all the ladies (although his wife gets beaten up and a girlfriend is killed), a sanctimonious romantic who is said to 'care about nothing but the truth', even though he and other Company men 'corrupt men, suborn women'. Christopher opens a Swiss bank account by quoting a line from one of his own early poems, meets a Soviet defector on Shelley's grave. In *The Tears of Autumn* (1975) he discovers who was behind the Kennedy assassination; *The Secret Lovers* finds him searching for an easily spotted traitor, and being torn between the Company and his wife Cathy. *The Last Supper* (1983) provides him at great length with a pedigree and fills in details about other Company men who enter the stories. All the books are written with great intelligence, which in the later ones is buried beneath the burdens of *I know you know* detail and of Christopher's love life. There is no doubt about McCarry's exceptional ability. One can only regret the course it has taken, and hope that before the next book Paul Christopher meets with a fatal accident.

(iv) The adventure story

To talk about the rise of the adventure story in the last decade may seem ridiculous. Haven't tales of adventure always been with us? If one had to make a simple 'yes or no' reply, the answer would be 'no'. In the sense that many Conan Doyle tales (not those about Sherlock Holmes) were adventure stories, such stories were very little written in the first half of the twentieth century. One exception is provided by the – so far as I am concerned – unreadable Dornford Yates, another by John Buchan, a third by Hammond Innes (1913–   ). Several of the Innes books, including *Campbell's Kingdom* (1952) and *The Mary Deare* (1956)[13] are adventure

13. In America *The Wreck of the Mary Deare*.

stories with a near-Victorian flavour which include an element of mystery or suspense. The element is always subsidiary, sometimes marginal. It is much more prominent, however, in the work of Dick Francis and Gavin Lyall, who certainly cannot be ignored here.

Dick Francis (1920–) would agree with this view of his books. 'I like to call them adventure stories but I usually have a main character who has to fight his way out of tight corners and this main character is discovering things all along,' he said with characteristic directness and clarity in an interview, adding that in his books things had to come out right in the end, and that 'I try to write so that they keep wanting to turn the pages over'. The immense and increasing success of Francis's books from *Dead Cert* (1962) onwards show how well he has succeeded. The often remarked sado-masochism of the stories is absent, or much less noticeable, in recent work, and too much has been made of it. A rare and enviable ability to drive a narrative along, combined with thoroughness in research of a given subject, are what makes readers keep wanting to turn the pages.

In his first books Francis used his knowledge as a professional jockey to produce convincing backgrounds. But dependence on horse racing lore obviously had its limitations, and later books offer much information about photography, flying, accountancy, smuggling of stolen horses, kidnapping. These background themes are almost always woven skilfully into the plot. With so much said, it must be added that Francis has been overpraised. The later books are better written than the earlier ones, but few offer characters of any depth, motives of any subtlety. The heroes are all very similar, the heroines are – heroines in adventure stories. These readable and enjoyable books are just that, and when Philip Larkin joins Francis with Thomas Hardy as two of his favourite novelists he does a disservice to literature generally, and to a modest man who perfectly understands the scope of his own talent.

Gavin Lyall (1932–) would also be likely to accept the adventure label. His first two books, *The Wrong Side of the Sky* (1961) and *The Most Dangerous Game* (1963) were written with the zest of a writer putting down exciting scenes on paper without bothering too much about whys and wherefores. In the tales that followed the research sometimes showed through too clearly in books like *Venus with Pistol* (1969), and one sometimes had the impression that the author was waiting impatiently until it was time for the shooting to start. Two recent novels, *The Secret Servant* (1980) and *The Conduct of Major Maxim* (1982) show a new direction. Major Harry Maxim, former SAS man, has been given a desk in 10 Downing Street and a rather mysterious trouble-shooting role as –

well, it's not exactly clear why he is there. Lyall, however, is a writer who evidently finds a central figure helpful. The plotting of these two books, especially the latter, is tight and cohesive, the style easy and sometimes humorous or sardonic, without any loss of pace. These adventure thrillers are the best things he has done.

Is it right to include Lionel Davidson (1922–   ) among writers of adventure stories? The fact is that no descriptive label fits him. His splendidly funny first novel, *Night of Wenceslas* (1960), was a spy story with several differences, including its oversize heroine. It was followed by *The Rose of Tibet* (1962), a tale of adventure that pleased Graham Greene but left its author dissatisfied. Other books, no more than seven in two decades, have given the impression of an author unsure what he wants to do with his considerable talent. Write about Israel (*A Long Way to Shiloh*, 1966),[14] or about the lingering echoes of Nazism (*Making Good Again*, 1968), or simply produce a mystery thriller (*The Chelsea Murders*, 1978)?[15] The most whole-hearted and successful of his novels have been those that in some way concern the various problems of being a Jew, and among them *Making Good Again* comes nearest to combining the excitement of a crime story with the moral intensity Davidson seems to be looking for. Perhaps the several elements in Davidson's work would cohere more easily if he acknowledged that he is a Jewish writer, rather than a writer who happens to be a Jew.

14. In America *The Menorah Men*.
15. In America *Murder Games*.

17

The Crystal Ball Revisited

(i) The past

The most spirited controversion of the ideas about crime stories advanced in this book was made by Jacques Barzun in 1958. In a lively article Barzun deplored the loss of the detective stories, chiefly represented by those here called the Humdrums, that embodied not only 'the entrancing facts about *rigor mortis* or the onset of arsenic poisoning ... but also certain abstractions – Intellect, Knowledge, and the workings of Reason itself'. What were we offered instead, he asked? Why, the swampy grounds of psychology, 'just what the older *genre* was created to avoid'. At this time Barzun had to wade through psychology knee-high, and probably he now finds himself in it up to the neck. Modern crime stories, he said, made him feel not only old but sold, for the whole point of the detective story was its specialized character. Delight in it accompanied 'the belief in greatness, intelligence and integrity ... the recognition of law and the directed curiosity of science'. In 1958 he found that it had 'lost its aim and possibly its place in literature', had 'ceased to give entertainment and proffered nothing in exchange'. Barzun in effect elaborated this point of view in the selection of entries for *A Catalogue of Crime* (1971), which he produced with Wendell Hertig Taylor, and in discussion of the entries. The works of John Rhode, mentioned here only as a name, are given nine pages of comment, and the almost similarly disregarded Henry Wade is called 'one of the great figures of the classical period' and awarded seven pages of considerable praise.

If you are rapturous about Rhode, worshipful of Wade, Barzun should be your guide. Obviously my point of view is so much opposed to his (what Barzun finds entrancing I think dull) that we have no common ground on which to argue. But it is interesting that his diagnosis of what has happened is similar to mine, except that what he regards as a flight from Intellect and Reason I should call an escape from self-deception and a move towards realism. It is interesting also that he makes no attempt at an artistic defence of the detective stories he most admires, beyond saying that they are 'dependable as entertainment and respectable as literature'. What are *dependable* and *respectable* in these contexts? The claim made for modern works is that the best of them are good novels and also interesting crime stories. There is much less difference between past and present than Barzun and others pretend. The gap only appears great from a point of view that considers Collins, Le Fanu and Doyle important chiefly as the precursors of 'the detective story', something that was truly 'classical' only from the early twenties up to the beginning of the Second World War.

The progression indicated here is a more reasonable one. The crime story as a literary form has developed alongside other fiction in a way shaped largely by social events, and its course has run roughly like this:

1   Stories about crime as a form of radical social protest, in Godwin, Lytton, Balzac. The criminal is seen as a hero, or a victim of social injustice.

2   Stories about detectives as protectors of society, or as intellectual Supermen. These began with Poe and were developed by Collins and Gaboriau.

3   The idea that the Superman detective alone might operate above or outside the processes of law, which began with Sherlock Holmes.

4   The commercially dictated change from short story to novel, and the emergence of women writers whose detectives followed the Holmes pattern, and whose work emphasized the importance of preserving the existing state of society. (The invention of the 'rules' could be related to this overriding social need.)

5   The attempts to break the 'rules', partly on the ground that their literary products were boring (by Iles), partly because they were silly (by Hammett and Chandler).

6   The development of crime novels, a bag of literary allsorts ranging from comedy to tragedy, from realistic portraits of society to psychological investigation of an individual, together with the flowering of the spy story as a literary form.

In the original (1972) edition of this book I made an attempt to look into the crystal ball and predict the course of crime stories during the following ten years. The answers I gave then are reprinted below, with italicized comments on how near the predictions came to what happened.

(ii) The future

What it seems to indicate, rather undramatically, is more of the same. The result may look something like this:

The detective story

A declining market. Some detective stories will continue to be written, but as the old masters and mistresses fade away, fewer and fewer of them will be pleasing to lovers of the Golden Age. The revival of 'entrancing facts about *rigor mortis*', or even about the unique nature of hairs and carpet threads, as the most important features of a crime story, seems very improbable. Clues of this kind are now, and will remain, the affair of the forensic scientist and not of the amateur detective. There will be no plans of the house and grounds, locked rooms will be passed over to writers of science fiction. If there are mysterious murder methods they will be up to date, being concerned with laser beams, poisons in frozen food or smeared on the elements of electric fires, and so on.

Yes, the market has declined, and few old-fashioned detective stories are written. Publishers lament the fact, ignoring the obvious truth that nobody who began writing after the Second World War could possibly write like Christie or Sayers. P. D. James is a case in point.

Spy stories

Also probably showing a temporary decline, in quality if not in number. Fewer stories about European spying, more about comparatively unexplored areas, particularly the Far East and South America. An upbeat tone seems likely after the le Carré depression. Why have the French written so few good spy stories? The form should appeal to them, and it would not be surprising to see some strongly nationalistic spy stories from France, Israel, Argentina.

Sadly astray. Any 'upbeat' tone tends to be unpleasantly contemptuous and even vicious, and little of interest has come from any writers outside Britain and America.

Adventure stories

A steadily rising market. Much of the talent that went into the detective story, with its nice uncomplicated view of character and scene, has now entered the adventure story. It is likely that more writers who don't want to take themselves or their readers seriously will move over to some kind of adventure story (men authors) or to Gothic novels with a mild mystery element (women). Considerable expertise is employed already here, as in Dick Francis's adventure thrillers based on his expert knowledge of horse racing. Why not similar books based on athletics, motor racing, swimming?

The last sentence awaits fulfilment, but the rest seems right enough. Women's Gothic flourishes, although it is outside the scope of this book. For comment on Dick Francis's development, see p. 231.

Police novels

Likely to provide more of the same, although in another decade that idea of running three or four cases side by side in one volume will surely be worn out. TV will continue to provide a visual rival to this kind of semi-documentary fiction, but there seems no reason why the two shouldn't exist side by side. Possible variations are more emphasis on laboratory work as already suggested, exploitation of a small town or country police force, and stories about police in countries apart from Britain and America. What are the cops of Tokyo's 87th Precinct like? It would be interesting to know.

The first two sentences are spot on. Other suggested developments await writers. Hill Street Blues *has blended police work and comedy with surprising success.*

Crime novels

Capable of any sort of development, according to the talents they attract. If 'the novel' continues to become even less concerned with realistic narrative, and still more with linguistic or science-fictional experiments or with states of mind symbolically seen (a tendency noticeable from Burroughs to Mailer to Murdoch), then 'the crime novel' may partly fill its place. It could attract writers who twenty years ago would have written novels, readers who would have read them. If this happens, we can expect the links with the detective story (what were six cat hairs doing on a saucer in the refrigerator?) to become more tenuous, story-telling to be more direct. But a lot of crime novelists will still be blending psychology, clues and social comment in the way that infuriates Barzun.

Yes, more novelists inhabit, or occasionally visit, the borderland between the crime story and the novel. Hugh Fleetwood and Francis King are two of them, and I'm sure there are others unknown to me. And the best crime writers when working at their best – like George V. Higgins and Ruth Rendell – are interesting novelists.

Who will write them?

There are some signs that British–American supremacy in crime writing, based partly on the social stability of those countries and partly on the fact that English is for readers a world language (in Scandinavia and Holland many people read crime stories in English for preference), may be challenged. There are some new Scandinavian writers, one or two French, at least one Italian, and their work is interesting particularly because it has a flavour quite unlike that of the Anglo-American product. The Wahlöo/Sjöwall and Dürrenmatt novels, for instance, have no counterpart elsewhere. In ten years' time there may well be a lot of new writers, not all of them Anglo-American, widening the field of crime fiction still further.

Partly true. In Sweden several writers have emerged in the wake of Wahlöo/ Sjöwall, although few have been translated into English. K. Arne Blom and Paul Ørum are two who have leapt the language barrier. There are new crime novelists in Spain, where the form has shown a resurgence of interest under a democratic government, in Canada and in France, although the French mostly follow paths alien to other crime writing. The Italian author I had in mind, Sciascia, proved to be not truly a crime writer. Upon the whole the new talents – for my money Higgins and Rendell are the most interesting – are Anglo-American. An Italian journalist suggested to me recently that one reason for the failure of Catholic countries to produce more than a very few interesting crime writers should be attributed to Catholic expunging of guilt feelings through confession. Hence, their attitude towards the whole problem of guilt which is at the heart of the crime story is quite different from that of anybody brought up under a Protestant ethic. This interesting idea would be worth detailed examination.

So far the crystal ball revisited. I am particularly struck by my failure to anticipate the immense and still growing academic interest in crime fiction during the past decade. Ten years ago the crime story was still a critical Cinderella: now, at least in America, Cinderella has become the fairy princess. The transformation must be welcome to those who, like me, have often complained that the best crime stories are treated with almost total critical disregard. Nevertheless much of the new criticism proceeds from a point of view that must be greeted with dissent by anybody prepared to say that some kinds of literature are more important than others.

Crime fiction has been one of the beneficiaries (science fiction and TV drama and documentaries are others) of a view that what is vaguely called 'popular art' is no less important than art which is less popular but more highly regarded. It would be over-polite to say merely that this view is mistaken. At the furthest extreme of infantility some people maintain that a long-running TV series, like the British *Coronation Street* or the American *Dallas*, must be treated seriously because it is so successful. The basic attitude behind the current critical attention paid to popular art, however it may be expressed, is a denial that one form of artistic expression is more important than another. The pop art of Lichtenstein may look like a comic strip, may almost *be* a comic strip, yet it has to be taken seriously because it hangs beside Picasso in the Museum of Modern Art or the Tate Gallery. Such a denial that any standards of excellence exist, or should exist, has also a connection with that aspect of structuralist theory which suggests that every book (even the word 'book' is replaced by the more neutral 'text') is different for every reader.

The stupidity of such ideas would be evident in any time less oppressed by a desire to deny the existence of standards. A sensible approach towards crime literature must begin by the acknowledgement that it has been, and will remain, primarily an entertainment created by popular demand. Most of it has little to do with literature, but is designed to give temporary pleasure – to Professor Barzun, to me, to old ladies using country libraries and young men buying violent stories in paperback. There is no contradiction between saying this and asserting also that a few writers in the form do more, and that their work has a claim to consideration as literature. There seems to me no doubt that since the end of the Second World War the crime story has interested more good writers than before, and that their approach has been more intelligent and varied, and their handling of criminal themes less trivial, than that of their Golden Age predecessors. Most crime writers produce too much, some exhaust their talent, but the best of the last decade shows that the vein still contains much gold. Yet it must always be said that the medium has limitations, and its writers have them too. In the highest reaches of the crime novel it is possible to create works of art, but because of their sensationalism they will always be works of a slightly flawed kind. *The Moonstone* and *The Glass Key* are fine novels, but the imaginations that created them are not those of great writers. Accordingly, articles about 'The Problem of

Moral Vision' in Hammett, and discoveries of archetypal qualities in Chandler's Philip Marlowe, are absurdly disproportionate. Hammett and Chandler (and of course other names could be added) were fine writers who for a long while received no serious critical attention at all, but they were not Tolstoy or George Eliot, nor were meant to be.

Yet in a world where Tolstoys and George Eliots are in short supply, or no supply at all, a defence of crime stories shouldn't rest there. The form has particular merits for our time, particular relevance to the age we live in. It is a truism, yet still true, that we live in a time of especial violence, and how can that be expressed better than in a crime story which takes violence seriously? Perhaps the public violence around us can be commented on most effectively through the private violence of individual crime. A really terrifying case like the British Moors Murders, or the American Manson killings, opens up questions relating to power and responsibility that go far beyond the crimes themselves. In the same way that Brecht asked 'What is the robbing of a bank, compared to the founding of a bank?' one might ask: 'What are a few private killings compared to the organization of murder in Vietnam and elsewhere by countries that pride themselves on their civilized qualities?' I am not suggesting that there is any single or simple answer, only that the questions may perhaps be better posed through the account of individual acts of violence than in a long novel that conscientiously tries to count the number of dead.

What the modern crime story can do, in short, is to say something of interest about our own time. The fine art of murder, as de Quincey called it, can tell us something about the world we live in, and about the best way of living peacefully in it.

· Index ·

Index

Index

Index

Index

Index